GRAND ADVEN TURES

GRAND ADVEN TURES

William Collins
An imprint of HarperCollins*Publishers*
1 London Bridge Street
London SE1 9GF

WilliamCollinsBooks.com

First published in Great Britain
by William Collins in 2016

21 20 19 18 17 16
10 9 8 7 6 5 4 3 2 1

ISBN 978-0-00-812934-7

A catalogue record for this book is available
from the British Library.

Publishing Director: Myles Archibald
Senior Editor: Julia Koppitz
Design and layout: This Side
Production: Chris Wright

The activities described in this book have risks and
can be dangerous, and many of the sites featured
are in remote locations. Please be prepared before
embarking on any adventures. The author and
publishers have gone to great lengths to ensure the
accuracy of the information herein, but they cannot
be held legally or financially responsible for any
accident, injury, loss or inconvenience sustained
as a result of the information or advice contained
in this book. Swimming, jumping, diving, cycling,
walking, sleeping outdoors or any other activities
at any of these locations is entirely at your own risk.

Colour reproduction by FMG
Printed and bound in Hong Kong

FOR MY PARENTS,
WHO TAUGHT ME TO SAVE UP, WORK HARD
AND MAKE STUFF HAPPEN.

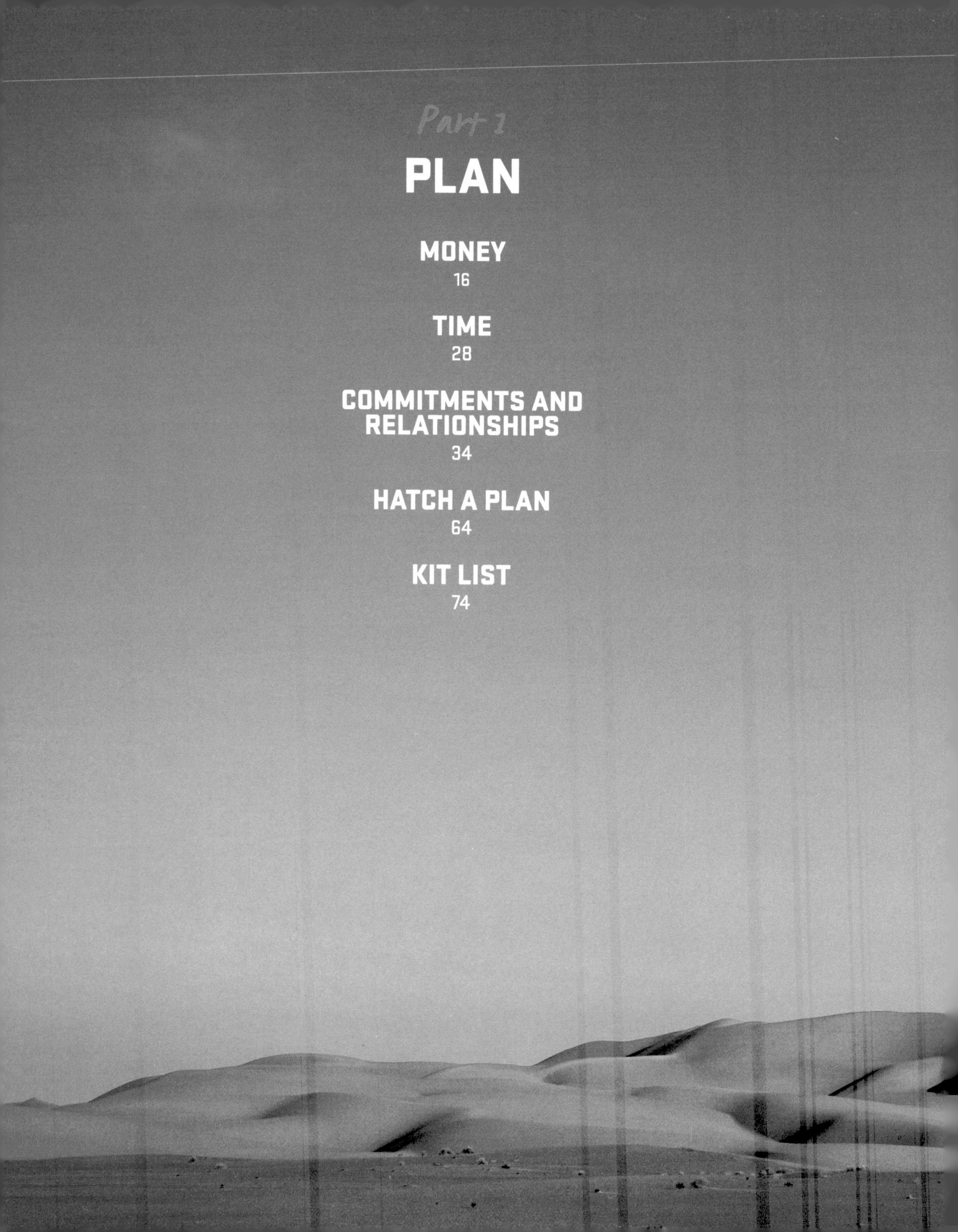

Part 1

PLAN

Part 2

CHOOSE

INTRODUCTION

Everyone loves adventure. Bookshops have bulging travel sections. Adventure film festivals are springing up all over the world. The web groans with exciting expedition blogs. I love adventure so much that I turned it into my job. I am a professional adventurer. It says as much on my business card, so it must be true. (Never mind that I made them myself in one of my many procrastinating-from-book-writing mornings.) I write books, give talks and make films about the adventures I've done, such as cycling round the world, crossing oceans or staggering through the heat of deserts. Enough people enjoy hearing these stories for me to earn a living from them. This means that more people read about adventures than go on big trips themselves. But this book aims to help you realise that grand adventures are within *your* grasp, that you can begin taking the steps necessary to make them happen for you, too. Why settle for reading about adventures when you could be out in the wild doing them yourself?

'Why settle for reading about adventures when you could be out in the wild doing them yourself?'

Many of my friends are also adventurers. They've climbed great mountains, trekked to the Poles, exciting stuff like that. These are special experiences. I love sitting in the pub with my adventurous friends, listening to increasingly far-fetched tales as last orders approaches. But here's an important thing: I know these guys and girls well enough to see that they are not particularly special people. They are ordinary people, but they do things that many people deem to be more than ordinary, even extra-ordinary. Being an adventurer is not a genetic gift. I know, for example, that I certainly am not brave, strong or athletic, yet I claim to be an adventurer. Usain Bolt was born fast. Albert Einstein was born brainy. Living adventurously, however, is nothing more than a choice.

When I left university I made the choice to make the best I could of my abilities and resources and see how far I could ride my bike. I didn't have a fancy bike. I didn't ride fast. I didn't spend much money. I got lost a lot. I napped under trees. I carried a bicycle repair book because I had little idea about bottom brackets or rear derailleurs. And yet I eventually succeeded in cycling the whole way round the world. I spent £7000 on the four-year trip. I did not choose

to do it on such a shoestring: it's just that this was the sum total of my worldly wealth. I preferred to get going and make it happen rather than saving and saving and never beginning. Four years of banana sandwiches was a small price to pay for eking out my money into so many memories.

When people dream of adventure they are generally not discouraged by the difficulties of the journey itself. Extremes of heat and cold; basic and uncomfortable conditions; the physical and mental struggle: these are actually often part of the appeal! The struggle, many of us feel, is preferable to boring routine.

So what is it that actually gets in the way, if not the hazards of the wild? Why do lots of people long for adventure and enjoy reading about it but not many actually get out there and do it?

I didn't think that it could be explained by a lack of practical skills, fitness or equipment. It's not as concrete as that. I guessed that what inhibits most people are the mental barriers in their head: it's too hard, too scary, too uncertain...

Through my blog, I decided to ask what it was that stood between people and the adventures they dreamed of. From around 2,000 responses, here are the most common issues:
— Time
— Money
— Family / partners / commitments
— Fear
— Society pressure
— No companion to go with
— Getting time off work
— Getting work afterwards

And these were mentioned, too:
— Solo female travel / safety
— Lazy / procrastination
— School holiday system
— Lack of knowledge
— Ideas
— The unknown
— Kit / logistics
— Lonely
— Fitness / health

I found it fascinating that not one person mentioned the worry of falling down a crevasse or getting eaten by a tiger. The greatest obstacles to people's adventures all lie *before the journey even begins*. In other words, getting to the start line is the hardest part!

Wrestling snakes, paddling rapids, tying a bowline with your teeth, pitching a tent in a typhoon: all this stuff is so much easier than

getting off the sofa, committing to action and beginning.

A similar example sometimes happens out on an expedition: leaving the tent when a blizzard is howling outside and your sleeping bag is snug can feel nigh on impossible. But when you do get out (it's usually a weak bladder rather than a strong will that eventually forces you into action), the world is never as grim as you'd imagined it to be from the safe cocoon of your sleeping bag. The raging blizzard you'd pictured is often just a bit of windy snow. Feeling sheepish, you pack away the tent and get on with the journey.

What's more, the practical preparations for launching a journey are also far easier than mustering the *cojones* to commit in the first place, to do something difficult and daunting and daring with your life.

There is a lovely Norwegian phrase that translates into 'the Doorstep Mile'. It refers to how hard it is to begin something, how hard it is to get out your front door and commit to action. This book helps tackle the Doorstep Mile.

'Do you dream of having a massive adventure but can't see how you will ever get the chance to do it? If so, this book is for you!'

The first half of the book tackles the barriers that make it hard to begin. The second half helps you choose which adventure is right for you.

Do you dream of having a massive adventure but can't see how you will ever get the chance to do it? Do you long to explore but don't know how to begin? Do you look enviously at other people's trips but think it's not what 'people like you' do? If so, this book is for you!

My aim is to help you commit to begin planning your dream adventure, to get you in motion. That's all. After that, the rest is easy – and up to you.

This book helps you shine a spotlight on what is getting in the way of the most amazing, life-changing, career-enhancing, personality-forging, memory-making adventure of your life. If you really, truly want to experience a big adventure, you *can* do it. *You* can do it. You can. *Grand Adventures* looks at the obstacles stopping you and shows that there *are* ways round them, *if* you choose to do it. Will you?

I spent an absorbing year interviewing many adventurers for this book, seeking hard-won wisdom from people who have been there and done the kind of trips we all dream of. I'm only sorry there was not space to include them all. (The in-depth interviews are all available to read on *www.alastairhumphreys.com/GrandAdventures*.) They've done it all: Everest, the North and South Poles, the Amazon and Sahara, all seven continents, the oceans – even going up to Space! All of them once took that huge step of committing to their very first adventure. I hope that you will take inspiration from them because they were once just like you: itching to hit the road but nervous about how to make it happen.

There are stories and photographs from men and women who have travelled by boat and boot, car and kayak, bike and motorbike, home-made raft and hi-tech spaceship. People who had one great trip then returned to normal life. Those bitten so badly by the bug that they devoted their life to the pursuit of adventure. There's youngsters and old folks; men and women; mates, couples and families; fit, fat or disabled. Extraordinary, inspiring people. People like you.

The only thing that stands between you *dreaming* of adventure and you *being* an adventurer is committing to it. Together, we'll show you that, whether it's cycling to the Sahara, walking across Australia or rafting the Amazon, the longest journeys really do all begin with a single step. They are, in fact, nothing more than lots of tiny, easy steps. Tiny, yes; easy, yes, but you've still gotta take 'em. Are you ready? Let's begin.

Part 1

PLAN

Most people cite money as one of their big worries in life. It's certainly seen as the largest obstacle to adventure. When people say to me 'I'd love to do a big adventure, but...' it is usually money that appears to be stopping them.

People who daydream about winning the lottery often say, 'I'd go and see the world. I'd have an adventure!' But you won't win the lottery. That's not the way the world, or probability, works, alas! (Especially if you're not wasting your money on lottery tickets in the first place and instead are saving for an adventure.)

Will you just accept that because you won't win the lottery you won't have that dream adventure? Or maybe you'll settle for doing something when you retire? (Gambling on the hope that you are not dead or decrepit by then...)

Before you do, there are two vital things to realise about money and adventures:

Adventures can be much cheaper than you might imagine. Not only that, it's relatively painless to save enough money without having to rely on a lottery ticket.

If I can demonstrate that the biggest hurdle is easy to get over, hopefully it will convince you that any other obstacles in your way can be fixed, too.

When it first dawned on me, this simple little sum stopped me in my tracks – for its simplicity, and for its implications.

If you put aside £20 a week, within a year you will have saved £1,000. One thousand pounds. In all its glory, a thousand quid...

£20 is not a particularly large amount of money for me, and that's probably the case for many of us who are in the privileged position in life of even being able to dream of adventures. I spend £20 in the pub, or on a meal to cook for a few friends. £20 is within my financial comfort zone.

But £1,000 *does* feel like a large amount of money to me. For much of the world, of course, it's an impossibly vast sum. For some people it's mere loose change. But I imagine that most people

reading this book are, approximately, on a similar financial level to me: £1,000 sounds like a lot of money, but it's more or less achievable if I set my mind to saving £20 a week.

I know from experience that £1,000 is enough to fund a phenomenal trip. I once flew to India, walked from one coast of the country to the other, and then flew back home for far less than that. I have cycled thousands of miles through extraordinary places for £1,000, a grand adventure. Almost all of the trips I have done – including canoeing the Yukon, crossing Iceland and cycling round the world – I funded by saving up my own money and then doing the trip as cheaply as I could manage.

If you travel under your own steam, eat inexpensive food and sleep in a tent then expeditions don't cost much once you've bought the essential equipment and plane ticket.

Some of my more recent trips, in places such as Greenland and the Atlantic, have required sponsorship, because they're beyond the depths of my wallet. But I'm a strong believer that you should walk before you run. Building up a solid CV of expeditions will help you secure sponsorship further down the line, but the best thing to do is begin with exciting projects that you can pay for yourself. Some of the journeys described in this book are expensive, but the lessons you can draw from them will help with any debut, budget expedition.

Saving a little bit of money regularly and seeing how that accumulates into a large amount is a handy metaphor for everything in this book. Things that seem daunting at first are not nearly so bad once you begin chipping away. Start small, but do start. Start rubbish, then get good along the way.

I have chosen £1,000 as a pretty arbitrary figure upon which to hang the adventures in this book simply because I loved the neat simplicity of putting aside £20 a week then hiking off into the sunset a year later. You can do something amazing for less than £1,000, although many journeys will cost

more than that. It doesn't really matter; this is not the book to help you with detailed budget planning. It's simply the spark which, I hope, will light the fire inside you and get you to commit to the journey of a lifetime. After that, you're halfway there.

A more useful way of thinking about expedition budgets than absolute figures such as '£1,000' is to consider how long it takes you to earn the money. There is the absurd social convention of spending between one and three months' salary on an engagement ring. (If anybody ever proposes to me I would far rather they spend that money on a grand adventure for the two of us than a highly squashed pebble.) So rather than focusing too much on the notional figure of £1,000, perhaps you should try to think about what fraction of your income you're able to save for an adventure.

Throughout this book, never think, 'I can't do that'. Instead, try to think of a way round

the difficulty that still fits within your particular circumstances. If you can't afford to save £20 a week, save £10 instead: you'll still get there in two years. Just put aside what you can when you can. More often than not, replacing the words 'I can't do that' with 'I choose not to do that' will give you an honest insight into how much you truly want to make something happen. Are you really in the position of saying 'I can't save £20/£10/£5 a week' or is it more like 'I choose not to save £20/£10/£5 a week'?

If I gave you £1,000 to go on an adventure, what would you go and do? Grab a pen and write a list of ideas. Physically write them, don't just think it – you're more likely to make stuff happen if it's set down in black and white.

I am not *actually* going to give you £1,000. I'm a Yorkshireman. However, I *am* going to help you begin saving it. If you can save up that much money and therefore eliminate the biggest perceived barrier that stops people having the adventure of their lives, what else can stop you making this thing happen?

HERE ARE A FEW SUGGESTIONS FOR IDEAS OF ADVENTURES YOU COULD HAVE FOR £1,000:

'I would go south, hitch-hiking into Africa.'
Steve Dew-Jones, hitch-hiked to Malaysia.

'I would leave the front door with my camping kit, and I'd just walk. It'd be really interesting to walk without a destination, away from home day after day. It wouldn't be very expensive, so that £1,000 might last a very long time.'
Hannah Engelkamp, walked 1000 miles round Wales with a donkey.

'I'd jump on a skateboard and go around India.'
Jamie McDonald, ran 5,000 miles across Canada.

'I'd go climbing illegally in China – it's the permits that cost so much. Or I'd go somewhere you don't really need permits, like Kyrgyzstan or Tajikistan.'
Paul Ramsden, climbed 'lots of big mountains'.

'I'd cycle to Istanbul. If I made sure my bike was fairly worthless, I could leave it there and then just fly home for £70 at the end.'
Tom Allen, cycled, packrafted, walked, hitch-hiked and rode horses on five continents.

'I like the idea of sea kayaking from Finland to Sweden through the archipelago.'
Karen Darke, Paralympian and expeditions by bike, sea kayak and sit-ski.

'I would sail out to the West Face of Ball's Pyramid and climb it: it's only 2,270 foot high, but 312 miles off the east coast of Australia.'
James Castrission, kayaked the Tasman Sea.

'I'd like to walk to the midnight sun. Set out from home and walk north up to the Arctic Circle.'
Sean Conway, first person to complete a 'length of Britain' triathlon.

Some people may consider spending £1,000 on adventure to be a flippant use of money. I know that it is not saving the world, but I suspect that, when I'm on my death bed, I'll be more grateful for the experiences that adventures have given me than for spending that amount of money on things like a massive TV or a trendy handbag.

You know that when you are old and looking back on your life you'd prefer to remember a bike ride through Borneo or a train journey across Tibet rather than the extra work you did and the extra £1,000 you're going to have to pay death duty on. So why don't you get out there and do it?

THERE ARE TWO WAYS TO GET MORE MONEY IN LIFE:

Earn more. Or spend less. I'm definitely not the right person to advise with Point 1, but here are some ideas to help you begin spending less money.

Remember, in order to save £1,000 for your adventure you need to save less than £3 each day for a year.

Think about all the ways you spend money and where you can make some savings. Consider the small changes you can make which will help lead to a big adventure and a big change in your life. I'm not advocating anything drastic, just tiny tweaks that won't hurt day-to-day but will accumulate into big piles of cash. If you think you'll struggle, try writing down every single thing you spend in the course of a week – you might be surprised where you can make some savings for your Adventure Fund.

If you're serious about saving money, do some Googling: there are blogs more knowledgeable and specific on the subject than I could ever pretend to be. But I hope this section will get you thinking. All the examples below are worth trading for the adventure of a lifetime, especially as they generally make your life healthier anyway.

— **Daily routine:** Cut out a daily takeaway coffee and you've almost made it to £1,000 in a year already. Take a packed lunch to the office and you're really saving.

— **Commuting:** Can you work from home occasionally? Can you share a lift or cycle one day a week?
— **Home bills:** Turn your thermostat down a notch and put on a jumper. Wash your clothes at a lower temperature. Have an occasional cold shower (they are good for the soul, the environment and your bank balance!). Sell your telly.
— **Entertainment:** Eat out less often or search online for restaurant discount vouchers.
— **Alcohol:** A pint in a London pub often costs £5. One fewer pints a week and you've saved almost 25 per cent of your £1,000. If you're tempted for 'just one more', consider that the price of that drink can easily equate to a day on the road in some of the world's wildest, cheapest and most exciting regions. Which would you rather have? Beer tastes better on a beach in Belize anyway!
— **Smoking:** Stop it.
— **Eat more veg:** An average UK family spends £5,300 per year on food. A moment's Googling leads me to a site of recipes that will feed a family for just £1,168 per year.
— **Stick to essentials:** Only buy stuff you really need. We all suffer from 'stuffocation'. Look around your house and ask, 'Do I need this?' When did you last use or wear some of it? Would you miss it if it were gone? Sell ten things on eBay and transfer the proceeds to your Grand Adventures fund. eBay is a great place to buy all the kit you need for your adventure, too. You can save a fortune this way.

I hope I've demonstrated that saving £1,000 is achievable through taking small steps. Remember that the same metaphor applies to all the other obstacles standing in your way. Overcoming inertia, generating momentum, getting out the front door, beginning: if you want it enough, you can do it.

Tiny steps. Grand adventures. Are you in?

WISE WORDS FROM FELLOW ADVENTURERS

JAMIE BOWLBY-WHITING
HITCH-HIKED THOUSANDS OF MILES, RAFTED THE RIVER DANUBE AND WALKED ACROSS ICELAND

It is possible to travel entirely without money by a combination of free camping, Couchsurfing and foraging.

HANNAH ENGELKAMP
WALKED A LAP OF WALES WITH AN ECCENTRIC DONKEY

Money-wise, if you do something that involves walking and camping, it's likely to be an awful lot cheaper than ordinary life. Really, it's a matter of getting your head around stopping what you're doing now and just doing something completely different.

DAVE CORNTHWAITE
MADE 25 NON-MOTORISED JOURNEYS

I learned to just downsize my life and limit my outgoings, which I think is a nice lesson overall.

ALICE GOFFART & ANDONI RODELGO
CYCLED ROUND THE WORLD FOR SEVEN YEARS

During those years, including having two children on the way, we spent less than €50,000. That's what some people spend on a car, and nobody asks them how they did it.

ANTS BOLINGBROKE-KENT
NUMEROUS VEHICLE-POWERED EXPEDITIONS

My money diet mantra was 'no unnecessary spending'. The only clothes I bought were off eBay or from charity shops (difficult as a lover of fashion). I made sure my saving didn't overly impact on my relationship, though. This adventure malarkey can be rather selfish and I wanted to save cash, but that couldn't mean becoming a miserly bore.

GRAHAM HUGHES
VISITED EVERY COUNTRY
IN THE WORLD WITHOUT FLYING

When asked how can I afford to travel so much, I feel like retorting with: how can you afford your rent? To keep a dog? To have children? To smoke? When I travel, I have no rent to pay, so 100 per cent of the money I have can go on travel.

JAMIE MCDONALD
RAN 200 MARATHONS ACROSS CANADA

I spent three years saving up for a house. The only reason was because everyone else was doing that. I

was just choosing it for someone else's sake. So I bought a second-hand bicycle for 50 quid out of the newspaper and I flew to Bangkok. And then I cycled home back to Gloucester.

ANDY KIRKPATRICK
BIG WALL CLIMBING & WINTER EXPEDITIONS

Before my first trip to the Alps I was working in a job where I got £100 a week, and just the bus ticket from Sheffield to the Alps cost me £99! I saved one week's pay, spent it on the ticket and packed in my job. Every penny we spent was considered.

JASON LEWIS
SPENT 13 YEARS CIRCUMNAVIGATING
THE PLANET BY HUMAN POWER

I ended up in the clink [prison] in east London

for trying to run out the door of the chandlery there with our shit bucket and a scrubbing brush, coming to the total of £4.20. I was rugby tackled by security guards at Woolworths. So yeah, we were just desperate.

MATT EVANS
TRAVELLED OVERLAND FROM
THE UK TO VIETNAM

I bought a big ceramic savings pot that needed to be smashed to get all the money inside. Every day we came in from work and put all the loose change in our pockets into it. No excuses. This might sound silly but after a while it became normal, and when we finally had a grand 'Smashing of the Jar' ceremony, we had £962.28 in it. That's quite a lot of money for a small daily ritual that didn't seem to take much effort. The funny thing was, once we'd saved up the money without living like hermits or living on beans on toast, we looked at each other and wondered why we hadn't been making these changes to our lives since we met. We hadn't felt unduly broke, we hadn't lost any friends, and we didn't feel as though we'd worked our fingers to the bone. Yet somehow we'd saved enough money to have the adventure of a lifetime. All it took was a little thinking, a few tweaks and a bit of willpower.

SEAN CONWAY
FIRST PERSON TO COMPLETE
A 'LENGTH OF BRITAIN' TRIATHLON

I don't have much money, so I just got loads of credit cards. That kind of got the funding out of the way initially.

KEVIN CARR
RAN AROUND THE WORLD

Unless what you're considering is crazy expensive, it's probably much less hassle to work a part-time second job/overtime than it is to chase sponsors.

PATRICK MARTIN SCHROEDER
TRYING TO CYCLE TO EVERY COUNTRY
IN THE WORLD

I know this: travelling made me richer, even if I have less money. The slower you travel, the less money you spend. Money is probably not the thing stopping you, but the fact that you have to leave your comfort zone. That you have to do something scary. Once you step over that line, once you are on the road, everything gets easier.

CHRIS MILLAR
CYCLED TO THE SAHARA

I worked as a rickshaw driver to save some pennies, get fit and learn the basics of bicycle maintenance.

NIC CONNER
CYCLED FROM LONDON TO TOKYO FOR £1,000

We realised with our pay cheques it wasn't going to be too much of a budget we were going to be living on, so we thought, 'Right. Let's work *with this* and make it a challenge.'

JAMES KETCHELL
CYCLED ROUND THE WORLD, ROWED
THE ATLANTIC, CLIMBED EVEREST

I was working as an account manager for an IT company. I moved back home with my parents; this made a big difference to my finances. Not particularly cool when you're in your late twenties but it goes back to how much you want something. I took on an extra job delivering Chinese food in the evenings.

BEGIN SAVING £1,000 TODAY

Here is an easy way to save your £1,000 Adventure Fund. It requires zero willpower or prolonged organisational skills, nor should it cause too much daily hardship in your life.

1. Open a new bank account.
This is the only hassle of the whole plan, but it's not much of a hassle at all. I hate doing stuff like this, but even I set up a new account online in under 15 minutes.

2. Set up a standing order to transfer £20 to the new account from your main bank account each week.

3. Persuade a friend to do the same.
It's easier and more fun to stick to a resolution if you've got a mate doing it too.

The hardest part is over. Now it is time for the second phase of the scheme: Tell everyone that a year from today you are going to cycle to Sweden or run to Romania or hitch-hike to Hanoi. It's vital to tell people of your plans, so that they can hold you to account, encourage you when you flag and tease you if you wimp out. Make a note in your diary for a year from today. 'Begin Adventure!'

You now have one year to sort out the rest of the adventure (commitments, equipment, fitness, time off work etc).

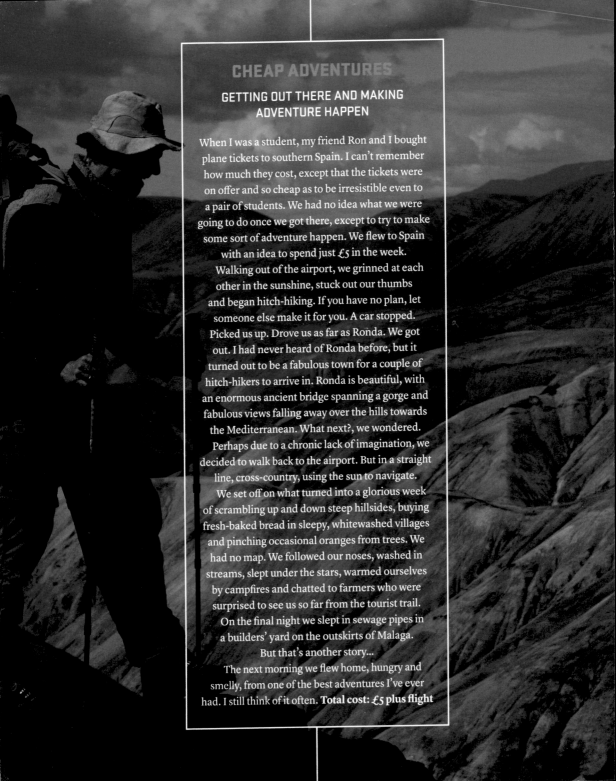

CHEAP ADVENTURES

GETTING OUT THERE AND MAKING ADVENTURE HAPPEN

When I was a student, my friend Ron and I bought plane tickets to southern Spain. I can't remember how much they cost, except that the tickets were on offer and so cheap as to be irresistible even to a pair of students. We had no idea what we were going to do once we got there, except to try to make some sort of adventure happen. We flew to Spain with an idea to spend just £5 in the week. Walking out of the airport, we grinned at each other in the sunshine, stuck out our thumbs and began hitch-hiking. If you have no plan, let someone else make it for you. A car stopped. Picked us up. Drove us as far as Ronda. We got out. I had never heard of Ronda before, but it turned out to be a fabulous town for a couple of hitch-hikers to arrive in. Ronda is beautiful, with an enormous ancient bridge spanning a gorge and fabulous views falling away over the hills towards the Mediterranean. What next?, we wondered. Perhaps due to a chronic lack of imagination, we decided to walk back to the airport. But in a straight line, cross-country, using the sun to navigate. We set off on what turned into a glorious week of scrambling up and down steep hillsides, buying fresh-baked bread in sleepy, whitewashed villages and pinching occasional oranges from trees. We had no map. We followed our noses, washed in streams, slept under the stars, warmed ourselves by campfires and chatted to farmers who were surprised to see us so far from the tourist trail. On the final night we slept in sewage pipes in a builders' yard on the outskirts of Malaga. But that's another story... The next morning we flew home, hungry and smelly, from one of the best adventures I've ever had. I still think of it often. **Total cost: £5 plus flight**

A SHORT WALK IN
THE WESTERN GHATS

I once walked 600 miles across southern India because I wanted a challenge but didn't have the time or money to walk 6,000 miles. I was trying to understand what drives me to go on all these adventures I feel addicted to. In order to understand, I felt I had to push myself really hard...

Head thumping, heat shimmering, sun beating. The loneliness I felt in crowds of foreign tongues, staring at one foreign face. Bruised feet, dragging spirit, bruised shoulders slumped. Can't think. Can't speak. Just walk. The monotony of the open road.

These are common complaints on a difficult journey. I often get them all in a single day, and I know there will be more of the same tomorrow. Most days involve very little except this carousel of discomfort. It doesn't sound like much of an escape.

Yet escape is a key part of the appeal of the road. All my adult life I have felt the need to get away. The intensity and frequency of this desire ebbs and flows but it has never gone altogether. Perhaps it is immaturity, perhaps a low-tolerance threshold. But there is something about rush hour on the London underground, tax return forms and the spirit-sapping averageness of normal life that weighs on my soul like a damp, drizzly November. It makes me want to scream. Life is so much easier out on the road. And so I run away for a while. I'm not proud of that, but the rush of freedom I feel each time I escape keeps me coming back for more. Trading it all in for simplicity, adventure, endurance, curiosity and perspective. For my complicated love affair with the open road.

Escaping to the open road is not a solution to life's difficulties. It's not going to win the beautiful girl or stop the debt letters piling up on the doormat. (It will probably do the opposite.) It's just an escape. A pause button for real life. An escape portal to a life that feels real. Life is so much simpler out there.

But it is not only about running away. I am also escaping to attempt difficult things, to see what I am capable of. I don't see it as opting out of life. I'm opting in. **Total cost: £500, including flight** (Extract from *There Are Other Rivers*)

CROSSING A CONTINENT

With three weeks to spare, my friend Rob and I decided to cycle across Europe. We flew to Istanbul and began riding home. The maths was quite simple: we had to ride 100 miles a day, every single day. We had £100 each to spend (plus money for ferries), which meant a budget of £5 a day.

I remember the stinking madness of the roads of Istanbul. I remember our excitement as we made it out of the city. I remember reaching the Sea of Marmara and how refreshing it felt to run into the water to cool down. Then it was back on the bike and ride, ride, ride.

Cycling 100 miles a day was really tough for me back then and this was a gruelling physical challenge. But that was what we wanted. We were invited into a family's home for strong coffee and fresh oranges. We peered at a dead bear beside the road. I waited for my friend for ages at the top of a winding hairpin pass in Greece. I was annoyed at his slowness. But then he arrived with his helmet full of sweets – like a foraged basket of blackberries – that a passing a driver had given him. Those bonus free calories tasted so good!

I remember the satisfaction of seeing the odometer tick over to '100' each day. I remember the simple fun of finding a quiet spot to camp, in flinty olive groves as the sun set over the sea. Those were good days. **Total cost: £100 plus flight**

IS £1,000 REALLY ENOUGH MONEY FOR AN ADVENTURE?

There is an assumption that adventures have to be expensive. They need not be. This is particularly true if you overcome another assumption: that you have to fly far away in order to have an adventure. Hatching an adventure that begins and ends at your front door is not only cheaper, it's also satisfying. It creates a story that is easier for your friends and family to engage with and get involved with, and it leaves you with fond memories every time you leave your front door in future.

Here's a cursory budget outline to help you start making plans and to realise that trips are neither as complicated nor as expensive as you might fear.

— Boring but important stuff: insurance, vaccinations, first aid supplies: £200.

— Equipment that you don't already own or can't borrow from a mate: £400 will get you a lot of stuff from eBay.

— Costs along the way: ferries, repairs, visas, an ill-advised piss-up in a dangerous but exciting port: £200

— Daily food budget: £5 per day. You could easily live on half this amount, or twice this amount, according to how you like to travel. But £5 will buy you pasta, oats, bread, bananas, veg and a tin of tuna, even in an expensive part of the world. Never pay for water. Just refill your bottles from a tap, purifying the water if necessary.

With £200 remaining, you have enough for 40 days on the road at £5 a day. If you set off from your front door and cycle a pretty leisurely 60 miles a day, and have one day off each week, that still amounts to an impressive 2,000-mile journey. You could cycle from London to Warsaw and back, San Francisco to Vancouver and back, or Copenhagen to Marseille and back. New York to New Orleans and back is a bit far, but York to Orleans is definitely do-able... If you choose to walk, run or swim you won't travel so fast but your equipment costs will be lower so you will have more days on the trail.

You might choose to spend a bit more or a bit less on different things. You'll probably find your own budget spreadsheet to be a little more complicated than mine here. But I hope you are starting to realise that the financial element of an adventure is within your grasp.

So, if you are trying to do a big trip for less than £1,000, I recommend cutting the expense of a plane ticket. Cycle away from your front door on whatever bike you own or can borrow and see how far you get.

However, you can get some great bargains on plane tickets. For example, if you decide to commit £200 of your £1,000 to a plane ticket, a website like Kayak (*www.kayak.co.uk/explore*) shows enticing options of where you can go for that amount of money. Writing this now, I had a look at the website. I could fly from London to Nizhny Novgorod for £190. I have never even heard of Nizhny Novgorod but instantly my mind starts to fill with ideas...

If you are in the fortunate position of even being able to dream of undertaking a big adventure, getting hold of £1,000 may not be the biggest hurdle. After all, it's less money than many holidays, kitchen upgrades, wedding dresses or TVs cost. But not many people have both plenty of money *and* plenty of time (at least not whilst they are still young enough to climb Rum Doodle without their knees hurting).

For many, the scarcest resource in life is time. That is why I wrote *Microadventures*, a book about squeezing local adventures into the confines of real life. Microadventures challenge you to look at how you spend the 24 hours you have each day and to try to re-prioritise things a little bit.

But grand adventures require more than 24 hours. If you're yearning to cross a continent, chasing the days west until the sun sets into the ocean before you, you'll need to find a bigger chunk of time. There is never an easy time to find that time. Too many people are willing to settle for waiting until they retire, and this always makes me sad. The actor Brandon Lee's grave is inscribed with these words:

'Because we don't know when we will die, we get to think of life as an inexhaustible well. And yet everything happens only a certain number of times, and a very small number really. How many more times will you remember a certain afternoon of your childhood, an afternoon that is so deeply a part of your being that you can't even conceive of your life without it? Perhaps four, or five times more? Perhaps not even that. How many more times will you watch the full moon rise? Perhaps twenty. And yet it all seems limitless ...'

Have a look at www.deathclock.com; it's one of my favourite websites! You add various parameters about your life (age, weight, gender, whether you smoke) and it will calculate the date you are likely to die. A big, unstoppable clock begins counting down the remaining seconds of your life.

I have the date of my predicted death scheduled into my diary. Morbid, perhaps, but it takes deadlines to spur most of us into action, and that non-extendable deadline scares the hell out of me. I have so much I want to get done before 8 September 2050!

Life, they say, is what happens while you're busy making plans. Time is ticking, life is short. These days everyone is busy. We're racing time, always chasing time. Bragging about how busy we are is one of our era's favourite things to do. But, as the pithy viral Tweet said, 'We all have the same 24 hours that Beyoncé has.' It's up to us to carve out time to make bootylicious stuff happen. When I was younger I would simply think of a trip, then go and do it. Now that I'm older and busier it's more often a case of making a chunk of time available and then coming up with a plan that fits into that time slot.

There is no simple solution. This book will not solve the lack-of-time conundrum. I'd be rich if it did. But it might get you excited enough to resolve to solve it yourself: to begin the conversations with the people in your life – your family, your boss, yourself – about how it might be possible to pause the racing rhythm of daily life for long enough to do something different and really memorable. After all, each hour that passes, each dreary commute, each bleary Monday morning – these are hours on the hamster wheel that you have spent and will never be able to recoup or spend again. So spend them wisely.

One of my favourite feelings on expeditions is how much time I have. I don't have more time, of course, I've just freed it up to do stuff that feels important to me. I wake at dawn, the diary is empty and the day stretches long before me. I drink tea and watch the sun rise. All I need to do today is make some miles. And then I will sit again, weary but satisfied, in some place I have never been before, and watch the sun set. The days are not busy, but they are full and fulfilling. I cherish spending that time. At home my days feel short and hurried. Yet at the end of most of them I've accomplished nothing memorable. What a waste!

I hope that this book persuades you to find a way to find time to fill your days with what feels important and worthwhile to *you*, not with the stuff that conventional society deems you ought to be doing.

'The sooner you begin to get into this mind-set, the sooner you will have that big juicy chunk of time inked into your diary and the adventure can begin'

The first task is to think carefully about how you use your time now, and how you might be able to make some time for adventure. This isn't about stirring your porridge into your coffee, sleeping in your work suit or other handy tips like that. For a big adventure you'll need to clear a swathe of time – weeks at least, months, maybe even a year or two.

Begin by asking yourself these questions. I know they are hard, but try to answer them as positively as you can rather than instantly dismissing them as impossible in the circumstances of your life.

What is the biggest chunk of time you might be able to carve out for an adventure? Is this long enough to do what you'd like to do? Squeeze another week on at either end. Is that long enough? How much time do you need?

When in the next year might you have time? Can you block off a non-negotiable chunk of time in your diary? It might be quite far in the future, but once it's in the diary you can treat it as sacrosanct.

What are your time constraints? Why can't you go away?

If it's work, do they truly need you all the time? Could your colleagues cope without you for a while? How much loyalty and time do you owe them? Beware of misplaced loyalty. Talk to your boss about how you might be able to free up some time. Don't just second-guess them by saying 'it'll never happen. They can't do anything about it'.

Have the conversation. Tell them how important this is to you, explain the benefits it will have for you and your work performance.

Imagine you were suddenly bedridden for a couple of months. Would the world cope without you? How would it manage? Could you, therefore, bugger off on an adventure for a couple of months without the world collapsing?

Could you take a sabbatical from work? Maybe you could work from the road. If you resigned, could you get your job back when you return? Could you quit, then seek a new job when you return? Or apply for a new job now but agree not to begin the position for a few months?

If you are too financially constrained to stop working, are there ways you can free yourself a little? Can you clear your credit card debts, downsize your house or rent it out, or even take out a loan? Richard Parks' parents re-mortgaged their house to help him accomplish his expedition dream of climbing the Seven Summits and bagging both Poles. Extreme measures, perhaps, but it is important to reflect upon how important this experience is to you. You can get more money in life, but not more time.

On expeditions you often need to take bold, decisive decisions that will have a significant impact on your chances of success or staying alive. You have to be confident, clear-headed and brave enough to back yourself. The wilderness is a place for positive decisions, pushing forwards and making shit happen. The sooner you begin to get into this adventurer's mind-set, the sooner you will have that big juicy chunk of time inked into your diary and the adventure can at last begin.

WISE WORDS FROM FELLOW ADVENTURERS

SEAN, INGRID AND KATE TOMLINSON
CYCLED THE LENGTH OF THE AMERICAS

Kate was eight: the perfect age – old enough to remember and benefit from her experiences, but not yet a reluctant stroppy teenager!

HANNAH ENGELKAMP
WALKED ROUND WALES WITH A DONKEY

Often I'd get people saying, 'Oh, well, I'm glad you're doing it now while you're young, while you can', and they'd be people in their fifties. Sometimes I'd just think, 'Oh, for heaven's sake, you're just giving yourself an easy excuse.'

ROSIE SWALE-POPE
RAN AROUND THE WORLD IN HER SIXTIES.

You're a long time dead, so you might as well get on and do it whilst you are alive!

JAMIE BOWLBY-WHITING
RAFTED DOWN THE DANUBE

It's not the days in the office that we'll reflect upon with nostalgia when we are old.

SARAH OUTEN
TRAVELLED ROUND THE NORTHERN HEMISPHERE BY HUMAN POWER

Treat it as you would any other project. Identify what the project is, break it down into bits and put a time frame on it, then suddenly it can happen. Monitor your progress as you go along and learn stuff on the way. I think so long as you're flexible in that plan and willing to change and adapt, then it's not rocket science.

COLIN WILLOX
BACKPACKED THROUGH EUROPE

People are often paralysed by fear at the difficulties of making an adventure happen ('where will I keep my car?'). There is no perfect time to go. So tie up the loose ends you can in a reasonable time, and leave. It will be messy. You'll screw up. There are no guarantees. Remember that this is what you want, it's why you're going. If you didn't, you would stay home.

PAUL RAMSDEN
TWO-TIME WINNER OF THE PIOLETS D'OR AWARD

It's really hard [to make the time]. I'm busy. It's hard to find the time to get fit. The most important thing is that I get the dates in the diary maybe a year in advance. It's then non-negotiable – if I get work offers or party invites I can then say 'sorry, I'll be in India'. It's a bit brutal. There's no compromise. It's massively important to set those dates, otherwise it would be much easier just not to bother.

ROLF POTTS
CIRCLED THE GLOBE WITH NO LUGGAGE OR BAGS

I'd say that procrastinating about the journey is tied into the core fears that keep us from travelling. We keep thinking that there will be a better time, a time when we have more money or fewer obligations, or when the world feels safer and more open. In truth it doesn't take as much money as most people think, obligations are something we can manage, and the world is far safer than you might think from just watching news headlines.

KIRSTIE PELLING
FOUNDER OF THE FAMILY ADVENTURE PROJECT

We made a decision to go freelance to make time to spend with the children. We started a website to record our adventures. If you voice your ambitions out loud you are more likely to achieve them.

MENNA PRITCHARD
CLIMBER

[Things like time], they're not the reasons – they're the excuses. Aren't they? I really believe that if you want something enough then you will find the time, scrape together the money, and overcome your fears... But it's all about priorities. And I know because I'm completely guilty of it myself. Ever since I became a mum, I have used it as an excuse. An excuse for not having the adventures my heart desires. There comes a time when we have to say to ourselves, 'stop making excuses'. That if something means so much to us then it's worth working towards, it's worth fighting for – and, dammit, it's worth the struggle. I don't want life to be about the battles I never fought, the barriers I never overcame, the excuses I made.

HELEN LLOYD
LONG-DISTANCE JOURNEYS BY BIKE, HORSE, RIVER AND ON FOOT

My job in engineering, although it started as a career, is now a means to an end. It's how I earn money to do the things I really want. I now work short-term contracts, live cheap, save up and plan another journey. For me, the mix of travel and engineering job satisfies all my needs, which I couldn't get from just one.

GRANT RAWLINSON
HUMAN-POWERED EXPEDITIONS BEGINNING AND ENDING ON INTERESTING MOUNTAIN SUMMITS

I have a full-time job as a regional sales manager based in Singapore, travelling around Asia spending lots of time eating very nice meals with customers and staying in beautiful hotels. All of which I do not appreciate as much as a lukewarm cup of instant soup in a freezing snow cave. What is wrong with me?!

SCOTT PARAZYNSKI
ASTRONAUT AND MOUNTAINEER

[A lack of time] can probably be viewed as a cop-out on many occasions. A couple of times in my life, I've had the opportunity to take a leave of absence and do big things. Both my trips to Everest required some creative work-arounds at my day job, banking vacation time, initially. There are all sorts of really cool adventures that can be done on a shorter scale too.

ANT GODDARD
ROAD-TRIPPED ALL OVER THE USA

I have a young kid and a pregnant wife, so I'm in a good position to tackle the regular excuse given by people that 'the timing's not right for adventure now, I'm too busy, life's too complicated.' It's an interesting thought because it's kind of similar to the dilemma of if/when to have kids. The timing will never be perfect. If you wait for the perfect time you'll miss out. Mostly everything you think you can't leave will still be there when you get back, and travelling gives you a lot of time to think about those complications and put them in perspective. There are very few things that are honest blockers to just getting out and having an adventure, no matter how large or small the adventure is. You may feel like there are a lot of 'what-ifs' preventing you doing something adventurous, but the scariest one in my mind has always been 'what if I never go? What if I stay here forever?'

ANDY MADELEY
CYCLED FROM LONDON TO SYDNEY

I realised that we only have this life to get everything done. That outweighed the fear of the unknown and gave me the momentum to bust out from the rut I found myself rolling down.

COMMITMENTS AND
RELATIONSHIPS

This much is true: expeditions have cost me time, money, relationships and messed with sensible life plans and pension prospects. They do not make my life easy. They are selfish. But I do not regret any of them. Indeed, I regret a few that I have not done. Adventures have enhanced my life and – this is important – they have ultimately enhanced most of those things I just mentioned, too, despite the initial pain, suffering, worry, compromise and hassle. In other words, my journeys have been worth it in the long run.

When I set off to cycle round the world I did not have a job or a mortgage. I had no monthly bills to pay. So long as I did not spend all the money I had saved, I was free to do whatever I wanted, wherever I wanted, for however long I wanted. My life was simple. I look back at that younger me with enormous envy!

If you are young, free and single, now is the time to head for the hills and go do something extraordinary. Life will never be so simple again, for you are not yet entangled in the mesh of commitments that grows over the years. Save up a bit of cash, whatever you can manage, and then go do something crazy. It will enhance your CV and teach you more than most expensive tuition fees will ever do. If a future employer isn't more inclined to give you a job because of your experiences then they're not the type you want to be working for anyway. Skip this chapter and go now! You have no excuse.

Money and time constraints make life complicated, but with planning you can free yourself from some of the muddle. Far more binding are our relationships: husbands, wives, boyfriends, girlfriends and families. If your other half is also itching for adventure, then things should be straightforward and exciting. You just need to start saving and start planning today. If you both save £1,000 and are happy to share a tent then you've got double the money and fewer outgoings.

If you're in a relationship and both wish to travel but you have children, adventure planning becomes more complicated. But if your brood are young enough not to have an opinion, or even if they are able to express an opinion but you can still get away with saying 'because I told you so', then adventures are still quite achievable.

Ingrid, Sean and their 8-year-old daughter, Kate, cycled the length of the Americas. Ingrid and Sean were accomplished kayakers and trekkers before they began. This may not appear to benefit a transcontinental cycling journey. But it does in one important way: they knew what life in the wild and on the road was like, and they wanted more of it. They had the appetite. They had momentum and confidence. Theirs was not a standing start. Overcoming the inertia of normal life and generating momentum is very difficult. It can feel overwhelmingly daunting to say 'we are going to change our life. We are going to go and do something big and bold. We will begin on this date. And right now we are going to begin to get ready by doing x, y and z.' It's a lot easier just to put the telly on and watch Bear Grylls.

Ingrid and Sean had to face the challenges of arranging for Kate to miss school, dealing with the concerns of well-meaning friends and family about taking a small girl on a big adventure, and managing their plans to make them compatible with helping an eight-year-old achieve a journey that most adults would be extremely jealous of!

There are challenges and potential difficulties in taking your family down an unconventional route like this, but what an education for Kate! What an achievement! What a glorious shared adventure for the whole family to remember and savour for the rest of their lives. That is worth the hassle.

Perhaps the most potentially difficult scenario is that you desperately wish to travel the world but your other half does not, and cannot be persuaded. If you're lucky you'll be given their blessing and the freedom to head out and do your own thing, reuniting afterwards in a lovely cocktail of happiness, rainbows and fluffy kittens.

But you may have a partner who – wonderful though they may be – does not want to join you on a trip, and does not want you to go either. This is where things get tricky. I'm not sure my dubious Agony Aunt skills will be much help, but I shall try my best!

You'll need to mull over a few questions to help everything proceed as amicably and smoothly as possible. This is a kind, decent thing to do, of course. But it's also your best option for being able to wangle another leave pass to go on an adventure again in the future!

Is it the time away, the money, the risk, the person you'll be going away with, or the inconvenience of being left to juggle everything back home by themselves?

If it's the length of time you will be away that is the problem, can you negotiate something that is acceptable for you both? Make the best of the time you're granted and hatch a plan that is suitably short and sharp. This will rule out cycling round the world, but won't eliminate everything.

After cycling round the world for four years, it took me a while to learn that duration is not the key measuring stick for a 'good adventure'. There are many other ingredients to a great trip, and time is not critical to the recipe. It took me 45 days to row across the Atlantic, and a week to walk round the M25. Both were memorable experiences. I personally feel that six weeks is a good minimum amount of time to do something really significant and rewarding. Jason Lewis suggests six months – but then he did spend 13 years on his adventure! Meanwhile climbers can get up and down something special in a couple of weeks. Ultimately, it's better to do something short than nothing at all.

If it's not so much the absence of your lovely personality that is the problem but the absence of your useful role in sharing life's daily chores, can you think of ways to equal up your balance sheet before or after the trip? Bear in mind that you will be perceived to be in debt on this account for the rest of your life, even long after you feel the debt has been settled! It's the price you'll have to pay.

If money is the stumbling block, work out

between you how much money you can justify spending, then set that as your limit for the trip. You'll still be able to do something great: doing stuff on a daft budget often makes it more fun anyway. Try pointing out how rich Bear Grylls has become from his adventures. Do not mention that almost nobody else has, though!

If it's the risk of the adventure that's causing friction, focus on an idea where the risk (or the perceived risk, at least) is lower. Perceived risk is an interesting concept; people often suggest to me that rowing across the Atlantic in a little boat was very dangerous. But so long as you don't fall off the

boat, it's really not very dangerous at all, for you are in control of most of the risks. Keep the hatches closed, keep yourself tied to the boat: chances are you'll be fine.

You might know that what you are planning is pretty safe, but the person who loves you may not. A little thoughtful compromise in this department need not dampen the adventure. There is an element of risk in every adventure, of course, just as there is some risk in driving to work each day and massive risk in sitting in front of the TV for years until your heart packs in. The most epic adventures *do* entail danger. The most prolific

adventurers *are* selfish. It's up to you to decide where you and your trip are going to lie on the spectrum.

Your choice of expedition partner can be a cause of friction. This is usually for one of two reasons.
1. Your beloved thinks your expedition buddy is a Grade A lunatic who will get you into all sorts of scrapes.
2. Your partner is jealous of your expedition partner, either because you spend waaaaay too much time chatting to each other about your impending adventure and which multi-fuel stove you should buy, or because your expedition partner is worryingly attractive.

Do your best to point out that on an expedition people are smelly, don't change their pants for weeks, and are too tired to want to do anything except sleep when you squeeze into that too-snug tent in an evening after watching the beautiful sunset slip behind the mountains, just the two of you out there, away from the world, nobody within a thousand miles of you... Be aware that whatever you say will be construed as protesting too much. Of course, you can always suggest to your partner that they can solve this particular problem by coming along with you instead!

Finally, failing that, you're going to have to split up. You won't have to endure Pizza Express Couples' Evenings on Valentine's Day ever again. You can do all the adventures that you dream of.

But don't blame me when you're out in the wild, freezing cold, deeply uncomfortable, starving, scared, stinking, lonely and you find yourself questioning your dramatic decision...

WISE WORDS FROM FELLOW ADVENTURERS

SCOTT PARAZYNSKI
ASTRONAUT AND MOUNTAINEER

There are huge personal rewards in exploration, but they aren't always enjoyed by your family, and certainly they worry for you deeply when you go away to do these kinds of things. So there is a certain selfishness, I suppose, in exploration. But if it's done for the right reasons, if there's some social benefit, some educational benefit... I've always tried to have some kind of educational outreach with the things that I've done. There can be some broader good as well. There's nothing wrong with having personal satisfaction with your exploration, either. And when we do go and explore, we come back better people as well. We come back reinvigorated, I think. I came back a better parent, more appreciative of the planet, a better steward of planet Earth.

SATU VÄNSKÄ-WESTGARTH
WHITEWATER KAYAKER TURNED LONG-DISTANCE CYCLIST

[When I was pregnant] the yearning for something, a proper adventure of sorts and the need to hold on to some pieces of the old 'I used to have a life before the kids too' kept burning. 'Are you really going to be away from your kids that long?' It was an inevitable question but one which I wasn't prepared for when it first came my way. Not so many people wondered how *my* main worry, the biking, would go. They wondered how I would survive without the kids. Or the kids without me.

Well, we all survived. I felt more alive than I had for a while, away from the sleep-deprived life of a parent of young kids. I enjoyed being me. Not the mum of so-and-so. Just me. And most mornings I would join my family at the breakfast table at home, virtually, via Skype. 'Mum goes biking

today?' my little girl would ask. Yes, Mum goes biking. And apparently she was going biking too. To be a good parent or a mum, I don't have to be with the family 24-7 every day of the year.

The kids need security, love and an example of how life could be lived. The best example I can give them is the one of the true me, the one who dreams of adventures, and goes after her dreams. The one who comes back excited with stories to tell and then takes the whole family on microadventures.

JAMES CASTRISSION
KAYAKED THE TASMAN AND TREKKED TO THE SOUTH POLE AND BACK

I looked at the managers at work who were five years ahead of me, then the partners who were 10 or 15 years older than me, and I looked at the lives they were living and I thought about what was really important to me. I just couldn't see myself living like that. Conformity has always freaked me out a little bit, so kayaking the Tasman was a way of identifying who I was and what I was capable of doing – and just seeing a bit of the world.

Even at the time, it was the hardest decision I'd ever had to make in my life. If I had to decide now, with a young family, I don't know if I would have had that will.

I come from a Greek family and my mum and dad had invested so much in my education and had it all planned out for me, really. You go to school, you go to uni, get a good job... To turn my back on that was almost like a bit of a slap in the face for them. Not living up to their expectations, no one understood why I was doing it. That's what made it so difficult.

SEAN, INGRID AND KATE TOMLINSON
FAMILY CYCLING EXPEDITION FROM ARCTIC CANADA TO PATAGONIA

Sean, our daughter Kate and I cycled from Arctic Canada to the southern tip of Chile on a single bike and a tandem pulling two trailers. We were always

inspired by the idea of making a very long journey. We wanted arriving somewhere new and unknown to us every evening to become part of our daily lifestyle. We feared that if we left it a few more years Kate would not want to miss out on school and her social life. This has turned out to be one thing that we were dead right about. We are lucky to get her to ourselves for one day every other weekend now and I'm glad we made the most of her pre-teen years!'

Kate offered this perspective on their adventure: 'My parents took me away because they are crazy. They have been taking me off on adventures for as long as I can remember, although this was the longest.

'Some of the toughest parts were also the best. The places where we had the hardest times are the moments we look back on with the fondest memories'

If I hadn't wanted to do it, though, it wouldn't have happened. I always get a say in the plans. I love looking back on the trip and I often think about it. It was just a way of life for two years. Some of the toughest parts of the trip were also the best parts. Like the places where we had the hardest times or felt scared are the moments we look back on with the fondest memories. I think the trip had a positive effect on my work. My Mum did schoolwork with me for about an hour every day and I had her all to myself. My Dad practised times tables with me on the bike and then asked me questions like how long it would take to get to somewhere depending on how fast we were going. As for subjects like geography and history, well, we didn't need books because the real thing was right there in front of me. My advice to other parents if you want to travel with kids is try to do it when they are fairly young. I am 13 now and the idea of going away and leaving

my friends for two years sounds much harder than back then. I think [the idea that children are not tough enough for a big adventure] is rubbish: I can tell you I was a lot tougher than my Mum and Dad!

CHRIS HERWIG
TRAVELLER AND PHOTOGRAPHER

With the arrival of our second child came the opportunity to take leave. A time for caring for our new bundle of joy, feeding him, changing his diapers and rocking him to sleep. But nowhere was it written that this could not also be a time for a bit of adventure. So we sublet our New York apartment and the four of us hit the vagabond road for a sixmonth, eleven-country round-the-world trip.

Over the six months our eleven pieces of luggage slimmed down to a large backpack and a carry-on as we slowly explored the wonders of Vietnam, Cambodia, Burma and New Zealand by train, boat, car, tuk-tuk, foot, bike, elephant and horse. We learned a great deal trying to overcome some of the challenges that came with travelling with two young kids, some of which were scary, some frustrating, but mostly fun. What to pack, where to go next, how to get there, how to make a three-year-old happy, how to keep all of us (especially the baby) safe while also having a bit of fun ourselves and proving the point that life does not have to change completely as soon as kids arrive.

KIRSTIE PELLING
6,000 MILES OF FAMILY CYCLING ACROSS THE GLOBE

An adventure is much more fun when you have kids along – in fact, in our experience they are the key to getting to know the world. They're also often better at things than you are, as we recently found out in the Pyrenees when the kids left us way behind on the mountain.

MARK KALCH
PADDLING THE LONGEST RIVER
ON EACH CONTINENT

Something like the Upper Nile and the Yangtze, which I'll have to paddle, are two rivers that are ridiculously difficult. They have an element of danger. Decisions based on how this might affect my kids or my family will certainly have to be taken. But most of the time I am paddling in nice weather, eating as many chocolate bars as I want to, meeting really cool people and essentially just having a paddling holiday.

PAULA CONSTANT
WALKED FOR THREE YEARS FROM
THE UK TO THE SAHARA

I was married when I left London. My husband and I left together. We walked the first year together. A month into the trip through the Sahara our marriage broke up. Gary left and I continued walking on my own. I don't have a fixed opinion on whether one should do a trip with a romantic partner or not. I think it entirely depends upon the couple, the expedition, and everything. I think there are virtues to both. The first year, it meant the world to me to have a partner to walk with. And I'm not sure to this day whether or not I would have had the courage to leave on my own. Having said that, I was absolutely and utterly frustrated by the time a year had gone past. And, I would say, travel certainly heightens any trouble with a couple.

RIAAN MANSER
ROWED FROM AFRICA TO NEW YORK
WITH HIS WIFE

When I look at the rowing now, I just think that [going solo] would be a step too far for me. On the topic of taking a friend with me: I think I romanticise the idea. I love the idea of taking a buddy, but that buddy would have to be a really good friend because I know what you have to go through. I'm actually glad that I took my wife, Vasti, because we did something special together. If I were to choose again, without a doubt I'd take my wife.

ANT GODDARD
DROVE AROUND THE USA WITH HIS YOUNG FAMILY

I've been able to work remotely while travelling, so some days I'll have to sit in a park or coffee shop working while my wife and son get to enjoy the local sites, but work has been super-flexible and that's definitely helped fund the trip.

GRANT 'AXE' RAWLINSON
HUMAN-POWERED EXPEDITIONS BEGINNING AND
ENDING ON INTERESTING MOUNTAIN SUMMITS

I treated my wife even more like a princess than I normally do until she gave me permission to go on the trip!

MATT PRIOR
DROVE TO MONGOLIA IN A £150 CAR

Family-wise, my dad didn't talk to me for a while. He thought I was being an idiot taking this risk when I had a good career [as a fighter pilot] laid out in front of me. I put this down to a generational thing: he's used to it now and I always come back in one piece so it can't be that bad!

TRAVELLING SOLO
OR WITH COMPANY

Most of my journeys have been solo, but I have
also had many great experiences when travelling
with a friend. If I had to choose, I'd go by myself
for character-building and pride and I'd go
with someone else for fun. Overall, though, I'd
encourage people to be brave and go by themselves.
But which is better? Here are a few thoughts
to help you weigh up the pros and cons of
travelling solo or with company.

ADVANTAGES OF GOING WITH SOMEONE ELSE:

- It's safer.
- It's cheaper (sharing rooms, taxis etc.).
- It's less stressful. You can share the haggling with touts and answering the same questions a million times from curious locals. You can keep an eye on each other's bag while one of you nips into a shop.
- You create shared memories to reminisce over when you are old.
- You have someone to laugh with.
- It's less daunting and scary when heading to strange and unknown places.
- There's less gear to carry. You can share a tent, guidebook and medicine.
- It's easier to ignore the weirdo on the 24-hour bus ride who is determined to sit next to you and tell you their life story.
- It's less boring or lonely.

ADVANTAGES OF GOING SOLO:

- It's more of a challenge.
- You meet more people.
- There's less bickering.
- You can do what you want when you want.
- It's more exciting.
- You're more immersed in the experience.
- You realise you are capable of more than you imagine.
- It's great for self-confidence.
- There's less faff and trivial discussions about what flavour jam to buy.
- There's no scaffolding – you succeed or fail alone.
- The joy of solitude.
- Strangers are kinder to you.
- A sense of real freedom. Arriving in a place where nobody knows a thing about you is liberating.
- A greater sense of achievement.
- There's more peace and quiet, time to think, to read, write and take photos.
- It's easier to tell outrageous lies about your adventures in order to impress others…

SOLO OR WITH FRIENDS? WISE WORDS FROM FELLOW ADVENTURERS

SEAN CONWAY
SWAM THE LENGTH OF BRITAIN,
CYCLED ROUND THE WORLD

I think the benefits of travelling alone include...
The freedom to change plans whenever you like
and you get to live the adventure you want to live.
If I had to choose, I prefer travelling alone
because I often like to do long days, which isn't
for everyone.

SHIRINE TAYLOR
CYCLING ROUND THE WORLD

I think the benefits of travelling alone include...
Learning more about yourself and gaining a sense
of independence. When you are alone you realise
that you can get through any situation. You are also
able to truly figure out who you are and what you
want when you are solely focused on yourself.

Whilst the advantages of going with someone
else include...

It's impossible to explain to an outsider how it
feels to sleep in a slum, or to cycle up a two-day
pass, so it's nice to have someone alongside you
who gets it.

You have someone to cuddle up with at night!

If I had to choose... That's a hard one. I
absolutely love travelling alone and will definitely
be doing more of it throughout my life, but now
that I have found 'my person' I wouldn't give him
up for the world. I think it's important for everyone
to travel alone at least once since it's such an eye-
opening, incredible experience.

ANNA HUGHES
BOTH CYCLED AND SAILED 4,000 MILES
AROUND THE COASTLINE OF GREAT BRITAIN

I think the benefits of travelling alone include...
People tend to offer help more if you are
travelling alone.

Whilst the advantages of going with someone
else include...

Sharing the views makes them more real,
somehow. If I had to choose, I would go alone,
because I am fiercely independent and want
to do things my way! And the satisfaction of
accomplishing something by yourself is wonderful.

JAMIE MCDONALD
RAN 5,000 MILES ACROSS CANADA

I think the benefits of travelling alone include...
Embracing the adventure, and everything around
you more. You only have to focus on one person:
you. Selfishly, that can be nice.

IAN PACKHAM
CIRCUMNAVIGATED AFRICA
BY PUBLIC TRANSPORT

I think the benefits of travelling alone include...
Gaining a much better, deeper insight into and
interaction with locals and local life.
 Whilst the advantages of going with someone
else include...
 Adopting new ideas and picking up new skills
from that person. Sharing costs!
 If I had to choose, I would go alone, simply for the
ease of being able to go without any pre-planning.

DAVE CORNTHWAITE
SKATEBOARDED ACROSS AUSTRALIA

I think the benefits of travelling alone include...
Faster decision-making and less scope for quarrels
or bother.
 Whilst the advantages of going with someone
else include...
 They're always going to be better at me than
some/most of the things I'm capable of, which can
make a difference to certain elements of a trip.
 In the right team, two people can do the work of
three (sometimes six can be less effective than one,
though).
 If I had to choose... I'd go alone. All things
considered, I've enjoyed my solo trips better,
and most of the unhappy memories I have from
my journeys have been due to other people. I've
done two trips with support teams. The first one,
by skateboard, had three vans. I still don't have a

HELEN LLOYD
ADVENTURES BY BIKE, HORSE,
RIVER AND ON FOOT

The advantages of going with someone else
include...
 It's safer to go places that would be difficult
or more dangerous alone.
 If I had to choose, I would go alone because
of the freedom, but it's still easy enough to find
someone to do stuff with if I want to. So it's the
best of both worlds.

driver's licence at the age of 34, but I bought my first three vehicles when I was 26! I don't think I'm ever again going to do a thousand-mile expedition with a big team. It can be quite problematic. So I'm going to keep it small or solo from now on.

SARAH OUTEN
ROWED THE INDIAN OCEAN ALONE

I think the benefits of travelling alone include... You are in charge and you make it happen your own way, at your own pace.

You only have your own cabin farts to endure.

The beauty of solitude and peace is sublime.

Whilst the advantages of going with someone else include...

You do not have to make all the decisions, although compromise is required.

There's someone else to help keep you safe, and having someone to focus on in times of need is a positive thing for me.

If I had to choose... Alone is your journey, in your style, and your pace and you can be totally open to the magic that will happen. Together can be magical, too. For me, it depends on the journey and goal and what's needed to make it happen.

BEN SAUNDERS
SOLO TO THE NORTH POLE AND A 2-MAN RETURN JOURNEY TO THE SOUTH POLE

The hardest thing about solo expeditions – big, long ones – is the knowledge that no one else can ever, or will ever, know what it was like. In some ways, that's very precious and very special, but in other ways, it's frustrating when you try to explain the experience to others.

TOM ALLEN
LONG-DISTANCE CYCLIST AND FILM-MAKER

I think the benefits of travelling alone include...

Allowing your mind to unwind entirely from the utter lunacy of everyday life.

Whilst the advantages of going with someone else include... Having another person there to take photos of you looking heroic.

If I had to choose, I would go alone because an experience that is entirely your own will be a better teacher.

When we – I say 'we' because it was me and my best mate at the start – set off together it gave us the confidence to set off at all. That was definitely the biggest thing about planning it with a friend: we gave each other moral support, we enabled each other to get started. I can't say if I would have done it if I'd been alone. I like to think that I would have done, because my life circumstances at the time were either to go travelling or suffer miserable, unfulfilling office jobs for the rest of my life.

But I did end up on my own as well and the experience couldn't have been more different. Of all the things you could change about an experience, the difference between being alone and being with someone else is the biggest.

I think if someone's too nervous to start something on their own, finding a friend to do it with will definitely help. I would just say be very careful about making sure that the friend has the same overall expectations for what the trip's about, because it's when people have differing expectations that things start getting difficult.

JASON LEWIS
FIRST HUMAN-POWERED CIRCUMNAVIGATION OF THE WORLD

Travelling alone is wonderful because you can do exactly what you want. If you want to travel or you want to ride your bike five miles and then stop and take the rest of the day off, you can. I've travelled

alone for long periods, and I think I've come to the conclusion that I'm not very good on my own, I actually unbalance.

I do prefer to be at least with one other person. Three is the ideal number, I think, because you get to share the experience. When you're on your own, it can become quite morbid, but it's a little too indulgent, I think. After about a month of being alone, you have no real way to appreciate, perhaps, what you're seeing, what you're experiencing, because you don't have another mirror near to you to reflect some of what you may be taking for granted.

LEON MCCARRON
LONG-DISTANCE CYCLIST, WALKER, FILM-MAKER

I think the benefits of travelling alone include... The vulnerability of a solo traveller often encourages more people to come and speak to you, while a pair or a group can look self-sufficient.

Whilst the advantages of going with someone else include...

Having a creative and decision-making sounding board, another perspective and opinion, and someone to see things you may be blind to.

If I had to choose, I would go with someone else because I like the company, and as someone who tries to film adventures, having a second person is invaluable logistically and creatively. I have no real

desire to do very long trips on my own anymore. When I was young and wanted to prove myself (to myself and to the world) I needed to travel alone, but now I mostly find myself very dull.

STEVE DEW-JONES
HITCH-HIKED THE AMERICAS

I think the benefits of travelling alone include: More space to think. Learning to be alone.

I find travelling solo quite lonely. Whenever I go somewhere new, I want to be able to share my thoughts with someone and to see if they feel the same way about the place. And I hate eating alone.

MATT PRIOR
ADVENTURER, FORMER FIGHTER PILOT

I think the benefits of travelling alone include:

Freedom to attach or detach yourself to or from groups without any ill-feeling. It's easier to take risks.

Whilst the advantages of going with someone else include:

You don't have to always introduce yourself and tell people the same story day in, day out: this gets old after a while.

If you're on a road trip, it's definitely worth going with a friend. Saying that, this can make or break your trip, so choose carefully. Doing a trip with someone else can create a very strong bond for life, but I have also known of best friends return and never speak again. There are people all over the place who are keen for randomness, so don't think if you can't find someone straightaway that you're going to be lonely!

TIM MOSS
MOUNTAINEER, ADVENTURER, CYCLIST

I think the benefits of travelling alone include:

For me, travelling solo is a much more powerful experience. That sounds a bit melodramatic but there's something about being on your own all the time, making every little decision by yourself and living through all these experiences without anyone around with whom you can share them.

Whilst the advantages of going with someone else include...

The highs and lows are mellower by virtue of being shared and, generally, I'd say it is easier and a lot more fun.

If I had to choose... I don't think recommending one over the other is illuminating. If you want to test yourself, push yourself and have a deeper experience, I'd suggest going solo. If you'd rather enjoy yourself (assuming you have a good partner) and have your problems halved, go with someone else.

OLLY WHITTLE
CANOED DOWN THE MEKONG

I do most of my adventures alone and I think it's actually more of a challenge to do them in a group, so that's what I might plan next. Also, I think a pair is completely different from alone and a group. A pair may fall out big time, which I think is less likely in a three or more.

I think the benefits of travelling alone include:

It's easier to actually get started.

No responsibilty for others' safety (if you mess up, it's only you that's in trouble).

You don't have to worry whether everyone is enjoying themselves (adventures are rarely pure fun).

It's scarier, there's a bigger sense of stretching yourself.

If I had to choose for my next adventure, I would go in a group because I've already done loads alone so it will give me new challenges. I probably wouldn't choose a pair.

DOM GILL
CYCLED THE AMERICAS ON A TANDEM,
PICKING UP PASSENGERS EN ROUTE

I still love the idea of doing solo journeys. There is
something very viscerally primeval about them. I
like the introspection. And actually, I become a little
addicted to the sort of low-level depression that I
experience on those trips. You get very lonely, and
when you're lonely, you think very profoundly about
all sorts of aspects of life. It may be depressing, but
I'm able to think creatively and write and expand
upon ideas. I love that aspect of solo travel. And
there's always the bravado aspect of getting through
it, getting through to the other side and talking
about the fact that you did it on your own. Especially
as a male, I think that's a little attractive. Doing
stuff with companions ,I think, is more conducive
to learning life lessons. Having to mix with all these
new people who moments ago were strangers gives
me a very refreshing understanding of people.
And I like to think that increases my ability to
communicate with the world around me.

COLIN WILLOX
BACKPACKED ROUND EUROPE

There is an unwritten bond between lone
travellers. It's called 'Holy shit, let's be friends',
and its participants are not those who turn their
head away when you walk in the door, but the ones
who keep looking and maybe flash you a smile. You
make friends so fast on the road. It's unbelievable.

ANDREW FORSTHOEFEL
WALKED 4,000 MILES ACROSS THE USA

I felt less lonely than I thought I would. But there
were times, of course, when I felt lonely, when
you're having these moments of, 'Oh my God, I
can't believe I'm experiencing this' and I don't get
to share it with anybody. I think maybe as human
beings there's this natural desire to communicate
and tell our stories to each other and revel in these
experiences together. Not being able to do that
in the moment was hard sometimes. But I think
it made those moments when you could share
something with somebody much more special.
I think the solitude and sometimes loneliness –
but just that aloneness – really accentuated those
times when I was hanging out with people.

JESSICA WATSON
SAILED SOLO ROUND THE WORLD, AGED 16

Sharing adventures with friends is really amazing

NIC CONNER
CYCLED FROM THE UK TO JAPAN FOR £1,000

My friend gave up in Russia. We're still really good mates. It doesn't really matter how fit you are, it's the mental determination, and I think he wasn't as committed as I was. He did well – he cycled to Russia and then he cycled home. In the time it took me to get from Moscow to Tokyo, he had cycled home via southern Europe, met a girl, moved in with her and started a business with her. John was an experienced cyclist and had done a lot of tours so it was great to have him around, especially in the first couple of months. But, if it was tomorrow, I'd start by myself.

JAMES CASTRISSION
KAYAKED THE TASMAN SEA

Some advice I got back when I was having a big difficult patch with [my expedition partner] Jonesy, a friend said to me, 'Look, even if you are responsible for 80 per cent of the project, 80 per cent is not going to get you to the start line.' And that's with me operating 24 hours a day. So if Jonesy only did 20 per cent that was enough. But on the trip itself, that's really where Jonesy's strong point is. He more than made up for everything out on the trip itself.

and a good way to get to know someone well, but there's also something very special about having an adventure all to yourself. Maybe it's a little selfish but there's something wonderful about a special moment being all yours.

TIM HOBIN
PADDLED THE GANGES IN A £50 KAYAK

When I think back now, highlights include pushing off onto the river through the cool and fragrant early morning mist as the sun rose and the delicious solitude that solo travel brings.

KYLE HENNING
TRAVELLED FROM THE LOWEST POINT IN AFRICA TO THE HIGHEST

I called the trip a 'solo' expedition, but part of why I did it was to meet people whom I would end up depending on. Welders, mechanics, waiters, drivers and simply kind-spirited people along the way made the expedition possible. I didn't realise it until afterwards, but I was seeking that connection in my life.'

IT MIGHT BE EASY FOR YOU, BUT FOR ME...

'It's OK for you to go off on these big adventures,' I sometimes hear people cry. 'I'm not as male, fit, rich, young or handsome as you.'

OK, I made the last bit of that sentence up, but the rest I do regularly hear. And it's probably not a coincidence that most of the people who do really big, really crazy adventures are male, fit, young, single and not poor.

But I do believe that anyone can do big and bold journeys. I *know* that you do not need to be athletic, brave or rich, for I am none of those things myself!

Women frequently ask my opinion on whether an expedition is suitable for a female to do. Here are reflections on that subject from some of the adventurers I interviewed who are more qualified than me to answer:

HANNAH ENGELKAMP
WALKED ROUND WALES WITH A DONKEY

Partly, I think that if you go out into the world wide-eyed and enthusiastic and smiley, people respond in that way. Nothing bad happened to me but, you know, I was in Wales and there are much scarier places that one could adventure.

CANDACE ROSE RARDON
DROVE AN AUTO-RICKSHAW 1,900 MILES ACROSS INDIA

What I say to other women who are thinking about going travelling on their own is, 'The concerns never go away. You never stop thinking about things that could go wrong.' You know, I really enjoy it. I think being on my own is an invitation for people to connect with me. I think when they see a woman on their own, people generally want to help you and protect you.

SHIRINE TAYLOR
TWO-YEAR CYCLE TOUR THROUGH ASIA AND SOUTH AMERICA

As a woman you may be afraid to embark alone, either camping or to a foreign country, but once you begin you realise just how much easier it is for us girls. The reason I have been taken in by countless families in every country is because the women in those countries don't see me as a threat, but as a friend. I absolutely love adventure, and being a female will only spur me on, not stop me.

KERRY O'NEILL
RODE THE 'GRAND TOUR' FOR A GRAND

I am quite a wuss but because I did this one thing one time, now people think I am some kind of intrepid explorer, and I am truly not. I thought I would be scared camping on my own. That was my main fear, but it turns out that I wasn't at all. It was always somewhere gorgeous. Food was basic because I was on a budget, but having some peace and quiet at the end of a night in a tent was absolute bliss and I didn't worry about kidnap or anything.

TEGAN PHILLIPS
CYCLED THROUGH SPAIN AND AFRICA

Being female was sometimes helpful and sometimes infuriating. People were definitely more willing to let me into their homes and help me when I needed help – I think if I had been a guy people would have been a little more suspicious. This is the upside of gender stereotypes. At the beginning there were times when I felt like there were certain things that I couldn't or shouldn't do because I was a girl travelling alone and that feeling was incredibly frustrating. I had one really terrible harassment experience and I was a bit shaken after that, but as I grew more confident in terms of figuring out how touring and camping actually worked it became much less of an issue.

Otherwise, being female had nothing to do with anything – it turns out adventuring has no gender.

ROSIE SWALE-POPE
RAN ROUND THE WORLD

It's rubbish! For any age, any gender, some things are more doable than others. But I believe that a woman travelling alone is safer. You have to obey the laws of the wild, certainly – to be polite and tidy, to pay your own way, to act unafraid. I've had murderers in Siberia teach me how to light fires. I've been to places far too dangerous for men to travel to – they'd have been shot. But I'm not a

threat, so again and again I have been OK. And I'm happy, too, and that radiates to people. There are lots of great lady travellers – Freya Stark and so on – it's not a man's game. Life is anybody's game. Whatever you choose to do, you just need to start. I met a man recently; he was longing to travel and I just said, 'Go on then! Get going!'

SARAH OUTEN
CYCLED, KAYAKED AND ROWED ROUND
THE NORTHERN HEMISPHERE

I guess I do meet women, quite a lot of women, who ask, 'Is it safe? Did you feel safe? I can't do it', and I think, compared to guys, women are often held back by the negative chatter. Mostly people are very friendly and keen to help you. There are no hurdles to stop people having adventures, apart from being dead, really. I think that's true of anything in life, isn't it?

PAULA CONSTANT
WALKED THE SAHARA WITH CAMELS

Being a woman is an advantage. In many, many cultures around the world it will help, so don't be afraid to be a woman. Don't get me going on this! But one thing that many women do in adventure is try to compete with the boys. Well, we're women. We travel differently. Embrace it. In most parts of the world, it works to your advantage to be not only a woman, but a beautiful woman, as feminine as you like. Don't play on that. Don't be a victim, but rather, stand in your magnificence, I would say. Nomadic cultures have nothing but the greatest of respect for strong women. If you can remain smiling and gentle, but strong at the same time, you are at a distinct advantage to your male equivalent, whom the local men will see as a threat. They'll see you as something to be fascinated by. And that can usually be an advantage. Yes, occasionally you're going to be sexually harassed, like every other day. But it all comes down to how you deal with that. And dealing with it, the biggest piece of advice I would give you is the same the world over. You're polite and civil, but you're much like a Jane Austen novel, with Mr Collins, you know, you're polite but firm.

HELEN LLOYD
CYCLED THE LENGTH OF AFRICA

I find it amazing that in today's society we still make such a differentiation between the sexes. What I do is no more dangerous than if I were a man. Mostly, the risks are the same and as long as you take sensible precautions (as anyone would when travelling) then there shouldn't be any problems. Of course, you may get unlucky and end up in the wrong place at the wrong time, but being a woman shouldn't make any difference. The only additional risk as a woman, is that of 'unwanted advances' from men, but that isn't necessarily a problem confined to the realms of travel. Actually, in many ways, I think being a woman is an advantage. Most people in this world are good and want to help. Perhaps they see me as a woman and think I may need help, or protecting. As a woman, I am sure I appear more approachable, less intimidating, than a man. And in some cultures, being a woman means you'll be invited into all kinds of situations that a man never would.

JESSICA WATSON
AROUND THE WORLD SOLO SAILOR

I like to think of myself as first a person and second a girl. Maybe it's because I'm young and grew up in a family that never treated my sisters and me any differently to my brother. But I struggle to understand why women shouldn't go on as many adventures as men.

Some of the most inspiring people I spoke to were elderly. Granted, their physical fitness may be beyond the norm for 'old-age pensioners', but their enthusiasm and spirit are inspirational for anyone who fears that their adventuring years may be behind them:

KU KING
EXPLORING THE PLANET WITH A PROGRESSIVELY SMALL BACKPACK

One of the things that we have noticed in many years of travel is the increasing number of older independent travellers on the road. Travel is no longer the domain of gap-year students. There are people of all ages out there creating their own unique adventures all around the planet. Nowadays, the economic situation means that redundancy (often with an attractive financial package) is an option for many. Instead of investing in a new kitchen or adding a conservatory, some people are grabbing life by the throat and booking year-long round-the-world tickets. When you are in your twenties, the years stretch ahead of you like a blank canvas. You have all the time in the world. When you hit your forties, and more so your fifties, you become aware that time is limited. We still have an abundance of travel dreams to realise, and we are determined to make them come true before arthritis sets in!

ROSIE SWALE-POPE
RAN ROUND THE WORLD IN HER SIXTIES

Age is one of the worst things. Most of my friends now are younger than my daughter. But as people get older they need to ask themselves 'who am I?' and 'what do I want?' Life is not a rehearsal! People just give up. There are so many real barriers in life that we should stop making false ones. Don't make yourself get stuck. It's a well-off people's problem: poor people in the world just get on with life when they are older. We give up. Of course, people are different biologically and there's a reality to ageing. When Paula Radcliffe is old she won't be able to run as fast, but she can do something different and amazing instead. I'm 68, but I'm overjoyed to be the age I am, to be who I am. You can be 21 *and* 68. I haven't grown up yet!'

SVEN YRVIND
75-YEAR-OLD SAILOR, ONCE SAILED ROUND CAPE HORN IN A 20-FOOT BOAT

When I was young I worked 8am to 10pm on my projects. But I'm getting older now, so I am slower. But that's OK: I am enjoying building the boat. It's interesting. I'm more knowledgeable now, more patient as well. The mind wanders. I try new things [design details for the boat]. They often don't succeed. I try again, I try something else.

At the opposite end of the spectrum, young people often worry that they are too inexperienced to set out on a big journey. Everyone needs to begin somewhere, though, and these adventurers demonstrate that age is no barrier to accomplishing extraordinary feats:

TEGAN PHILLIPS
CARTOONIST AND CYCLIST

I am 21. I think my age actually worked to my advantage because, for me anyway, one of the biggest parts of adventuring is *un*learning a lot of things that you didn't even realise you had been taught. A lot of the time I would think things like, 'Oh no, I can't wash my hair in a restaurant bathroom, it just isn't done'. And then I would think, 'why the hell not?' Where did I even get all of these silly ideas from in the first place?

ANDY WARD
WALKED ACROSS EUROPE, FROM THE UK TO ISTANBUL

You've got to start somewhere. You don't need experience. Everyone has walked a certain distance, chatted to random people they meet along the way and set up a tent in the ditch, or asked a farmer to camp in their field. It's just a case of getting up and getting on with it. I'd been a little worried about getting a job afterwards until I was halfway through my walk and I got two emails from two different investment banks in London. Both asked me to come and work for them. I've never applied for a job with a bank before. They had just heard about the walk and the blog, and they got in touch. I spoke to them and said, 'Why on Earth would you want me? You don't even know my CV or anything else.' They said, 'We've got enough Cambridge students. We want interesting people. We want people who can talk to clients and talk about interesting things.'

SARAH OUTEN
ROWED THE INDIAN OCEAN

I guess there's a bit of naivety that comes in at the age of 21. You think you can take on the world, all of these things. I saw it very simplistically. I can't think what the right word is, but I looked at other big expeditions and I thought, 'Well, this isn't rocket science. It's just a big project and if I chopped that project down then I can make it happen.'

JESSICA WATSON
SAILED SOLO ROUND THE WORLD

It's incredible how low our expectations of young people can sometimes be. As I was preparing to sail around the world I constantly came up against people who just assumed that a young girl couldn't do such a thing. I don't know why we automatically think something's not possible rather than looking at how it might be achieved.

ANDREW FORSTHOEFEL
WALKED ACROSS THE USA

I graduated from college with a ton of questions, unsure of what I wanted to do, and figured I'd try to create around myself a situation that would help me engage those questions. I thought I might go abroad for a little bit but then I got fired from a job and didn't have the money I thought I would have. So I figured I'd just start walking and keep it simple. I wore a sign that said, 'Walking to Listen'. The idea was to get people curious and hopefully they'd stop and share a story or a piece of advice. And that was pretty much it. I had a few basic rules: walk every mile that was possible to walk. And camp out more often than not because that's all I could afford.

Jessica Watson

BELINDA KIRK
ROWED AROUND BRITAIN

I had towed the line, worked hard at school and felt that I had done what I was obliged to do for my parents, friends, society, etc. So, completely against my parents' wishes, I told them I was going to Africa to study monkeys and have an adventure for a year before getting back on society's merry-go-round and going to university and all that jazz. It was without doubt the best step I've ever taken, bar none.

Some people say the first step is the hardest. I think it can also be the easiest. Because really it's a no-brainer if it's what you want to do more than anything else. I started as part of an organised expedition. I paid to be there – when you have zero experience to offer anyone then I think you should expect to pay to build that experience. I also knew I wanted to be part of some zoological fieldwork and couldn't have done anything meaningful on my own.

KELLY DIGGLE
CYCLED A LAP OF ICELAND

I panicked at the realisation that, age 22, I was settling down to a life of conformity. It had just become a norm. I turned my back on pouring coffee for a living, sold the car, waved goodbye to my relationship and left Cornwall. I had no idea where I was headed. All I knew was that I had this burning desire to do something. I wanted to travel, to absorb culture, to meet all sorts of people and to purposely step outside of my comfort zone. After all, I was young, commitment-free and, let's face it, a little bit naive. So far in my experience, these three things have favoured me extremely well.

SVEN YRVIND
PLANNING TO SAIL ROUND ANTARCTICA

My advice for young people considering their first adventure is, don't trust the grown-ups! You need courage. You have to be a rebel.

A few years ago I rowed from England to France with Phil Packer, a disabled soldier. Two contrasting memories stand out from that experience. The first was that so many things that are easy for me – that I do not even think about – are either difficult or impossible for disabled people. Daily life is so much harder. On the other hand, disabled people are used to discomfort and difficulty, and this is perfect expedition training! I was on that row in order to help Phil, but I was so seasick that I was actually pretty useless and Phil did just about everything for me! If you think that your physical condition may limit your adventurous ambitions, read these interviews:

JIMMY GODDARD
HAND-CYCLED UP KILIMANJARO

About a month after the rock-climbing accident which left me paralysed from the chest down I was lying in my bed in Stoke Mandeville Hospital. What I really wanted more than anything else was to get back into the mountains and the open air and away from the 'disability' that surrounded me at Stoke Mandeville. Having a massive challenge to focus on again really got me moving forward. Travelling to Massachusetts to test-ride the bike and then later to Arizona to train with a friend on the moonscape terrain similar to Kilimanjaro, plus training here in the UK, gave me that sense of purpose and focus that I really enjoy. This was extremely cathartic after the accident. So many people have done so many extraordinary things these days that it's nearly impossible not to find somebody who has done something similar to what you might be planning. So get on the internet and look for inspiration. Don't be shy. Approach people and get advice. Most adventurers I've met make a point of being really helpful to new people trying to get into the scene. And finally, dream big but start small; learn the processes – kit, funding, planning – and work your way up to something epic!

KAREN DARKE
TWO DECADES OF EXPEDITIONS BY BIKE, SEA KAYAK AND SIT-SKI

I have no idea how my life would have been if I hadn't ended up paralysed all those years ago. Certainly I'm sure I would have got more into climbing and big mountain/greater range stuff, but who knows? It's a bit like that film *Sliding Doors* where one decision or incident totally changes the course of your life. I can't know what direction my life would have gone in if I had survived the climbing accident with my spine intact. The stuff I've done since becoming paralysed has been about who I am deep down as a person – with a love of adventure, sport and the outdoors. I think people find it more surprising or inspiring or something because I happen to be paralysed. But for me I just feel fortunate to still be able to do things I love (albeit in an alternative way), and for great friends and companions without whom most of the adventures I've experienced would never have been possible. There was a time when I was first paralysed when pushing my wheelchair around the hospital grounds was a big adventure (no joke) – kind of a mini-expedition. When I've felt really daunted by a forthcoming adventure, I find it helpful to write down all my fears of likely problems. Then I try to think of one thing I can do, no matter how small or silly it might seem, to make myself feel more optimistic. For example, on the expedition skiing across the Greenland ice cap, I bought a fish-tank thermometer which has two temperature gauges, so that I could keep an eye on the temperature of my foot and my hip [as I have no feeling there, I cannot know if they are becoming cold], and reduce the risk of getting frostbite. I also carried a rape alarm in case we met polar bears as I understood they don't like loud noises and I felt the most vulnerable of the team. Maybe they were crazy solutions, but they built my confidence, helped me overcome some fears and therefore made the whole adventure seem just a bit less daunting.

Many of the people I spoke to are serial adventurers – they've been doing this stuff for years and may even be able to make a living out of what they do. But everyone has to begin somewhere. We were all novices once. If you have not done a big trip before, don't be disheartened or feel that you need to limit your ambitions. Many, if not most, of the people I've chatted to in this book had very little idea what they were getting themselves into at the beginning. If you have the nerve to begin, the nous to learn and the capacity to persevere, you'll probably achieve whatever journey you set your mind to.

NIC CONNER
CYCLED TO JAPAN ON £1,000

The year before I went to cycle a bit of the Ridgeway – that was one overnight – but that was my only experience. It was quite a spur-of-the-moment thing to do. I like my sport, but I wouldn't call myself athletic. I certainly carry a bit of weight. You know, I have love handles, I like drinking beer, I quite like a burger now and then. I wouldn't say I have a nutritionist or am out at 5am every morning training.

INGRID, SEAN AND KATE TOMLINSON
CYCLED THE AMERICAS

Other than buying the bikes and trailers and our tickets, we pretty much made up the rest as we went along. I think with a trip like this there's only so much preparation you can do. If you waited until you were 100 per cent ready, and had researched everything you needed to know, you would probably never set off! We didn't have enough money to buy fancy cycling gear. When we first packed the trailers and pannier bags (in Inuvik itself!) we realised that we were hopelessly overloaded and had to give half our gear away.

TEGAN PHILLIPS
CYCLED THROUGH SPAIN AND AFRICA

I had no experience, no GPS, no set route, no sense of direction, no foresight and no coordination, which meant that I spent more time than not with absolutely no idea where I was. I fell off my bike at least once a day. I was attacked by wasps and thorn bushes and stationary poles. We never spent more than one night in any place. We camped under bridges, on private property (with permission), on private property (without permission), with friends of friends of friends, with people who just happened to be there when we couldn't go on any more. But in the end I turned up in Alicante, which shows that if I can do it then anyone can. All you really need to do is this: Cycle. Eat. Sleep. Repeat.

MATT EVANS
TRAVELLED OVERLAND FROM THE UK TO SAIGON

I guess that if I was giving anyone advice on how to make the trip of a lifetime happen, it would be to take a deep breath and do something concrete that means it has to happen. We can all talk about what we want to do and make it sound convincing, but until you've actually passed a tipping point to make it happen – something that can't be undone – then it's all just dreams and window-shopping. Personally, I find dreams unfulfilling and window-shopping frustrating. So, take the plunge. Do something permanent and immovable. Once you've done that, you'll find a way to make the rest fall into place.

OLLY WHITTLE
PADDLED THE MEKONG AND CROSSED FROZEN LAKE BAIKAL ON FOOT

I set out utterly bricking it. I had pretty much no canoeing experience. I hadn't been able to find a life vest and I had no idea if my canoe was river-worthy. It felt pretty unstable and it leaked more than I thought it should do. But I had half an old plastic carton to bail it out with – which later also served as a urinal on the go. The feeling of saying 'here goes nothing!' impossible to replicate back at home in our normal, sanitised, risk-free lives.

JAMIE BUNCHUK
LIVED WITH INDIGENOUS HUNTERS IN TAJIKISTAN AND MONGOLIA

The single most practical thing a person can do to make an adventure happen is to book their flights to that country. Then you're committed; everything else you'll just have to work out and hopefully get right. Don't wait for everything to be nailed down to the last detail before you commit, because an adventure can never be completely planned. At some point you're just going to have to jump into the deep end. Book the trip and you've already made the leap.

MARTIN HARTLEY
FOUR EXPEDITIONS TO THE GEOGRAPHIC NORTH POLE

It all happened by complete accident. I just seemed to get on this road and just kept on it. I entered an outdoors writing competition. The prize was to win a trek to Everest Base Camp. I was too late to post my entry so I cycled round to the given address to hand it in. I expected some old biddy man to open the door. And this skinny kid called Paul Deegan opened the door and he invited me in for a cup of tea. I was subsequently invited to the expedition HQ for an interview and it was only years later that Paul told me that my essay was poor but that he had

suggested to the expedition leader that the team needed a photographer and that I was a good bloke who could take pictures. That's how I got on to my first expedition. I sold all my photo developing equipment to pay for my flights to be on the trip.

JAMIE MCDONALD
RAN ACROSS CANADA

I really don't plan. I'm the naive one. I think that anywhere we go there are people there who live in that environment who will have the gear to survive there, so I just don't think about it. I don't look into brand clothing, I just go. That's kind of why I stuck a superhero outfit on. And people were great. They'd turn up on the side of the road giving me trainers, giving me warm clothes, to make sure I was all right, because I do it quite stupidly.

JAMIE BOWLBY-WHITING
RAFTED THE DANUBE

You don't need to know where you'll sleep, where you'll find food: all you have to do is keep going and you will find something. We must all stop worrying, because when we are scared, we put things off and end up doing nothing of value. I did this for much of my life. You do not need expensive equipment, past experience or excessive amounts of planning. All you need is a little bit of desire and the commitment to take that first step.

LIAM MARTIN
RODE A PIZZA DELIVERY BIKE TO GREECE

We tried to plan it. We'd get together with a few beers and pretend to plan. We did that quite a lot. We'd end up just talking rubbish. We rode down to Dover and it took us about seven hours. We weren't prepared for that at all. We got there and were like, 'Bloody Hell, this is going to take forever.' And that was definitely a reason for it working as well as it did because it meant that we had no expectations.

HATCH A PLAN

So you've decided you want to do a big journey. You've begun saving. You've allocated time in your calendar for the trip. Your family and boss know that you're doing it. Nothing is standing in your way. You have permission to smile smugly at this point.

What happens next? Well, next you need to work out what you are going to do and where you will go. It's time to make a plan.

You may already know exactly what you want to do – perhaps it was a childhood dream or something you've been mulling over for ages. If so, skip this chapter and get working on your to-do list.

But for many, the yearning for adventure comes before having any idea of what you want to do. Until you know something about travel and adventure it can be hard to work out what you want from your trip, or what ingredients are needed to cook up a decent journey. This was certainly true for me when I started out. I knew nothing about the practicalities of making an adventure happen. I didn't really know the ways in which my adventure would differ by heading to different parts of the world. I didn't know very much at all.

I knew only that I wanted to head far away from everything that was familiar. I wanted to do something physically difficult. I had no specific skills I could draw on. Wild places appealed to me, rather than cities. And it needed to be cheap. I didn't really care what I did: I just wanted to do *something*!

How then do you begin to narrow down your choices when the whole world is beckoning? I said that I had no idea what I wanted to do, but in fact, if you look again, I actually had quite a few parameters in place without realising. Though the world is huge, it's pretty easy to cut down your options:

I wanted to head far away from everything that was familiar. This ruled out exploring the UK or Europe.

I had no specific skills; so no climbing technical mountains then.

I wanted to do something physically difficult; so no vehicles or hitch-hiking.

Wild places appealed, rather than cities.

It needed to be cheap. That eliminated ocean and polar journeys. It also made sense not to do the trip in developed countries.

I could therefore write down my thoughts more clearly than I realised:

I wanted to do something difficult, but non-technical, in Africa, Asia or South America. It probably would be on foot or by bicycle.

I'd already been to Africa. Asia has better food than South America. Cycling sounded preferable to walking. And so, without much difficulty at all, I'd narrowed down my plan to cycling in a remote part of Asia.

It is important not to fret about all the adventures that get away. The previous paragraph, explaining the thought process that went into deciding on my bicycle ride along the Karakoram Highway, might sound glib and too easily dismissive of a thousand other opportunities. But looking from another angle, it was a series of decisions based upon both pragmatism and aspiration that led to one of the best rides I have ever done. Don't worry about the ones that get away. That's a mug's game. I think often, and very fondly, of cycling over the 15,000-foot Khunjerab Pass border crossing between Pakistan and China. I could have done a hundred different rides instead of that one. Who cares? What matters is that I did something that I will always remember.

To help narrow down the sort of adventure that might best suit you, try answering the questions below. If you are planning to do the trip with someone else, get them involved now too.

If you already know the person you will be doing your trip with, take them to the pub and discuss the questions over a couple of beers and some pork scratchings. (I know I said in a previous chapter that you should stop going to the pub in order to start saving, but let's call this occasion a Vital Expedition Meeting, and therefore permitted.)

It is really important to be clear about your plans and goals for a trip before you begin. Dissonance and disagreement brew on journeys when your goals are not aligned.

— What is the maximum amount of money you'll be able to get hold of?
— How much money are you willing to live on each day? An honest assessment of the standard of living you are willing to endure is vital for working out how far you can go on the money you have available. Do you need a hotel and a pizza once a week? If so, you will probably be cleaner and plumper than someone willing to endure instant noodles in a ditch every night, but your trip will also be shorter.
— Are you up for the gruelling, lengthy battle of seeking sponsorship to supplement your funds? If not, you'll need to wave *sayonara* (for now) to oceans, Everest and Antarctica (unless you are considerably richer than most of the adventurers you'll meet on your travels).
— How much time do you have available for your trip?
— Do you wish to travel alone, with a friend, or in a group? Why?
— Do you want to travel quickly and go a long way, or would you prefer to have a more relaxed schedule with spare time factored in? Why?
— Do you want a motorised adventure (cars and motorbikes), a travelling experience (trains and hitch-hiking) or something human-powered? Why?
— Do you want to have fun (don't cycle through Siberia in the winter; do cycle through Sicily in the springtime), or do you want to punish yourself for some unknown sin in a former life and have a masochistic misery-fest in the speculative hope that at some point in an unknowable future this will make you happy? Are you searching for Type 1 Fun or Type 2 Fun? Why?
— Which appeals most: bicycles, walking, running, kayaking, rafting, climbing or something else altogether? Why? Which of those appeals least? Why?
— Which parts of the world appeal to you most? Which appeal less? Why?
— Which environments and climates appeal to you most? Which appeal least? Why?
— What time of the year can you travel? This will add some direction to where you can go, depending on what weather you're looking for. You can find summer or winter any day of the year, but only in certain places.
— Do you see this trip as a lifestyle choice (cancel your rent, quit your job, cycle into the sunset), or as a burst of madness away from the humdrum real world we spend most of our lives in (or should that be a burst of reality away from the mad world we spend most of our lives in?), in which case something shorter and more dramatic is probably a good choice?
— Do you have any useful skills? Are you a medic or can you crew a yacht? Can you earn money along the way somehow? Are you a magician, a mechanic, a linguist? Does learning something new appeal to you as part of the plan?
— Are you looking for the heady excitement of a world-first journey? Why? If so, you'll need primarily to think of something that appeals to the media rather than to you. Are you looking for something that is difficult and groundbreaking but meaningful only to you? If so, you can come up with any idea, so long as it gets you so excited that you lie awake at night thinking about it. You'll have to pay for it yourself – nobody else will care about the trip – but perhaps that is OK for you.
— Are you a novice or a veteran adventurer? Ask yourself this question only so that you can remind yourself it really doesn't matter. Of course, if you want to climb a difficult mountain and not merely be hauled up it by a guide, you've got a lot to learn. But whatever trip you do there will be lots to learn, so don't let that

put you off. Some trips require more expertise and experience than others, but that does not necessarily make them 'better'. I have greater admiration for a young person who walks alone from Land's End to John O'Groats than one whose parents pay for them to do a guided last degree North Pole trip for a few days.

— Do you enjoy learning new things and putting together complex projects? If not, you might want to stick to something simple like walking or cycling out of your front door and seeing how far south you can get.
— Are you more interested in a journey (going from A to B) or a challenge (climbing something, going from A to B in a difficult way, as fast as you can, or some other self-imposed criteria)?
— Which adventures that you have read about excite you the most? Why?
— What idea can you not get out of your head? Why?
— What will make your friends back home most jealous? Why?
— What, if anything, is still preventing you from doing all this? Why?
— What date are you going to begin?

Hopefully this will help you start to get a better idea of what you might want to do. You know you want to go on a big adventure. You're excited. You're making plans. It's actually going to happen!

This is a good time to pause and reflect on the reasons why you are going on the trip and what you hope to get out of the whole project. Many of the reasons for tackling big adventures are intangible, and I'm certainly a fan of just saddling up and heading off out into the world with no fixed objective, time frame or destination. It's a wonderful way of watching life unfold and shaping it to be more memorable, colourful and transformative than just staying at home.

But if you are travelling with somebody else, if your trip has sponsors (and therefore commitments to other people), if there is a specific destination or

aim for your trip, if you'll be doing research, trying to get your trip to reach an audience, or if your trip may be dangerous, it would be sensible to reflect upon these questions.

Better still, discuss them in another VEM (Vital Expedition Meeting in the pub). Better still, write down your answers so that they are really clear and you can refer to them later. It's much easier to do this before you get out into the wild, where your answers will blur and shift and change according to your daily mood.

— Why are you doing the trip?
— What is the objective of the trip?
— What do you hope to get out of it?
— What will constitute 'success'?
— What will constitute 'failure'?
— How much does success or failure matter?
— Does your adventure benefit anyone else but you?
— Do you have enough time to do the trip justice?
— What are you willing to sacrifice for this trip? (cash, time, safety, friendship)
— Why are you going solo/with someone else? If you are going with someone else, are you going with the right person?
— How will you deal with one person in the group being faster/slower, happier/sadder, richer/poorer, healthy/sick, etc.?
— If stuff goes wrong, can you cope?
— Do you have the skills, fitness, paperwork, contingency plans and emergency procedures necessary?
— What will you do with the trip afterwards?

CREATING AN EXCITING, REWARDING, CHALLENGING EXPEDITION IS BOTH EASY AND DIFFICULT

Here is how I go about making stuff happen when I'm trying to launch a trip.

— Block off the biggest chunk of time possible in my diary. Guard this jealously; time is so precious and demands on it so numerous. I can always earn more money; I can never reclaim lost time.
— Sit and daydream. Think of all the places I have not been. Pore over an atlas as I pour the coffee. Browse my bookshelves for inspiration. Drool over Google Images, Pinterest, Instagram, Flickr and Sidetracked.
— Try to think of trips that feel fresh, novel, difficult and different.
— Draw up a shortlist of the plans that excite me most.
— Narrow this list down against criteria such as cost, season, time frame and potential partners available.
— More or less settle on one preferred option.
— Faff around for a while.
— Send out an email/meet up with somebody/ do something that tips me over from day-dreaming about how fun this would all be to actually making it happen. The tipping point is often small but significant: walking across India was solidified merely by having dinner with a friend's parents, for example. Their enthusiasm for India convinced me to buy my ticket.
— Buy a plane ticket or whatever is the single most expensive, painful, committing action to take. This is without doubt the most significant and difficult stage of the entire process (hint: it's far harder than the scary expedition you are worrying about). This single act of commitment is what differentiates dreamers from doers.

It's not hard, but it is bold.
— Run around like an idiot realising that I have grossly underestimated the time and expense involved in making the trip happen. (NB: I have never looked back at a trip and regretted how much it cost. I have often looked back and regretted not taking a trip. If you want to do something and it feels important, find a way to pay for it. Make it happen. Or do it cheap and embrace the ensuing hassle and suffering.) Because I am committed to the trip, I know that it will happen. It might not be 100 per cent perfectly planned for, but that doesn't matter too much: I have momentum.

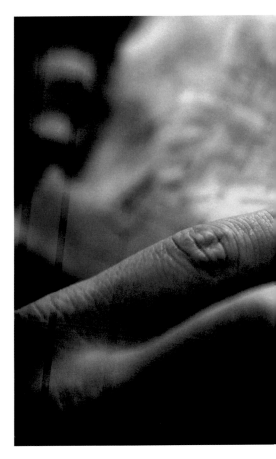

WISE WORDS FROM FELLOW ADVENTURERS

TOM ALLEN
CYCLING ADVENTURER

I chose to cycle because I was interested in exploring countries, meeting people, discovering cultures, and I wanted as much versatility in my means of transport as possible. With the bicycle you can carry everything you need. You've also got a massive range of distance that you can cover in a day, from as little as you like to up to, on a really good day, maybe a couple of hundred kilometres.

JOFF SUMMERFIELD
CYCLING ROUND THE WORLD ON A PENNY-FARTHING

I cycled as a kid, but then I didn't touch a bicycle until I was an adult. My first bicycle tour was a way of having a cheap holiday when I first became self-employed. Setting out, I didn't realise that I was going to have the epiphany which sent me on the path to my current lifestyle.

DOM GILL
GLOBAL TANDEM CYCLING AND CLIMBING EXPEDITIONS

Climbing is still my passion, but I begrudgingly realised when I thought about making a documentary that if I was into storytelling, I had to mix with other people of some kind. In order to make an engaging story, generally speaking, you have to mingle with communities. And what climbing does, by and large, is take you away from communities into isolation and into your own head, into your own struggles. And cycling, because of the nature of it taking you along relatively major thoroughfares, does the exact opposite and you stand a very good chance of meeting some interesting characters. So that was really the reason why I did my trip.

ANDREW FORSTHOEFEL
WALKED ACROSS THE USA

I chose walking rather than, say, cycling because I wanted to slow down. I had all these questions and I didn't feel like going onward with my life at the rate I had been would do anything to help answer those questions. So slowing down, walking, was just a great metaphor for that. I like the simplicity of it. I didn't know a whole lot about bikes and bike mechanics.

ANDY WARD
WALKED FROM LONDON TO ISTANBUL

My friend and I were always inspired by Patrick Leigh Fermor's trilogy of books about when he walked from Rotterdam to Constantinople. That gave us the idea of walking. It seemed to be the cheapest and simplest form of travelling. You didn't need much – a rucksack, a tent, a little cooker, and then you're pretty much on your way.

TIM COPE
RODE ON HORSEBACK FROM MONGOLIA TO EUROPE

The idea of the horse journey came to me when I was cycling across Asia. Some horsemen appeared from nowhere. I realised that the horse opened a world without boundaries: 6,000 miles without a fence.

OLLY WHITTLE
RAFTED THE MEKONG

Most of my adventures had been pre-planned and organised expeditions. I felt as if I needed to do something that I had created myself, where I would set off completely oblivious to what lay ahead, and with no one to report to, no targets or objectives to complete. I tried to build a raft and paddle a river in China but was thwarted by the police, so I headed south to Laos where I thought the rules might be a little more relaxed. I found the Mekong and thought 'this is the river.'

HENRIK FREDERIKSEN
RAFTED THE AMAZON ON A HOME-MADE RAFT

Cycling around the world – that's what I wanted to do and I really, really enjoyed it. I loved it. It was a beautiful way of travelling. But once in a while, I must admit, there was a little voice in the back of my head that said, 'There could be other fun ways of doing adventures as well.' What made the Amazon adventure actually happen was that I ran into a Bulgarian dude who was cycling the Americas and we became really good friends and started talking about other options for adventure. We got really worked up with this idea of maybe building a bamboo raft and floating down the Amazon. I quickly realised that the greatest courage for me was to follow exactly what I was passionate about doing, and that was the raft, at that moment. It's important to move out from your boundaries and to try something else.

LEV WOOD
WALKED THE RIVER NILE

I've always had an interest in Africa, and about four years ago, I drove from England down to Malawi. I followed parts of the Nile along the way and it just got me thinking that it would be great to explore this in more depth and do a bit of photography and a bit of writing. I just thought, what's the best way for me to really explore the countries and meet the people? Walking is the way that humans left Africa all those hundreds of thousands of years ago. And I thought it would be a really raw and visceral way of meeting the people along the way. And finally, it did also play quite a good marketing pitch for the people who wanted to make a film about it as well!

DAVE CORNTHWAITE
SWAM 1,000 MILES DOWN THE MISSISSIPPI

I think a good idea for an adventure starts with just that little fizzle of chemistry in your gut, when you wake up one morning and go, 'My God, this is it. You know, I just have to do it. It just feels right.' I find that if you go with your instinct, 99 times out of 100 it ends up being a pretty cool thing. Then, for me, having a lovely A to B, a simple geographical/distance goal, I get excited about that. Then along the way there has to be a story.

LIAM MARTIN
RODE A PIZZA DELIVERY BIKE TO GREECE

One day, [my friend and co-worker] Jamie said that he'd like to ride a C90 to Greece. I got really excited about that because it just seemed like such a stupid thing to do and such a cool idea. I bought a bike off eBay. I think it may have even been the next day after we had that conversation, just in a total stupid eBay moment. And so it snowballed from there.

PAUL ARCHER
DROVE ROUND THE WORLD IN A LONDON TAXI

We were talking about maybe doing something big, a road trip somewhere, and then the idea just came in the back of a taxi one evening. 'What's the longest ever taxi journey?' Found out there's a world record. Decided to try to break it. The only taxi we could use was a classic London cab, so that's what we did. We bought one from eBay for £1,200 and off we went.

PAULA CONSTANT
WALKED ACROSS THE SAHARA WITH CAMELS

Deep down, [the explorer] Thesiger was my major inspiration. And he had done so much on foot. I was a total romantic. Still am, really. I think you have to be to some degree.

JON MUIR
SOLO UNASSISTED WALK ACROSS AUSTRALIA

My first passion was mountaineering. After many years climbing extraordinary new routes all over the world I had a sense that I had achieved the very best that I personally could in all fields of climbing. Also, it was time to stop mountaineering because it was getting ugly. People weren't working as teams so much. There was an increasing amount of hype about summits per se, rather than the experience

of the climb and the beauty of the mountains. Getting to the top at all costs was becoming more popular and I didn't enjoy being around that mind-set. Well, that's why I stopped guiding on Everest anyway.

Imagination! You've got to have it inside you first. No one else can tell you the ingredients of a great adventure. What does your heart long for? Ask yourself that question and see what comes up, and when you get an answer, act on it. Don't let anyone tell you your heart's desire can't be done. Just do it. I've gotta say, though, I suspect that if you have to ask someone else to tell you the ingredients of a decent adventure, perhaps adventure's not really your thing.

RACHEL BESWETHERICK
WALKED THE 'DEATH RAILWAY' IN THAILAND AND BURMA

We had both known a prisoner of war from World War II who had been forced to build the Thai-Burma Railway. Stan was part of the F Force who were forced to march a 200-mile route from Ban Pong to the Burmese border, where they then commenced work on the railway. We decided to follow the route of his working party.

BEN SAUNDERS
LONGEST HUMAN-POWERED POLAR JOURNEY IN HISTORY

'It is important to me to be doing something that isn't a contrived stunt. It was genuinely inching things forward in the field that I care about.'

JASON LEWIS
FIRST HUMAN-POWERED CIRCUMNAVIGATION OF THE WORLD

It wasn't my idea. It was my mate's idea and, honestly, it was not something that I would have thought of myself to do. But he was bored at his desk job in Brussels and thought of it. Steve had noticed that people had rowed oceans and bicycled across continents. But the ah-ha moment for him was realising that these trips had always typically ended at the end of a continent or the end of an ocean. And so, why not keep on going? And this idea, it was just so beautifully simple and it didn't seem like it was another gimmick. It was like, 'wow'. And you didn't need to be an expert. So that simplicity also appealed to me. It's a bit of a cliché, but I know that when Steve thought of this idea he was in a café in Paris and he wrote it on the back of a cigarette packet, this idea of going around the world by human power, which ironically was just above the words from the cigarette manufacturer, 'Danger to your health'. I wish he'd kept that cigarette packet.

ED GILLESPIE
TRAVELLED ROUND WORLD WITHOUT FLYING

I wanted to get away from work on a truly escapist adventure. I needed a break to recharge and reconnect with myself and my environmental work – seeing and visiting some of the amazing places I was trying to save. It was a chance to ground myself, change perspectives, open my eyes and breathe deeply of this wonderful, wild and crazy planet.

MARK KALCH
PADDLING THE LONGEST RIVER ON
ALL SEVEN CONTINENTS

After the Amazon, immediately I thought, 'What can I do next?' All too quickly it seems you have to think of the next thing. My girlfriend, Holly, suggested it might be a good idea to have some sort of focus, instead of just jumping around. It was actually she who suggested paddling the longest river on each continent from source to sea.

GRAHAM HUGHES
VISITED EVERY COUNTRY ON EARTH
WITHOUT FLYING

Travel isn't a question of being loaded, it's a question of priorities. Obviously if you want comfort and security, stay at home, work hard and maybe go on a cruise when you're 67 years old. If you're lucky enough to live that long. But if you want to see the world NOW, while you're young, rush headlong into the thrill and vigour of the unknown, wake up every day in a new place with new challenges and new friends, then the world is your dance floor – all you have to do is make the decision to *get out there* and strut your funky stuff.

CHRIS GUILLEBEAU
VISITED EVERY COUNTRY IN THE WORLD

My advice: make the first step very easy. The first step could be going to the bookstore and getting the guidebook for your planned destination, or researching online about the big idea you have. Then, right away, plan the next step. At some point, find someone else who's done something similar to what you plan and ask them how they did it. Most importantly, think ahead and ask yourself if you'll regret not taking the action you want. If the answer is yes, your next step may be scary, but you'll know you have to do it.

BELINDA KIRK
TWO DECADES FILMING EXPEDITIONS
IN JUNGLES, MOUNTAINS AND DESERTS

This is your adventure. You're organising it or paying for it. Don't do it because it will be good for your career, don't do it because your best mate is doing it and don't do it to impress a girl. Do it because it is the thing you want to do more than anything else.

KIT LIST

If I was told to pack, with ten minutes' notice, for a mystery adventure somewhere in the world, these would be the essentials I would fling into my pack every time.

If you do not already own these items, I'd urge you to buy quality used items on eBay rather than cheaper, less-good brand-new versions. These items need to be good, not shiny. Be aware that it is possible to spend vast amounts of money on kit that you really do not need. See kit as something to be bought with the spare money you have once you have budgeted for everything else in your adventure, rather than what most people do, which is buy a £400 raincoat and then lament that they now don't have the money necessary to cycle across Europe (which you could certainly do for £350 in a £50 raincoat).

A BACKPACK Take a smaller pack than you think you will need, otherwise you will fill it full of heavy superfluous items which weigh you down, physically and psychologically. Just bear in mind that you will need to add food and water, so ensure you have space for that. In other words, take a bigger pack than you think you'll need, but when you are packing try your best to pretend that it's a small pack. Still following?!

STOUT SHOES Is there a less glamorous, less exciting coupling of words in the English language? But your footwear will take a pounding, so it needs to be up to the job. As this will be your only pair of shoes, you'll find yourself clumping up mountains in them, strutting your stuff in a random nightclub or brushing off the dirt and dust as best you can to look smart as you try to impress a visa official or attend a wedding you were spontaneously invited to.

MERINO BASE LAYER Warm, breathable, cosy, not too smelly when not washed for weeks. Get one that will look vaguely acceptable at the aforementioned mountain summit/nightclub/embassy/wedding.

ZIP-OFF TROUSERS Giving 'stout shoes' a run for their money in the ugly clothing category, I nonetheless find zip-off trousers (the legs zip off into shorts) to be phenomenally useful and versatile. It is possible, just, to find brands that do not look utterly ridiculous (be particularly cautious with the shorts).

A BUFF Versatile as a hat, a balaclava under a helmet, a neck warmer, a sweat band, a hair band and an eye shade for sleeping in light places. Versatility is the key criteria for a good bit of adventure gear. Always try to choose things that can serve more than one purpose.

SLEEPING BAG Get the smallest one that will keep you alive at the coldest temperatures that you think you will experience. Far better to have a small sleeping bag and wear all your clothes to keep warm than to lug around a vast sleeping bag you do not need. You'll have to decide whether to take a down bag or a synthetic one. Climate, weight and cost will determine your answer.

SILK SLEEPING-BAG LINER Adds warmth to your sleeping bag as well as being useful on its own in hot climates. It stops your sleeping bag from getting smelly and requiring washing and is also useful when your bed is full of fleas.

THERMAREST Unless you are on an adventure that includes beds (lucky you!) or a lot of thorns/sharp rocks (in which case take a foam sleeping mat), a sleeping mat like this is lightweight, low volume and makes a giant difference to your quality of sleep. Worth the cash. Get a three-quarter-length one not a full-length one.

A RAINCOAT The climate and type of journey will determine what kind of jacket you take, but you'll want some sort of waterproof layer for almost every adventure.

A ZIPLOCK BAG To keep your passport and cash dry. Take a few different credit cards and don't keep all your cash, credit cards or eggs in one place/basket.

TOOTHBRUSH AND TOOTHPASTE

Personal hygiene is not a strong priority for most adventurers – ugly beards flecked with dinner are common – but brushing your teeth always boosts morale. Plus, nobody likes a tent mate with halitosis. If you're really lucky it might even keep you kissable (if you can persuade someone to ignore the ugly beard, stout shoes and zip-off trousers). Consider whether you want your tent mate kissing you...

BEER-CAN STOVE A quick Google will teach you how to make this stove in just a few minutes.

ANY MEDICINES YOU REQUIRE

SUN HAT, SUNCREAM AND SUNGLASSES

MULTI-TOOL SUCH AS A SWISS ARMY KNIFE OR LEATHERMAN

PASSPORT AND APPROPRIATE VISAS

FLIP-FLOPS Not necessary for Polar journeys.

HEADTORCH I'd recommend one that uses AA batteries if you're going somewhere remote where AAA batteries might be hard to come by. Every village on earth sells AA.

JOURNAL AND PEN If you think you are the sort of person who does not write diaries, think again. You really should jot down some thoughts and memories on the road. One day you'll be glad you did.

READING BOOK Take one that will last until the end of your journey, but not something so weighty (in grams or content) that you can't be bothered with it. I prefer re-reading poetry rather than novels.

CAMERA Though do not feel compelled to photograph everything and experience nothing.

DOWN JACKET Not quite essential, but if I was going anywhere cold and I had the cash to afford one, I'd pop a down jacket (or a down bodywarmer)

into my pack every time. Budget and temperature will determine your choice.

AN OPEN MIND, PATIENCE AND A HEALTHY SENSE OF THE RIDICULOUS

Other things to consider, depending on where in the world you are going: VACCINATIONS MALARIA PILLS, MOSQUITO NET

WATER PURIFICATION Research which option works best for you – chemical, filtration or sticking to bottled water.

INSURANCE Specific to the location you are going to and the activity you will be doing.

One of my favourite adventure memories is of a three-month trip I took to the Philippines. I left my home wearing shorts, T-shirt and flip-flops and shivered my way to the airport. In my carry-on-sized backpack I had a mosquito net, a silk sleeping-bag liner, a sarong to use as a towel and a base layer for when kipping on buses and to wear when I washed my clothes at night. I had suncream, sunglasses and sun hat (the curse of being semi-translucent), a raincoat for the monsoon, and a toothbrush, diary, camera, passport, credit card, iodine for purifying water and a reading book. I had everything I needed in life. The blissful simplicity of that journey remains in my mind as one of the highlights of the adventure, along with winning my first ever bike race, riding on the roofs of crazy buses, and being given the dubious honour of killing a pig with a stick in a remote village I stayed in for a few weeks.

WISE WORDS FROM FELLOW ADVENTURERS

NIC CONNER
CYCLED FROM THE UK TO TOKYO

I did my kit stuff the week before. There was a big sale in Covent Garden in the outdoor shops, and I just kind of went along and thought, 'Oh, that looks interesting. I'll buy it.' I got stuff I thought might be useful, which I actually ended up not using at all. If I were going tomorrow, all I would take is two pairs of cycling shorts, two shorts, two T-shirts, food, a tent and my sleeping bag. That's all you need, really.

TOM ALLEN
ADVENTURE TRAVEL WRITER AND FILM-MAKER

All kit-buying decisions should depend on how many days on the road it costs. You have to be realistic about what the bare minimum is going to be to achieve what you're trying to achieve. Nice gear is nice, but it's not essential. If the choice is between having crap gear or having nice gear but not being able to afford the trip, then it's obvious you should just take what you can and live with it. You know, deal with a bit of discomfort.

MARTIN HARTLEY
POLAR PHOTOGRAPHER

Ideally you need a camera that you can change lenses on. Zoom lenses are great but unreliable in the cold or in dusty places. So definitely a camera that has a manual function, and one you can drop a few times and it still works. You can do anything on a 24-millimetre lens; you can do landscapes and portraits. That would be one lens I would always carry in case everything failed. A 35-millimetre lens is a classic reportage lens and then a long lens just so you can shoot things from far away, even portraits – nosy, voyeuristic shots of people!

JAMES KETCHELL
CYCLED ROUND THE WORLD

I was using a second-hand bike that I purchased for £300 from a friend. I did actually have the budget to buy a new bike, but I really liked the idea of cycling the world on a second-hand bike, so that's what I did! You don't have to have the biggest and the best of everything to go away on an adventure. My bike performed amazingly and I don't believe a brand-new bike would have made any difference. So don't worry too much if you don't have the money for expensive kit, it's not always necessary.

LEV WOOD
WALKED THE NILE

The moment you've got cameras and fancy equipment, it makes it a lot more difficult and you're more of a target for people who think they can make a bit of cash. So, yeah, it's about making yourself look as rugged and scruffy as possible really. People just think you're a bit of a hippy and don't have any money, which is ideal.

JAMIE BOWLBY-WHITING
CYCLED ACROSS EUROPE

I had spent time reading about long-distance cycle journeys, but neither of us had the money to purchase nice bicycles. In a little village in England we found a couple of bicycles being sold by a friendly old man in his garden. We bought them for £30 each. We attached cool boxes as budget panniers. Daniel, my Slovakian friend, decided to join us, so we drew a rough line from my family home in Norfolk to his in Slovakia, then we cycled it. It was a 1,000-mile journey during which we camped outside for free every night, foraged wild fruit almost every day and cooked on an alcohol-powered beer can. We washed in lakes or rivers, and on many occasions people were kind enough to offer us food, accommodation or even a ride on their horses.

COLIN WILLOX
BACKPACKED ACROSS EUROPE

I can suggest that you only bring what is *absolutely* essential; don't buy anything if you can help it. Try to get down to one bag. Be ruthless.

KEVIN CARR
RAN ROUND THE WORLD

If using equipment, learn how to fix it at home. Have you ever changed a spoke before? Fixed a puncture wearing a head torch in the driving rain? Don't wait to learn how when you're at the side of a busy road with your hands shaking from the cold!

SUZIE WELFORD AND ADAM JONES
CYCLED ROUND ICELAND

You don't need fancy new equipment; a mountain bike will work as a touring bike. Slick tyres would actually have been a good idea, but knobbly ones helped get us legs of steel!

KRISTEN ZIPPERER
TREKKED IN NEPAL

'Depending on your budget, it may be worth waiting until you get to your destination to purchase things, because they are often significantly cheaper than at home.'

TOM LLOYD-SMITH
CYCLED TO INDIA

I got the bike through my employer's cycle-to-work scheme, and the other big-ticket items (tent, stove) I acquired over quite a long period. By working out what I needed to get early, I knew what the budget required was and was able to keep an eye on eBay and pick up all the kit I needed at a reasonable cost.

TO-DO LIST

As your adventure plans gather momentum, you'll find yourself deluged with to-do lists. You will never, ever get through them all before your day of departure dawns. You will *not* get as much training done as you intended. You *will* be up packing at 3am the morning you are due to leave.

It's important not to get consumed by the fun items on the list ('buy massive penknife') and neglect to deal with the items that are actually essential for getting you to the start line. To-do lists can grow so enormous that they terrify you and inhibit productivity. So here is a minimal to-do list which will help get your plans galloping forwards.

Begin with the urgent and important stuff. Work down the list from the top – do not skip any of them just because they are boring. This stuff needs to get done!

1. Start saving and plan your finances.
2. Cut down on your spending.
3. Discuss your plan with the people it will have an impact on: family, colleagues, friends.
4. Make a plan and put the dates in your diary.
5. Tell people what you plan to do and when you will begin.
6. Book your flight to the start line (or do something similar that commits you irrevocably to action).
7. Work out the things you need to do without which the trip will not happen. Do them.
8. Look into bureaucracy, transport and logistics.
9. Make plans for healthcare while abroad.
10. Emergency and safety planning.
11. Organise your equipment. Focus on the stuff you need rather than the stuff you'd quite like to have.
12. Only now should you begin doing all the fun bits: buy a massive penknife, create a website, etc.
13. Begin!

Part 2

CHOOSE

BICYCLE

The bicycle is where my adventuring heart lies. It's the most versatile, all-purpose accessory to adventure ever invented. A motorbike may be faster; walking may be slower (there is a time and a place for both fast and slow adventure). Kayaks, canoes and crampons may get you to wilder places, living and working in a foreign land may immerse you deeper into a culture, but a journey by bike does a pretty good job in every one of these aspects.

Riding a bike is one of the most joyful aspects of childhood. Every eulogy to cycling trots out that cliché, but it remains true: riding a bike is fun. If something is fun, why not do more of it? Certainly it's possible to have too much of a good thing. I have buried myself deep in pain and exhaustion on long days in the saddle. These days are classic Type 2 fun (hideous at the time; glorious retrospectively). But a bicycle gives you a choice. You can choose to pedal furiously around the planet in just six months like Mark Beaumont. Or, as Heinz Stucke did, you can set out in search of a life more fulfilling than a 'boring and monotonous job'. Heinz wanted to take charge of his future. Fifty years and 370,000 miles later, he is still cycling round the world! Proof, if nothing else, that there is a lot of world to be seen out there. You'll probably pick a pace somewhere in between the two. But that's the point: a bicycle journey gives you the freedom to do it however the hell you choose.

When I think of my bicycle journeys, large and small, I have a variety of happy memories. I think of the wild places bicycles have taken me to. The sheer variety of them makes me smile, whether it's snowy mountain passes, deserts shimmering with heat, or bumpy single-track paths leading to isolated Scottish bothies.

Travelling by bicycle can be as simple as tucking a credit card, passport and toothbrush in your pocket and making your way between cafés and hotels. Bikes can also be a small miracle of self-sufficiency. I've loaded my bike so heavy with food and gear that I couldn't lift it an inch off the ground. Progress is slow like this but it's liberating and rewarding to be able to cross swathes of desert or mountain without caring whether or not you meet another person or find a shop along the way. I've carried food for ten-day stretches, cycling through a Siberian winter, spending hours each night melting enough snow for the next day's drinking water. I once carried all I needed to make it right the way across Turkmenistan without stopping because I'd faked the visa dates in my passport and I did not want to linger. In the high mountain deserts between Argentina, Chile and Bolivia, I've cycled without speaking to a soul for more than a week, battling the icy wind and sandy tracks all alone.

But bike journeys are not just about leaving the world behind. I have also enjoyed riding amongst hordes of bicycles during rush hour in Beijing, or weaving through the chaotic streets of La Paz. Bike journeys are a superb way of meeting people. When you arrive somewhere on a bicycle you don't get bracketed as an Annoying Tourist or a Rich Foreigner. You're just a person riding a bike, and an interesting person at that.

'Where are you from? Where are you going? On a bike? You're crazy! Come meet my family!' is the standard opening exchange when arriving almost anywhere on Earth on a heavily loaded bicycle. I have been welcomed into mosques and churches, yurts and embassies, mud huts and mansions. And in every one of those places people want to talk. 'Tell me about your adventures!', 'Tell me of the things you have seen.'

Buying a bike is not expensive (correction: it *need not be* expensive) and anyone can participate in a cycling journey. If you strapped a tent to the back of any old bike and began riding tomorrow, you could reach another continent in a few months' time. You certainly don't need to see yourself as a 'cyclist' to consider this as a serious proposition. I've spent five years travelling by bike but I am not a 'cyclist'. The bike was always just a tool, an adventure-enabler. A bicycle is the greatest

Willy Wonka-style Golden Ticket to Adventure that has ever been made. It opens up the world to absolutely anyone.

Proper cyclists are often dismayed about my lack of knowledge or interest in how many sprockets my chainset has, or that I do not shave my legs. None of this matters to me. The late Anne Mustoe, a retired headmistress who pedalled round the planet a couple of times, could not fix a puncture. She would rely on the effective, if incongruous, combination of feminine charms and headmistress-ly authority to persuade a local man to help her whenever the need arose.

A bicycle journey can be an appetite-whetting weekend away, a couple of weeks riding from Land's End to John O'Groats, or a transcontinental epic. I find it beguiling that anyone who is able to ride a bike and read the instructions for how to pitch a tent has all of the skills necessary to cycle from New York to Los Angeles, from Cairo to Cape Town, or from London to Singapore. As you read these words now, dozens of very ordinary, very humble and laidback folk are currently cycling thousands of miles through every terrain on the planet, having an adventure that they will never forget. You could, too. I have never met anyone who regretted their big bicycle journey, but I have often met people who regretted not taking one when they had the opportunity.

This book began with the claim that you can have a grand adventure for £1,000. I chose that figure simply because it was a nice round number, cheaper than a week's family holiday, which I knew was more than enough money to do a great expedition with.

As money is perceived to be the greatest obstacle between people and their adventures, I wanted to scupper that perception right at the start of the book. After that point, I haven't really discussed the details of finances again because this book is about garnering the inspiration and the motivation to do a big trip, not the detail. However, I did especially enjoy interviewing Nic Conner for

this book. A novice adventurer and not much of a cyclist, Nic cycled all the way from London to Tokyo as a challenge to see how far he could ride for £1,000. He had £15 left and a head full of stories by the time he reached Japan. What perfect proof that the £1,000 adventure works! Kerry O'Neill also framed her own ride around a budget of £1,000 – setting out to ride the route of the classical Grand Tour for less than a grand.

You can go on a cycling adventure by yourself, with a friend, on a tandem, on a tandem by yourself and pick up passengers along the way, on your honeymoon, as a family, or as a couple and return as a family. These are all things that our interviewees have done. You don't need to be fit and strong (though you soon will become that). You don't need to be rich (indeed, I believe that

the more basic your bike journey, the longer it will linger in the memory). You don't need to be tough. You don't need to be clever, or skilful or practical. You don't need to serve years of apprenticeship before tackling something huge. If you want to cycle 200 miles in a day, you'll soon be able to. If you want to snooze off a long lunch of Romanian homebrew underneath a tree, you can probably manage that right away.

In other words, a bicycle journey can be whatever you want it to be.

If you are interested in adventure on any scale, I would urge you to consider going for a bike ride. Do not discount yourself on the grounds of age, gender, disability, fitness or a dislike of camping: the adventurers in the coming pages should make that abundantly clear.

WISE WORDS FROM
FELLOW ADVENTURERS

ALICE GOFFART AND ANDONI RODELGO
CYCLED AROUND THE WORLD FOR SEVEN YEARS

During the time we cycled round the world, our children were born. We had nothing to prove, nowhere to go, no agendas, no must-do. It was just us, on our bicycles. Going. Living the present as it came, going right or left depending on our wishes at that very moment. We were just there to enjoy ourselves and the present was the only thing we actually had, since we had never any idea of where we would be 15 minutes later. Maybe we would meet someone... Maybe not...

We wanted unlimited time, we wanted to be able to cross a country without restriction, slowly making sense of it all. Our bicycles would give us the perfect excuse for why the hell don't we stay in that village in the middle of nowhere?

Just go, you'll have plenty of time to learn and adjust yourselves to what works for you.

NIC CONNER
CYCLED FROM THE UK TO TOKYO FOR £1,000

We only came up with the idea of going about six weeks before we left. I was having a phone call with my mate where we both said, 'I'm bored. I'm fed up.' He said, 'Look, we've been chatting for a year about doing something. Let's just do it. Let's get a date. When's the first time we can hand our notices in and just go?'

As a child, you always have those dreams of doing crazy stuff. So I've always wanted to do something. And it's always so much easier talking about it or daydreaming. It was time to just do it.

I want to say how hard it was, but I really have to say how easy it was if I'm honest, because that was the reality. I actually thought it would be much harder than it was. Food, especially when you got east, was very cheap. I would sleep in my tent, which was pretty easy, pretty much all the way. I never had a day of hassle.

I wouldn't change anything about it. It was the most amazing six months of my life. There were difficult bits, but those difficult bits were great, you know? They made the good bits worth it. I met some amazing people. My bike broke so many times, but people would help me fix it. They would pay for bits for it. So just meeting people was wonderful. If I had £1,000 again, yeah, I would probably do the trip again. It was brilliant.

It's not as hard as people think. It's just a case of doing it. That's the hardest thing. It's just pushing my feet around and cycling. It's not as frightening as the crazy stuff your mind makes up. Do it.

KERRY O'NEILL
RE-CREATED THE GRAND TOUR ON
A BUDGET OF A GRAND

I re-created the Grand Tour (when, between the 17th and 19th centuries, rich young men would go to see the sights of Europe) on my bicycle, just because I wanted to, because it was fun, it was summer and it was Europe, but also to prove that you don't have to be young, rich and male to have adventures.

I really enjoyed having lots of time to think about whatever I wanted and not feeling stressed to have to do anything particularly or get anywhere specific.

We used to have lots of time for that kind of thing, but people don't find that time in their lives anymore. It's nice to have nothing to do. Though some people might consider this an idle waste of time, it is actually fruitful and productive. Things you haven't had time to think about properly for years suddenly have space.

[My mum was worried about my safety], but the reality is that everyone around you on your travels is really helpful, really friendly, intrigued and interested about what you're doing.

The experience of Couchsurfing was amazing. Every host was better than the last, they would throw you parties, they would take days off work to show you around town, it's just phenomenal. It really restored my faith in human nature. I don't think I met one negative influence the whole time.

SATU VÄNSKÄ-WESTGARTH
CYCLING ADVENTURE DURING HER MATERNITY LEAVE

Bike touring, until this summer, was something that others did. Then I got pregnant for the second time. I was about to get huge and the day would come when I would be waddling on resembling a duck. I spent most of my time indoors, dreaming of adventures and fighting off frustration. It all started with an idea, a joke really. I thought about exploring the Wild Atlantic Way, a new scenic route in Ireland, maybe with a camper van and the family. My friend suggested I bike it. With a giggle, I texted my husband about 'the plan', of me biking 1,250-plus miles, leaving him and the kids home. What I intended as an entertaining joke, he took seriously.

And that was that, I thought I'd better take it and myself seriously, too. Hence I was now bound to end my maternity leave with a bang, to bike approximately 60 miles a day, five days a week for five weeks in Ireland with my friends while my family followed the journey virtually from home.

'I love the fact that you wake up in the morning and you have no idea where you're going to be at the end of the day'

Doing something I never thought about doing before definitely opened up new horizons, and joining the league of 'others' made me realise that being a mother, thirty-something at that, or having a certain full-time job or not having the confidence to kayak the rivers I once used to run are not factors that define me.

What defines me doesn't have to be definite. I can be or become whatever I choose to be. Be it mother today or maybe an adventurer tomorrow.

TOM ALLEN
SELF-UNEMPLOYED BICYCLE TRAVELLER, FILM-MAKER AND WRITER

I love the fact that you wake up in the morning and you have no idea where you're going to be at the end of that day, or what you're going to see or whom you're going to meet on the way. That's kind of what adventure means to me, anyway. It's the unpredictability and the surprises and the unexpected, and the knowledge that it's very, very rarely a bad kind of surprise. It's usually pretty positive stuff.

Before I set off I spent a year planning the first trip, which is way too much planning to be quite honest, but it got me to begin.

I did no training whatsoever. I didn't even finish building the bike until the morning I left. I didn't have time, because the last few weeks of preparation were so frantic in terms of getting the stuff, getting the gear together, that I didn't actually have any time to test any of it. The funny thing is, for shorter trips training makes more sense because you're more time-restricted and your ability to pull the trip off depends more on your fitness in the first place. Whereas if you're going off for months or years, you'll be as fit as you'll ever be within the first month, regardless of how fit you are to start with. I figured that by the time I actually did clear Europe, I'd have enough experience to deal with whatever came up next.

I desperately needed someone to tell me that flexibility is the most important part of putting a plan together. You need to have an attitude that in a real adventure there are unknowns, and unknowns are going to involve challenge, and challenge is going to mean that you learn new things. So you've got to have flexibility. I was guilty of over-structuring what I was doing, definitely. When I changed my plans, I had to spend a lot of time and effort deconstructing all of that. I had a lot of apologising to do to sponsors and I had to face the music when it came to telling all the followers I'd got on the blog that actually, 'I'm not going to do this. I'm not going to cycle around the world anymore. I'm going to go and cycle in a way which is more relevant to me.' So it would have been better to have had a much looser plan and fewer obligations.

And that's why I now advise people not to bother with the whole sponsorship thing. If you've got an external cause, which is why you're doing the trip, then fine, get sponsorship. You've got strings attached anyway, so a few more won't hurt. But, otherwise, just keep it really simple.

IMRAN MUGHAL
FIRST BRITISH-PAKISTANI TO CYCLE ROUND THE WORLD

I always had the need for travelling, but I didn't know what to do; I didn't know where to go. I got into cycling quite a few years ago. But it wasn't until I met a Dutch guy who was cycle-touring Europe with his big, loaded bike, and that's when I was like, 'Ker-ching, this is it! This is what I want to do.'

I watched him in fascination, because here he was with all his bags, his tent and everything. I just looked, thinking, 'My goodness, I have got to do this. I just have to do this.' So really, that day was kind of like a turnaround point, I guess.

Whenever I tell folks what I've done, they think I'm superhuman. But I say, 'Listen, I'm not superhuman. You have the same properties as I have.'

The highlight was Iran, without a doubt. Anybody who's been through Iran always talks about how unbelievable it is. Being a Sunni Muslim, I've always heard nothing but negativity about the Shia Muslims. So I was apprehensive. People are scared of the world because they buy into fear. In my opinion, Iran is the safest country with the most hospitable people. The world is generally good and that's what I got. I mean, obviously there were heavy [bad] incidents, but I can count them on one hand. But the mad hospitality, love, generosity and kindness were just overwhelming.

A year or more prior to the journey, I had been made redundant. I used to work in a call centre for a subsidiary of the NHS. I couldn't find work. My father had been very ill for a long time and he passed away during that time. My whole preparation for the journey was all made while I was in turmoil, actually.

Culturally, this is not what we do [British-Pakistanis]. Ask any of my friends and they'd say you're supposed to settle down, get married. Because of my ethnicity, what I did is just unheard of. I think I may be the first British-Pakistani to have cycled around the world.

After my journey, I've had so many people from my culture thinking, 'I'm going to do what you do' and asking advice on doing stuff on a small scale. I got made redundant, and I was paid the minimum they could make for the redundancy. I knew I wanted to do a journey. I didn't know at that time whether I'd get around the world, although that was a dream.

I think the simplicity of the life is one of the biggest things I'll take with me for the rest of my life.

MARK BEAUMONT
RECORD-BREAKING ROUND-THE-WORLD CYCLIST

My overriding memory of the round-the-world trip was excitement. It was exciting heading off into the unknown. It still tops the chart of all the trips I've done because it was that one where I was wide-eyed, and very innocent, and exploring the world for the first time. The great thing about a bike, which I always harp on about, is just how much you can see from it. You're experiencing absolutely everything.

Every subsequent trip I've done I've got more experience. With experience comes a lot of good stuff, but it loses that excitement, that wide-eyed innocence that I experienced on the round-the-world cycle. I'd never pedalled outside Europe, so it was just wonderful, every mile that I went further away from home.

A few days ago I found my logbooks for the planning year up to my journey. I read of the mental state that I was in and, you know, it wasn't all rose-tinted and wonderful the way I like to remember it. It was bloody hard work and very demoralizing and I nearly gave up tons of times. But that's not the way I remember it now.

When I first put together the world cycle, I simply wanted to break a record and go on a massive adventure. I don't think most people wake up one day and just pedal around the world. You need to build confidence first. But so, so, so many people have big ideas. Getting to the start line to actually do it is where most people fail.

[You should start with] something small because then most of those questions, those what-ifs and those doubts will simply evaporate. It's not like you need to become a grand expert and suddenly become brilliant at it. I'm not even a grand expert at cycle touring. I know what I know and I bumble along. I struggle to put a bike together, that's for sure. I just hope it doesn't break. People assume once you've broken world records and done great trips you're some sort of Jedi master at expeditions. It couldn't be further from the truth.

Somebody emailed me this morning and said, 'I've got this epic trip planned to cycle through Europe but I just don't know where to camp and how to do it.' I'm like, 'Honestly? Europe?' That's something I would be thinking about as I got a ferry across the Channel. And maybe as I pedalled through my first day in Northern France, 'Where am I going to sleep tonight?' You know, you're never going to do anything, you're never going to step out your front door if you worry about those things.

KAREN DARKE
PARALYMPIC CYCLIST AND ADVENTURER

My ride through Central Asia was a long time ago, so tourists were almost nonexistent. The people just welcomed us and were so generous with their food, water and sharing their homes. As we didn't speak the same language I don't really know what they thought of the wheelchair. I remember they just welcomed us with open arms and were so incredibly warm and kind. The kids liked having a seat on the back of the tandem and a quick spin around!

Ultimately it's people – their characters, generosity, spirit and smiles – that I remember and that really stays with me and impacts me most. I think I prefer that sort of trip, where you are meeting people and learning so much more about a place, its history, culture and character, than being in the complete wilderness. Pure nature and wilderness offers something different that's harder to define, harder to place, but also very impacting.

TEGAN PHILLIPS
CARTOONIST WHO CYCLED, AGED 21, FROM THE UK TO SPAIN

I had the time and the means to go in absolutely any direction I wanted for as long as I wanted. That sensation of absolute freedom has no parallel and I think it's one of the main things that gets people hooked on adventuring.

It's sometimes hard to be good-humoured when you're dying from the heat and every single part of your body hurts and you're going uphill and really you would prefer to be going downhill. Without wanting to sound too dramatic, the adventure changed the way I see the world entirely. I started thinking about cycling and running as ways to actually get places, instead of just exercisey things to get outdoors and get nice legs.

I wish I had known how easy adventuring can be so I could have avoided the 'preparation panic' people often face before trips of any sort, where you somehow convince yourself that if you don't have this particular tool or tent or saddle or clothing then your adventure will be a disaster and you will probably die. As I discovered, whatever you are going to do, the chances are that somebody has done it with much less than you and somehow survived.

Also, I wish I had known what a difference it makes to take the smaller roads in terms of scenery and traffic and everything really.

And I wish I had known that the dark patches on a map means uphill. Significant uphill. This was a painful lesson to learn.

JOFF SUMMERFIELD
CYCLING ROUND THE WORLD ON A PENNY-FARTHING FOR THE SECOND TIME

I'm guessing it will take me at least a year to get to the bottom of South America, and there is so much to think about just in that stretch that thinking further ahead is too overwhelming. There are also so many different political and environmental situations that can make countries harder or easier to cross that the making of any hard and fast decisions now is impossible.

Before I started making the longer journeys I did always wonder how I was going to be received by people. If you watch the news you would never leave your house, as news is always bad news, it seems. Although I do have great faith in humanity, you can't help but be influenced by the surrounding media. When first setting out, I did wonder if all the bicycle travel books I had read were true, and were people that kind? Well, it turns out the people of the world, no matter which colour, race or creed, religion or beliefs, are wonderful. As someone travelling on a bicycle, people see you as being vulnerable, and are always willing to be friendly and help you out.

The bicycle, I'm sure, does indeed make you instantly innocent. Everyone across the world

'I started thinking about cycling and running as ways to actually get places, instead of just exercisey things to get outdoors and get nice legs'

rides bicycles, be they rich or poor – it's a universal connection between us all. When people see you arrive, road-worn and dusty with that cyclist's grin on your face, they cannot help but smile back. On one occasion in China I was getting a bit peckish so I stopped in a small rural village to get something to eat. There was a crude restaurant by the roadside. I pushed the bike inside so I could keep an eye on it. The owners were startled at

my sudden arrival, especially since I just stepped inside with a penny-farthing wearing a colonial pith helmet. But bless them, they made me some noodle soup and gave me hot water to drink from a jam jar. But when I came to leave and made the universal gesture of 'how much' they did seem a bit puzzled. It slowly started to dawn on me that this wasn't a restaurant at all, it was in fact someone's home! These lovely people had just fed and watered me after I had unceremoniously stepped straight into their living room with my bicycle. I'm sure it was the bicycle that made me innocent and sparked them into being so obliging. [Author's note: I have made exactly the same mistake – twice! Once in Pakistan, once in Costa Rica. Both had the same outcome as Joff's.]

DOM GILL
CYCLED THE LENGTH OF THE AMERICAS ON A TANDEM, BY HIMSELF, PICKING UP PASSENGERS ALONG THE WAY

My trip was about inclusive adventure. Using a tandem not only to have an adventure myself and explore new places amongst a whole new set of people, but also to invite people to join me on that adventure and perhaps push their own boundaries of what they can experience in life.

I started as many red-blooded adventurers do, thinking I wanted to prove to the world how tough I am and how I could get from A to B without the help of anybody. But I was also very interested in making this first journey a springboard into the world of documentary film-making.

Very quickly, within two or three weeks, I realised that the physical aspect of the journey, while it appealed to me, was massively secondary to seeing what I could learn from the people around me and seeing what they had to teach me.

I had the good fortune of deciding to do this journey before my salary was anything close to what I could earn at McDonald's. So it was like I had nothing to lose. That makes everything a lot easier. The biggest advice I would give to people is make a real effort not to plan too much.

Since doing that trip I've found that a lot of people ask me what equipment they'll need or what route they should best take. The experience was more meaningful on my trip because obviously I was relying on locals to guide me where they wanted to go really. But I would say leave time in your itinerary and your adventure, whatever it may be, for that chance meeting of an old lady who makes honey and wants to teach you how.

SEAN CONWAY
CYCLED ROUND THE WORLD

There's nothing more soul-destroying than a job that everyone hates, including yourself. I decided to just quit. I sold my business for a pound (I still have that pound, framed). So I was now 30 years old. I had no money, no spark, no desire to do anything. I just thought maybe I should go travelling, but I couldn't afford to go travelling. What could I do to get someone to pay me to go travelling? I was really miserable and depressed, and I thought, well maybe if I try something a little bit daft, a little bit bonkers, and a little bit completely out of my league, that would get me my confidence back and also allow me to go and travel, which I had never done before. And that's when I thought of the round-the-world cycling, because I'd always followed people like yourself, like Mark Beaumont and even, back in the day, Tommy Godwin, who did all those incredible rides. But through lack of confidence I always thought, 'oh that's what people with money do, that's what people who are superhuman do', which was all completely wrong.

Once I broke it down into baby steps, I realised that actually it was doable. I went and looked for sponsors, trained hard, then looked at bikes and, eventually, a year later, I was on the start line and cycling around the world. I sacrificed a lot for this race. Girlfriends dumped me, I moved back in with my mum and all that sort of thing. But I didn't mind because it was something I really had a drive for, and a spark. For the first time in ages I had this spark to achieve something I thought I could do. I met a lady in the Rocky Mountains, she must have been 70-odd years old, who has done 110,000 miles around the world so far in the last 20 years. And her pedals didn't even have the plastic on them, there was just the metal sticking out. She had wellies on, plastic bags for a rain jacket, and she only did 20 miles a day – but that was because she was 70, and she didn't really care much for pushing big miles.

JAMES KETCHELL
CYCLED ROUND THE WORLD

You cannot buy back time no matter how wealthy you are, so my appreciation of time has changed massively. Travelling the world and meeting people from different cultures, some rich, some very poor, will give you a good appreciation of the things that we actually have in our lives and how lucky most of us really are. One of the biggest things I've taken away from adventure is that, with the right mind-set, anything is possible and it's quite amazing how you will surprise yourself when you're prepared to put the hard work in.

Once you have made the decision, it's not uncommon for people around you to start telling you that this may not be a good idea. Quite often they will be your closest friends and family, but it's only a natural reaction as they want to protect you. I found that actions speak louder than words, and when I started relentlessly working on sponsorship and promoting the project, people who were anxious about my activities became my greatest supporters. Don't be put off by anyone telling you what you should or shouldn't be doing; this is why taking the first step is the toughest part. In all honesty, there is no short cut to turning your dream into a reality. It will take hard work and determination. However, that capability does lie within everyone if you want something badly enough.

Before I started going away on adventures, I didn't really like it when things didn't go my way or the outcome of whatever I was working on was not what I wanted or expected. Adventure and expeditions will teach you that sometimes things don't always go your way, and that is OK. It's a simple fact of life. I often found myself adjusting my route and itinerary as I cycled around the world for reasons that were beyond my control.

HELEN LLOYD
CYCLED THE LENGTH OF AFRICA

The reason I love to travel is to see new places and meet new people, to learn from other cultures and try to understand how we all fit together in this world. I chose to cycle because it struck me that this would be the ideal way to get about. By cycling, I hoped I would spend time in the places between the guidebooks' must-see highlights, and meet people like you and me. I guess, simply put, I wanted to see normal life, except there is no 'normal'.

Many people have said that they have a dream but are scared to make it a reality. It can be hard to make a change in your life, take a leap into the unknown, but what scares me more is living a life of regret, wishing I had had the courage to do what I dreamed. Of course, there are things that I have worried about with some of my journeys – anxiety and fear are useful tools and shouldn't be ignored – but I try to turn those feelings into something positive. Do research, plan, prepare, equip, quantify risk and minimise it. Risk is real, fear is an essential emotion, and if you can reduce the risk the fear subsides, too.

The best thing about the journey was all the great people I met – isn't that always the way...?

RIAAN MANSER
CYCLED THE PERIMETER OF AFRICA

If you come to Africa on a bicycle and are not expecting any administration issues, you're living in a dreamland. First thing to understand is that you're going to have some and you shouldn't be surprised by them. Secondly, there is nothing, nothing, nothing better in an awkward and difficult administration moment with border staff than to keep smiling. So, you just keep smiling. Act ignorant and keep smiling. If you're going to let little stuff like that get you down, it's going to get you down day in, day out.

If you look back now to when I began my ride – gel on my hair and all the clothing and stuff that I didn't need – then coming back you can see in my face it is a different human being who finished the journey two years later.

There's an ocean between saying and doing. Many people stand around the fire with a beer in hand and they talk big war stories about what they're going to do, and they never get round to doing it. Make the date, tell everybody around you. Your plane ticket is booked, set that day that you're going to leave and get going.

'I decided that before finishing my studies I wanted to see more of the world. Now I couldn't be happier. This adventure has turned into a lifestyle full of fulfilment and education'

SHIRINE TAYLOR
CYCLING ROUND THE WORLD, AGED 20

I'm currently cycling around the world, an adventure I plan to continue for the next three or four years. I have cycled across my own country, the USA, and have explored India and Nepal as a solo female. Throughout each of these three countries I have experienced unimaginable hospitality and kindness, and stayed with families in slums, big cities and small farming villages for weeks at a time. I loved staying in those remote villages where I would cook with the women, run through the fields with the children and experience daily life in a place so different to where I come from. Before starting on this adventure I was a nanny; a simple young girl making ten dollars an hour. I decided that before finishing my studies I wanted to see more of the world, and after hearing stories from others, I realised that cycling would be the perfect way to do so. Now, I couldn't be happier. This adventure has turned into a lifestyle, a lifestyle full of adventure, fulfilment and education.

As I am living on five dollars a day – a mere two thousand dollars a year (though with flights and visas, it ends up being a bit more) – I figured with fifteen grand I would be able to cycle and live for years on the road as long as I was living simply.

Though my parents were a bit concerned that I was not following the norm of college, career, retirement, they now see how much happier and more satisfied I am for living the life of my dreams.

The best advice I can give is don't over-plan. Maybe do some research about where you want to go, but just go for it, wherever it is. Pick a country, pick one randomly if you want, or do it in your own country. There's so much to visit in your own country. Just let yourself be free. And don't worry – everything always works out.

ANNA HUGHES
CYCLED A LAP OF THE BRITISH COASTLINE

You can go anywhere on a bicycle, and the riding itself is free. I cycled around the British coastline – a 10-week, 4,000-mile trip, which cost me £1,017 – roughly 25p per mile or £100 per week – cheaper than my London rent. I could have rented out my room while I was away and the trip would have paid for itself!

I am a huge advocate of exploring close to home, of doing something extraordinary on your own doorstep, of starting the adventure the minute you leave your house. One of my favourite parts was simply that I was exploring my home country and discovering new things each day, even somewhere that was so familiar.

90 MILE STRAIGHT
AUSTRALIA'S LONGEST STRAIGHT ROAD
145.6 km

PATRICK MARTIN SCHROEDER
CYCLED THROUGH OVER 100 COUNTRIES

I was 19 when I started. I had no idea what I was doing, I had little money, a backpack and only one goal: to go round the world. Little did I know how easy it actually is with today's means.

I was trying to come up with a long bike tour that I could do to challenge myself, so I headed towards Africa because I have never been there. I had a €100 bike and I made it to Israel before the bike literally broke apart. I finished the rest of the trip to Cape Town on a €400 bike from Israel that I built myself. It's impossible to be a pessimist, to be distrustful or racist if you have seen what I have seen. The locals have always been amazing. When I asked people in Sudan if they knew a place that sold food, they just told me to sit down and they would come back with a meal. I remember sitting in Peru playing chess with a shoeshine boy, and being cheered by Malawian schoolchildren while cycling up a steep hill. I have encountered so much goodness and hospitality.

Travelling has made me wiser, even if I have never been to university. And it has made me a happier person. It has made me someone who opens up and helps others more readily, instead of just living in a bubble. I recommend it to anyone. Give it a try at the very least.

I wish I had known that most of these supposedly superhuman things that explorers and travellers do are actually things that anyone can do. If you can ride a bicycle, nothing will stop you biking from Europe to China.

ZITA ZÁRUG AND ÁRPÁD HARKÁNYI
CYCLED ROUND THE WORLD FOR THEIR HONEYMOON

We always wanted to travel, to see the world. When my husband proposed to me, I said, 'this is the time to go'. He said, 'let's go by bike'. I said, 'let's make it as a honeymoon'. Then we said, 'let's go around the world'. This really happened; it was that simple. We started from Hungary one week after our wedding. We've cycled 21,000 miles through 38 countries in three years, nine months. But these are the numbers only!

There were glorious moments when we conquered our limits, like in Tajikistan, when we were cycling the Pamir Highway. We crossed the 15,500-foot-high Akbajtal Pass in early winter! Then there are amazing connections with local people, where they and us share many things, even without a common language.

My husband had done previous cycling trips, but I seldom did any sport. But this still didn't stop me setting out on this crazy journey. I wasn't completely out of shape, but I was far and away from fit and strong. I had to learn the golden rule: it all happens in your brain and in your heart, not in your muscles. I learned that if I want to do it, I will. This is my message to those who think that a place is too far for a bicycle. Nothing is too far.

We quit our workplace, we had our wedding and said goodbye to friends and family in Hungary. It was worth it, a thousand times, believe me – this is by far the best damn thing we have ever done, the best school we have ever been to, the most amazing dream we have ever made into reality. Just go! It sounds so simple, but this very first step is the hardest.

CHRIS SZCZERBA
CYCLED TO THE GAMBIA WITH HIS GIRLFRIEND

Countries get big when you cross them on a bicycle. What could be a ten-hour train ride becomes a two-week adventure. Despite the effort, I'd rather waste my breath climbing a mountain pass than on empty words or the sigh of resignation to a daily routine. You can't regret riding through a desert.

Indecision invites inactivity, so make that decision to go. Don't script your adventure before you leave, the story will write itself. Travel isn't a textbook, it's a series of short stories without endings.

And don't agonise over gear; cycle touring isn't income-dependent. Get a strong bike and rack, decent panniers, load them up and leave. You'll get fit on the road. Ease in gently and the miles will stack up. This trip took four months of our lives, opened our eyes wide, gave us sunsets, beaches, hard climbs and long descents. It was heart-warming and heartbreaking, exciting and mundane. It ignited emotions and fired the imagination. It took less than £1,000 out of our bank accounts, but in return it gave us quality of life, a value that transcends all currency.

SUSAN WELFORD AND ADAM JONES
STUDENTS WHO CYCLED A LAP OF ICELAND

We did the trip because we'd always wanted to see Iceland but could never afford to go. After five years of wanting to go it finally occurred to us to take our bikes for free pedal power and to take our tent because wild camping is allowed and all the stunning scenery is free! We were university students and had a month's holiday between our third and fourth years – the perfect length for an adventure. Since that trip we have realised that we can do anything as long as we get planning; expensive trips can be made cheap, you can cycle 75 miles a day even after spending the last three years living a slobby uni lifestyle (especially when fuelled by digestive biscuits!). Now if there's a trip we want to do we don't ask ourselves 'can we do it?', we ask 'how do we do it?'!

RAYEES RASHID
CYCLED THROUGH THE ANDES

Our panniers weren't big enough so we headed to a Peruvian market, bought some Tupperware and cable ties and set about constructing some panniers to tackle the Andes, laughing ourselves silly in the process. We loaded the panniers with vegetables and headed for the open road with a hand-drawn map on a scrap of paper.

TOM LLOYD-SMITH
CYCLED FROM KENT TO KERALA

I was living in east London working for a medium-sized government quango. I took a career break and rode a bicycle from Kent to Kerala with the idea of visiting some of the world's classic rock-climbing destinations along the way.

I get a thrill out of working hard and I enjoy my job. Even though I had no great desire for an alteration in life's course, and was content with the way that my career was progressing, I was aware that it would be likely to be increasingly difficult to undertake any grand journey as I moved into the next phase of my life. I could see that as I progressed up the career ladder, took on a larger mortgage, got married, had children and so on, travel for more than a couple of weeks at a time would be increasingly unrealistic. This was likely to be my 'last hurrah' in travel terms (for a few years at least) and I wanted to make it as ambitious as I could. I was single when I started planning the trip but met the woman who was to become my wife close to my departure.

There are some surprising parallels between managing the required resources associated with a long-distance bicycle trip and effectively managing a heavy workload and prioritising within a professional context. In simplistic terms, the hardships of long-distance bicycle travel can be minimised by effective resource management in the same way that marshalling the available resources is critical to performing well in a demanding job. To illustrate, it's not a disaster if you carry a dozen spare inner tubes on a bike trip, and in many ways it's very sensible, it's just not very good use of the limited (weight and

pannier-space) resource available. Working out the most efficient way to deliver a project or put together a deal, while sensibly managing all the associated risks, essentially involves the same set of fundamental skills as efficient and enjoyable bicycle travel. Personally, I feel better able to handle the pressures of a demanding job as a result of the experience of this trip. The skills learned and developed on that journey – such as coping with pressure, problem solving and building good relationships quickly – have proved useful to me in my professional life.

When I'm still in the office at 10pm I now try to remember that while I was on the bicycle journey I missed the camaraderie of work colleagues, the sense of shared purpose and the thrill associated with doing a big deal. To live life pining for something else is futile and, following this journey, I try harder to make the best of any situation that I find myself in rather than wishing I was somewhere else.

If I had understood the true extent of the forthcoming hardships prior to departure, actually departing (which was the hardest step of all) may have become too daunting a prospect. Ignorance, to a certain extent, is the mother of adventure. Similarly, it was impossible for me to understand fully what personal benefit and enjoyment I would derive from the journey and to understand how these would offset against the journey's hardships.

I think it's important to build in enough time to prepare mentally for an expedition prior to departure and to allow some time to wind down following one's return. Be aware that it's likely to be mentally quite burdensome to go from a demanding full-time job to a demanding expedition or vice versa without taking time for readjustment. For example, I found social situations really quite challenging for a few weeks following my return.

Had I not had a job to come back to, I would have been more anxious about returning to the UK, such that I probably would not have enjoyed the journey as much as I did. I would therefore recommend

having at least an idea of what will follow when you return from a 'big, life-changing expedition' rather than expecting a trajectory to be magically mapped out as a result of undertaking said challenge.

BRENDAN LEONARD
CYCLED ACROSS AMERICA

On a bicycle, I feel like everyone is interested in what you're doing and they think you're so harmless. They'll just come right up and talk to you at gas stations. They come over and they're so drawn by curiosity, that these two idiots were riding bikes across the country. We've met so many cool people that way. To experience the world at 11 miles per hour is an incredible thing. You have all this time and that's all you have. It's so slow and I had so much thinking time.

I don't remember getting a little bit behind on my bills, that sort of stuff, but what I do remember is cycling across America with my friend.

DAVE BOUSKILL AND DEB CORBEIL
MAKING THEIR LIVING FROM TRAVEL AND ADVENTURE, INCLUDING CYCLING THE LENGTH OF AFRICA

The first adventure that really kicked off our life of travel was cycling from Cairo to Cape Town. It was a 7,500-mile adventure through nine countries over 120 days. We had made a New Year's resolution to change our lives within a year. Two weeks later we saw an ad for an epic race through Africa and we decided to sign up. We put down a deposit right away so we wouldn't chicken out, then told all our friends, family and colleagues so that we couldn't back out.

We were looking for something epic to wake us up and shake us out of the rut we were in, working full-time and too hard on careers we didn't love. We had done a lot of travel in the past and wanted to figure out a way to make travel a career. We didn't know how we were going to accomplish that dream, but we knew that we needed to do something monumental to stand out from the crowd and get away from the regular backpacking thing we'd been doing. We needed some direction, and being a couple who tries crazy adventures together seemed like the right idea at the time. It was definitely the wake-up call we were looking for and it eventually all worked out.

This adventure completely changed our lives. We came home from Africa invigorated. We still didn't know how to make a living out of travel and adventure, but we knew that it was what we wanted.

It's never too late and you are never too old. Once you've decided what you want to do, make a plan and be patient. It takes time, but if you love what you do and continue to work on it, you will figure out a way to succeed.

We didn't know a lot about anything before that trip, but the ride has been a fun one. We've been learning as we go. Too many people are paralysed from having a great adventure because they think they need to know everything before they go. You can learn on the road. That's not to say go out blind and put yourself in danger, but don't be afraid to push yourself out of your comfort zone.

IAIN DENLEY
CYCLED EUROPE AND SOUTH AMERICA

I'm like you. I can't do incredible journeys or adventures – my knees won't take it, I can't afford it. What will my parents think? I'll be giving up a career, no one will give me another job with a *gap* on my CV. I might get hurt. I might not like it. I might even get wet, like really wet, and cold as well, wet and cold. I *hate* being cold and wet. So I'll just sit here and read another blog about someone else doing something amazing somewhere in the world. Then I'll go to bed and dream that it was me but I know I can't do it. It is not possible.

The problem was that itch, that nagging feeling that never went away. Scratching it with tales and photos of other people's adventures didn't stop it reminding me. Reminding me that it wasn't *me*.

You can sit at home and think, 'it's all right for him/her, they can do it because of this and that reason'. Truth is, these are your excuses, your manufactured excuses. You formulate reasons to back up why you can't do something amazing.

You are going to die, that is a given. Do you really want to be on your deathbed thinking 'I should have tried, I really should have tried'? At that moment no one will care one iota about what

confident enough of my plans. The problem with friends and family is that they will give you a lot more things to add to your lists before you know enough to realise that you don't need to add their worries and fears to yours.

When I knew what I was doing, why I was doing it and how I was doing it, I told people. That gave me the final motivation to push through the front door and begin. The shame of not then beginning would have been too much!

I set a date and I left on that date. I started my first ever cycle tour, heading for Spain via the Netherlands, Germany and France. Then I will fly to Ushuaia in Tierra del Fuego and I will head north to Prudhoe Bay in Alaska.

People whom I meet ask me where I am cycling to and I start off giving them the short version (Spain), and if the conversation goes on they get the long version (Alaska). I see it in people's eyes: the fear, the worry, the incredulity. I see them thinking, 'this guy can't do that, he doesn't know what he is doing. What he is saying is not possible for someone *like him*.' I see it in *their* eyes. I see *their* fear, *their* worry. I smile, my eyes say to them, 'it's OK, don't worry, don't be afraid, I don't have far to go *today*.'

I may never arrive in Alaska, but I know the day my time runs out on this Earth I will have a smile on my face because I chose to chase my rainbow. That is the greatest gift I can ask for.

you did with your life, apart from you. I don't want to die without trying to live a dream. To try to do something I'm possibly not capable of. To try to do something that only other people with more time, more money, more contacts, more equipment, more knowledge and more experience do. Those privileged people who dare to chase their dreams and live a life true to who they are.

I did something small that moved me a tiny bit closer to being able to fulfil my dream. I had lists of lists but I made sure I crossed something off each day.

The other thing I did was not tell anyone what I was doing. This was important to me as I wasn't

Having spent more than five years out in the world on my bike, I'm a fervent evangelist for two-wheeled adventures. I still believe it's the best way to have a grand adventure. Two things strike me about the testimonies you have just read. The first was how similar were their stories and advice – similar to me and to each other. The second was how different they all were as individuals.

The tales are not just from white, middle-class, young-ish, moderately fit blokes like me. Imran did it, despite expeditions being unheard of in the British-Pakistani community. One of the hardest aspects of beginning an adventure is convincing yourself that it is possible, acceptable and worthwhile. Doing that in a community that never contemplates, let alone encourages, expeditions, takes a good amount of self-belief and determination. This raises the bar on Imran's achievement. James's reminder that you cannot buy time is important, of course, but his observation not to be put off by anyone telling you what you should or shouldn't be doing is also crucial.

Sean and Ingrid did their huge trip with their 8-year-old daughter. Satu did hers on maternity leave. And Karen did it despite being paralysed. This is reassuring to me, for many of the people I talk to who are dreaming of an adventure are quite unlike me and yet I still always try to persuade them to travel by bike!

I wanted to cycle round the world because I was ambitious and angry. I was young, energetic and impatient. I wanted insecurity and strife. I wanted to have a hard time and drive myself to my limits. Fun was for wimps! Similar, then, to Dom who wanted to prove to the world how tough he was. But they are totally opposite reasons to Helen, who had many reasons to cycle through Africa, but 'for the challenge' wasn't one of them. It's interesting how different people, with different goals, can all take satisfaction from cycling across a continent.

I began cycling round the world because I wanted a physical challenge. I wanted to ride far and hard through places that would break me if I let them. But, like Dom, I realised that the physical aspect of the journey mattered less than what I could learn. I second Tom's observation that after a month on the road you'll be as fit as you ever need to be, capable of cycling distances which would have seemed unimaginable before beginning. The longer you ride, the more the journey becomes about the people, about the stories. Karen, who has done plenty of gruelling wilderness challenges, also preferred meeting people and learning more about a place on her bike trips.

Shirine was a low-paid nanny before she set off, aged 20, to pedal the planet. Imran had been made redundant from his call-centre job, whilst Tom had a successful city career which he enjoyed. It's pertinent that Tom enjoyed his job: adventure is not just for people looking for a change of direction in life. He was happy with his life but was aware that making the time for an adventure would only become more difficult as he grew older, got promoted and married. Mark's motivations, meanwhile, were clear cut and easy to act upon as young, single man: 'I simply wanted to break a record and go on a massive adventure.'

I've never personally been interested in speed or records on my travels – the slower I travel, the more satisfying the experience. But I do share most of my adventuring DNA with Mark, not least his observation that cycling round the world 'still tops the chart of all the trips I've done because it was that one where I was wide-eyed, and very innocent, and exploring the world for the first time'.

Indeed, the thrill of that first adventure, where everything is new and exciting, outweighs the downside of not really knowing what you are doing. Bicycle journeys are ideal for cutting your teeth. You are unlikely to find yourself, on Day 1, in a genuinely remote, difficult or dangerous part of the world. So you have time to learn. Tegan fell off her bike at least once a day, Mark had no idea how to fix his bike, and I carried a 'how to fix your bike' book with me for three years before I felt competent enough to dispense with it!

Many of those I spoke to raved above the sense of freedom, of unpredictability and of being solely responsible for your choices and progress. My first big trip, cycling the Karakoram Highway from Pakistan to China, taught me just how easy it is to go and do a big trip. By the end of that adventure I had already begun to dream about going bigger, going all the way round the world. Lots of these long-distance cyclists are my good friends now, so I feel able to say that most of us are really very normal, borderline incompetent people in the real world who just made the decision to get out there and chase the horizon. I laughed a lot at Rayees' description of buying Tupperware containers to make panniers. I know exactly how they will have giggled at the ridiculous-looking bike, and exactly how chuffed they will have felt when their plan worked.

Although I was young, champing at the bit and desperate to get out into the deserts and mountains and madhouse cities of the world when I first dreamed of adventure, many people feel the pull of adventure later on in life when things are generally more complex. Dave and Deb are fine examples that it's never too late and you are never too old. Cycling the length of Africa led them to a total change in life-direction and a more fulfilling career. They understood that they could learn on the road. Starting before you are ready is a super adage for most bicycle adventures. This is certainly true from my own experience. At times, riding through a desert, or haranguing an official for trying to rip me off, I have looked at myself in amazement and thought 'I can't believe that *you* are doing this!' I was not the sort of guy you'd expect to be taking the world in my stride. But you learn along the way, and you also learn that it's really not that difficult.

I look back now and am so thankful that I began before I was ready. I was exactly the same as Tom who did no training whatsoever and didn't even finish building his bike until the morning he left. Alice and Andoni's exhortation to 'just go, you'll have plenty of time to learn' is one that I wish I had received in the nervous weeks before my departure, when I'd have chickened out of the whole trip had I been brave enough to do so.

I didn't have the athletic prowess or the cash to cycle across continents. Nor did Nic. He was unfit, liked beer, and only had £1,000 to his name. Yet he looks back and reflects that he actually thought it would be much harder than it was. I feel the same way. One of the reasons I decided to try to ride round the planet was because I didn't think I could actually do it. That was part of the appeal. It excited me more than doing something I knew I could finish. But I surprised myself and managed to ride 46,000 miles all the way back to my front door.

I did not think I had enough money to get right round the world either, but I just decided to set off and figure that detail out later on. I soon learned that by sleeping wild and eating the cheapest food I could find, I *did* actually have enough money to get home again. Anna calculated that her trip cost less than her rent. When I look back now, my memories of cycling round the world definitely match Brendan's: 'I don't remember getting a little bit behind on my bills, that sort of stuff.'

Nic's trip also reminds us that it is OK for plans to evolve and change. Nic set off on the ride with a friend, they enjoyed riding together, but at some point his friend decided he had had enough and returned home. His friend's action is a good reminder that decisions about adventure are not irreversible. If you think you want an adventure, but fear it may not actually be for you, give it a go. Try it. If you hate it, you can always come home! It's not the end of the world. And far better to

realise that than not even to begin and be filled with regrets and 'what-ifs' for the rest of your life. Adventures twist and turn and change course. Not only is that OK: it's one of the best parts. To have an idea of where you want to get to, but to not really worry or mind quite how you get there is a lovely way to live.

Before the ride Nic was a normal guy with a normal job. Now, after the ride, Nic is a normal guy with a normal job. In other words, adventure can be compatible with real life. You don't have to see your plan as a choice between a normal life with friends, ties, salary and pension *or* life as a crazy wild-eyed lunatic who has dropped out of life to go chase the horizon. It is entirely possible to have a big adventure without ruining everything else that feels important or unavoidable in your life.

One of the great unrealised fears of my years spent cycling were the dangers I faced from my fellow man. I worried about cycling through the Middle East, yet encountered nothing but civility and kindness. I was frightened about Sudan, in the aftermath of decades of sectarian civil war, yet fell in love with the people I met. I feared Zimbabwe, then loved the ride. I dreaded Colombia before dancing happily through that joyful land. Joff noted that 'if you watch the news you will never leave your house.' Kerry found that 'everyone is really helpful, really friendly.' Time and time again my interviewees told tales of the kindness they encountered, the hospitality of countries like Iran, and just how welcome and safe they felt out in the world.

I look back on the years I spent cycling round the world as being the best and most educational of my life. They weren't always easy times, but I agree with Nic's reflection: 'There were difficult bits, but those difficult bits were great.'

Finally, perhaps my biggest motivation to forcing myself to be brave enough to swim against the tide of convention was the same as Andy's: 'I didn't want my epitaph to read: Here lies Andy Madeley, he sure knew how to turn on a computer.'

FOOT

Simplicity and slowness are core components of virtually all the best adventures. Walking is king of both these. Walking requires no expertise and can, if you prefer, entail zero training, preparation or planning. If you decided that you wanted to walk around the world, you could be packed and on your way ten minutes from now. It's that simple. Walking journeys require little gear, though it is worth spending money on lightweight kit if you can. You could fly to the start line of most walking journeys using only your carry-on luggage allowance on the aeroplane.

In many parts of the world you will stand out on your travels for being very rich. Rich enough to afford the time for your adventure. Rich enough to buy snazzy equipment, a plane ticket and a passport. Going for a long walk gives you a better chance of not being perceived in this way and to engage more naturally and equally with the people you meet. People will think you are crazy – that is a given – but they will at least not be covetous of your expensive bicycle. You will share the road with people walking to school, walking to work, walking to their fields, walking as a pilgrimage, walking because they are too poor to take the bus.

On the flip side, walking can be very monotonous – arriving at the horizon takes an inordinate amount of time. When you're hungry and thirsty the 'just a few miles' to the next town can last an eternity. Blisters, a heavy pack and a blazing sun can turn a walk into the most exquisite form of agony. I don't think I have ever done a journey as painful as one on foot. And the agony is not reserved for long journeys. I once walked a lap of London, a week-long walk with a friend who has also done a 3,000-mile walk. Rob still tells me that the pain on our stroll trumped anything he experienced trekking from Mongolia to Hong Kong!

I walked 600 miles across southern India. It was a tiny journey compared to the vastness of India as a whole. So I saw but a fraction of the country. And yet it was one of my richest travel experiences.

What I saw, I saw well. I wanted to walk, because walking is slow and simple and difficult. I decided to walk from the east coast in Tamil Nadu to the west coast in Kerala. I did the tiniest amount of planning I could do yet still have the nerve to commit to the journey. And then I set off. The most difficult, nerve-wracking part of the whole trip was landing in India in the middle of the night, getting to a bus station, finding the correct bus in the melée, then surviving the suicidal maniacal drive to the coast where my walk would begin.

I hated those first 24 hours. I always do. I find crowded foreign places lonely, overwhelming and frightening when I am by myself until I am established in a country. I invariably wish I'd stayed home and not bothered. It's only once I commit to the journey, and get moving down the road, that I can relax, and the joy and excitement and curiosity come bursting forth once more. I followed the course of a holy river through southern India carrying a tiny pack. I ate at street stalls, and at night I slept under the stars under my mosquito net, in cheap truckers' hostels, or with kind families who took me into their homes. It was a busy, noisy, crowded journey and I savoured it for those very reasons.

'In the time span you have available for your adventure, you will see the fewest places if you decide to walk, but the places that you do see, you will truly see'

Indeed, it was a very conscious contrast to a walk I had undertaken the year before when I crossed Iceland by foot and packraft. I chose Iceland for its emptiness and beauty. I travelled with a friend so I had none of that pre-trip worry and I could share any other concerns that I had. We didn't actually have time to worry: the night we arrived in Iceland we gorged on barbecued whale, knocked back vodka shots and danced the midsummer night away so effectively that we were too hungover to begin our expedition the next day. But 24 hours later, we were off. Laden with food for a month, plus cameras, crampons and packrafting gear, our 88 lb packs were a daily torture. We walked as fast as we could: move slowly and the trip would take longer, so our rations would be spread thinner still. My main memories of that journey are pain, hunger, incredible scenery, isolation and lots of laughter. It was a great trip.

You can speed up the slowness of your walk by running. And anyone can run; Jamie McDonald was

play to your advantage if you'd like to raise money for a charity during your trip, as Jamie did, running in a superhero costume.

All the long-distance runners in this book, including senior citizen superhero Rosie Swale-Pope, who ran round the world, have resorted to using some form of trailer during their expedition. It improves the efficiency of their run but reduces the minimalist simplicity. Karl Bushby is using a trailer for his multi-year hike – the longest human walk in history – and Leon McCarron and I took the cart idea to stupid extremes when we set out into the Empty Quarter desert with the worst cart in history (designed by the combined genius of both our incompetencies), laden with 660 lbs of food and water. Terrible though our cart was, when the terrain was good it was incredible how easy it was to tow such a vast weight.

If I were forced to choose, I would say that bicycle trips trump journeys on foot, except where the terrain would be impassable on two wheels or if there is some other reason why a bike would not work – for example, the load of our cart in Oman. I have done lightweight walks and walks laden with wilderness gear. I've walked with a big cart and I have run through the Sahara with my toothbrush sawn in half to save weight. It's hard to lump all these experiences into one category. There is one common thread, however: travel on foot is slow. It is the speed at which most of the human race experienced life for thousands of years, right up until the last couple of centuries. In the time span you have available for your adventure, you will see the fewest places if you decide to walk, but the places that you do see, you will truly see. And that is worth a lot.

a novice runner when he set out to run thousands of miles across Canada. I have never done a running journey, but I have run marathons and ultramarathons, including the 150-mile Marathon des Sables through the Sahara Desert. The memories are seared into my mind, perhaps from the pain, perhaps from the euphoric satisfaction of being very fit and churning through distance.

You cover miles more quickly when you run than when walking, so you can potentially do a longer journey. But you also risk greater agonies and need to travel even more minimally to reduce the weight of your kit. Every ounce counts. Injury risks rise. People will think you are doubly crazy, but this may

WISE WORDS FROM FELLOW ADVENTURERS

ANDREW FORSTHOEFEL
WALKED ACROSS AMERICA

I just wanted to try to meet people, you know? And so I spent a little under eleven months, a little over four thousand miles walking from Pennsylvania to New Orleans, and then to San Francisco.

The trip cost less than a thousand dollars, because of the way people helped me along the way.

I didn't want it to be framed in terms of success or failure. Like, if you don't make it to a certain place, you didn't do it. You didn't win or something. It's crazy. So holding the end point lightly was a nice strategy to appreciate the present moment and dig into what's here and now instead of focusing on what was maybe going to happen months from now. I'd do it the same way if I had to do it over again.

Another thing I would say to anyone who's aspiring to do something like this is that people would often say to me, 'I can't believe you're doing this.' They'd just express their disbelief and I would almost feel guilty in that moment because, in many ways, walking across America was the easiest thing in the world. These people who are supporting families and working these jobs, whatever the job may be, you know, it's so much harder. So that, I would imagine, could be a catalyst, realising that it's actually the easiest thing ever.

JAMIE MCDONALD
RAN ACROSS CANADA IN A SUPERHERO COSTUME

Before I started the run I had never really run before. I'm definitely not an athlete, I'm literally just like your everyday bloke. A go-to-the-gym-a-couple-of-times-a-week kind of human, really. I chose to take on a challenge because I felt like I had a shot at pulling it off.

I ran a marathon about seven years ago. I didn't do any training for it and I completed it, just. It took me about five hours. At the end I was in such a state and I was all, 'I am never, ever doing that again!'

For the first nine years of my life I spent most of my time in hospital. I've got a very rare condition called syringomyelia. I had epilepsy, an immune deficiency, sometimes I couldn't move my legs. And then, at nine years old, I started to move. I started to play tennis. And I'm really lucky that the symptoms disappeared, because they should've progressed. Lots of people end up losing their mobility and their life. Whether loving to move cured me or not, I don't know. But I feel like it did. And so I just carried on moving. I think you've only got to see a kid's face when they're moving and the first thing you see is that they're smiling.

I was quite inspired by the fact that my dad had been a bricklayer all his life. And while I was saving up for the house he came in and said, 'Do you know what? I hate what I do. I've been doing it for 25 years. Why am I doing it?' I said, 'Well, just quit.' So he did, and he started working with people with mental health and learning difficulties. And my mum has said all her life, 'I really want to foster children.' So together they went through the process and now they're fostering. My dad's on minimum wage but he's the happiest bloke on the planet. That goes for both my mum and my dad; they're so happy because they've chosen something that they just really, really love. And I don't think I recognised it at the time but I watched that whole process and then off I went!

My mum hated the fact that I was leaving. If she had had her way, I'd be living next door to her, married with kids. My dad is on the other end of the spectrum, and he's so passionate. He's like, 'Get out there and just love life.' My mum's supportive in her own way, she just worries about me. She's a mother – that's what mothers do.

I've realised that I like suffering. I like the challenge. I look at the run across Canada and it was so physically challenging that at the end of it all, I feel like it's more memorable.

The moment that I was able to take this challenge on was the moment that I accepted failure. We often try to avoid it, especially as we get older. You can't fail, you shouldn't fail, and it's a mistake if you do. But the truth of it is, failure exists. So once you accept that you might fail, I think that will give you a lot more courage to then jump on and do it. Having said that, once you start it, just don't bloody give up.

I didn't realise that actually just me being out there trying was enough to inspire people to hopefully do what they want to do out of life. I received an amazing message in the Rocky Mountains. I had been told that I shouldn't go. The rangers, the police, everyone said, 'Do not cross the Rocky Mountains. It's winter. You're going to die.' And then I received this message from a woman whom I'd met, her and her son, en route. She said, 'I just want to remind you what you're running for.' She said, 'Do you remember my little boy called Samuel?' And I remembered him like it was yesterday. And she said, 'His cancer has returned now and he's out of treatment options. As a mother I'm so, so worried for you. But as a mother that's about to lose her child's life, I just say keep going.' It brought me to tears. It didn't matter how much money I raised, it didn't matter whether I was succeeding or not. It just mattered that I was out there trying.

ANNA MCNUFF
RAN THE LENGTH OF NEW ZEALAND

There's just something so incredibly childlike about running. Pounding barefoot on a beach, lungs burning, a mass of blonde curls being tossed about in the wind – days like these left me feeling more connected and alive than I ever have. I thrived on the freedom and simplicity of travelling under trainer power alone. In being able to leave the trail to set up camp wherever I fancied, and in visiting areas of wilderness that I knew weren't accessible by car, or even by bike.

Over the course of six months I learned that endurance journeys are 90 per cent mental. Once you decide that stopping isn't an option, it becomes far easier to carry on. The fact that my core equipment was my own flesh and bones took the challenge to a new level. As the weeks passed I began to observe, understand and interpret my thought processes better than I have in 30 years of 'normal life'. I realised that no one understands your body better than you. If you listen to it, cajole it and gently but repeatedly beat it up – it'll catch on. We're not as far removed from our running ancestors as we like to believe.

KARL BUSHBY
WALKING FROM PATAGONIA BACK TO THE UK SINCE 1998

After a long haul on the open road it's amazing to reach civilisation. Then after a while in civilisation you need to get back into the jungle, or onto the mountains. For the most part I would avoid the bigger cities. If you are going to get yourself in trouble those are the likely places, but again, that's largely due to the way I travel, unique to my reality.

I did not have the resources to do what I did, but I was armed with a deluded – almost insane – sense of self-confidence that had been drilled into me as a paratrooper. I was bullet-proof. I had been pushed to my limits repeatedly over many years and I knew just what I could do. Confidence in my abilities took care of everything, it seemed. I had experienced a number of environments from desert to jungle to the Arctic and I 'knew' I could handle it.

And that's the defining element, that's what allows you to wander off on something so ridiculously overwhelming with little more than a cheeky grin.

Everyone's story is different, everyone's background is unique and we all bring our own [baggage] to the table. Remember one thing only: you live once. Confidence is a powerful thing. I told someone once, 'I have a superhuman power, just like the X-Men: my superhuman power is I am too ignorant to know I can fail'.

'Finding the time is the biggest fear of commitment that people have. They think their lives are too busy to get up and do things, but time is of the essence'

ROSIE SWALE-POPE
RAN AROUND THE WORLD.
NOW RUNNING ACROSS AMERICA

I spent four years running 20,000 miles round the world. I did the run in memory of my dear husband, Clive, who had recently passed away from prostate cancer. I wanted to raise money and awareness and also help me grieve and begin to move on with my life. The idea was crazy, of course, but you fight darkness with light. On my record day I covered 30 miles. On the slowest day, when I had to shuttle all my kit through deep snow so I was moving backwards and forwards, I only made 100 yards of progress. At times it was very cold, down to -62C in Alaska, although the damp cold of the two Russian winters I ran through at -20C often felt colder than that. It was wonderful!

You shouldn't have to grieve, or to lose a limb or something to be spurred into being forced to do your best. It's nothing to do with age or gender, it's just a frame of mind.

ANDY WARD
WALKED ACROSS EUROPE

I walked, with a friend, from London to Istanbul, which is the closest point of Asia. We began about 48 hours after coming up with the idea rather drunkenly in Somerset, bought a tent, quit our jobs, bought a map to get us to Dover, and beyond that the rest was a bit of an adventure, really. It took five and a half months, with a couple of breaks. I fractured my fibula, which slowed us down for a couple of weeks. It wasn't a race, just having fun.

Everyone was incredibly welcoming and interested in what we were doing. Though none of them believed that we were actually walking, they just thought we were trying to hitch-hike! Trying to get across that we were in fact walking, that we didn't need a lift and that we had really walked all the way from London was always quite amusing. Other highlights include waking up in a minefield, being shot at in Switzerland, free cupcakes in Italy and being granted special permission to walk across the Bosphorus Bridge in Istanbul, which is normally closed to pedestrians. If you're open and friendly to the people you meet you shouldn't get into much trouble.

I always saw the first month as training! We didn't need to keep up an enormous mileage, but the first day was quite big. We did about 29 miles, I think, and that almost broke us in the pouring rain. From then on, once the feet healed and the blisters got better, it was just like a day job. Just have to walk for seven hours a day and get it done…

Once you have made that decision to do it, things are a lot easier. It's just a case of organising it and getting on with it. Finding the time, I guess, is usually the biggest fear of commitment that people have. They think their lives are too busy to get up and do things, but time is of the essence. Turns out, walking to Asia was one of the best things I ever did. I was offered several jobs because of it, because people thought I was an interesting person. Yet my fear of going off walking was that I was ignoring having any career, job or anything else.

If I got to do it again, I'd take more photos and definitely do a few more detours and take the time to enjoy the nice spots.

LEON MCCARRON
WALKED 3,000 MILES FROM MONGOLIA TO HONG KONG

Walking is ultimately so much harder than cycling and there are rewards within that because you do manage to immerse yourself even more. But the more I walk, the more I realise I wish I had done more cycling!

When I set off on my first big adventure, I wanted it to be really long. I wanted it to be indefinitely long because I felt I needed that, and I wanted all the challenges, and I didn't really want to be able to see an end point. I wanted to keep pushing myself and see what would happen. And I wanted it to be really cheap and miserable. I wanted not to be able to spend much money, and just to force myself into action in all sorts of senses. But now, I don't necessarily want really long trips because I quite like all the comforts of home and everything else. And you're absolutely right, you can get the same highs, the same lows, the same emotional responses from a few weeks, perhaps even a few days away.

The only thing you can't get is that real rite of passage, testing yourself against the world. If you're young and angry, you need to go and do a long trip. But other than that, or unless you like the nomadic lifestyle where every day is a new location, then shorter trips provide all the same results.

ROB LILWALL
WALKED 3,000 MILES FROM MONGOLIA TO HONG KONG

Well, before I started walking expeditions, I had this very romantic idea in my mind of walking across valleys and mountains and it being a wonderful way to travel. But the reality of walking was really hard.

I think walking can be really cool, but you have to be less ambitious. I'm not saying don't do walking trips, I think you just have to be careful not to be too optimistic about how far you can travel. You need to allow a lot more margin for rest and to not have to catch up distances. And, if you get lost, it's a major hassle on foot.

I think the best is a walking trip where it's more of a ramble rather than a hardcore expedition to get from A to B and you've got to do 30 miles a day. Those sorts of walking expeditions are hard work, but a nice rambling walk where you're just being a wild man, and camping out, and not carrying too much stuff... that kind of walk can be really cool as a first trip.

I think the two obvious things we should have done differently is, one – allowing ourselves more time. I think if we'd had a year to do that expedition it would have been pretty cool, but doing it in six months was pretty hard. And the other thing was just taking seriously the need to take time out to study Chinese. We could speak a bit, but it would have been a much more interesting trip if I had taken a three-month crash course in Chinese, rather than just trying to teach myself on the way. Those two things would have made a big difference.

It's so magical, isn't it? Your first trip – especially your first trip outside your home continent. You never get that again.

KEVIN CARR
RAN ROUND THE WORLD

I ran 18,000 miles around the world, aiming to become the first runner ever to circumnavigate the world fully self-supported. Along the way I witnessed a massive display of the Northern Lights for the first time in my life, and having run every step of the way to reach that spot made the experience all the more special.

I also loved the feeling when, after a few thousand miles of running, I turned around to face where I'd come from and realised that it was too far to go back. This meant it finally dawned on me that it felt right to say, 'I am running around the world' rather than 'I'm trying to run around the world.' When you're only a few hundred miles from home it's hard to feel that it's really under way.

A few tips I'd pass on would be don't waste time on the internet sweating over the small stuff... what kit to use, what's the best food to take, is a route through this area safe, practical or even possible? All this sort of stuff, you can waste hours a day on forums and easily get sidetracked. Also, language barriers usually aren't barriers at all, just an opportunity for you to swallow your pride and feel a bit silly. As long as you show willing, most people will try to understand you and help where they can.

JON MUIR
WALKED ACROSS AUSTRALIA,
THROUGH THE OUTBACK, UNSUPPORTED

In extreme environments, whilst attempting extreme challenges, even if the objective isn't reached, if you've got home safely you've succeeded. The early attempts at both Everest and my unsupported crossing of Australia were enormously rewarding. I learnt so much about myself, about the terrain that I was negotiating, about my gear and how to improve on it. Those early attempts were my life unfolding, I was living every moment of them, not focused on just the end goal, and they were intensely rewarding because of that. Failure to me is simply not having a go in the first place.

Throughout the early decades of my career I was looking for something that would really push me to the limits of my endurance. The rock climbing, mountaineering, sea kayaking and polar journeys never took me close. The unsupported desert walks were in a totally different league than all my previous expeditions. Every day of the 128 days on my continental crossing was more difficult than my summit day on Everest. I thrive on that intense challenge. I love the desert country, too. It's so clean and wild and ancient. It has amazing presence.

You know, I never really assume I'm going to complete any project. Sure, you gain skills and knowledge from previous attempts, and a degree of confidence in yourself, but every moment of everyone's lives are unique moments so it's best not to assume too much about how things might unfold.

When I'm really pushing hard I start to draw on an inner reserve that's only accessible through adversity. I like the absorption in the moment that place allows me. It draws out a part of myself that is more powerful than the usual concept I hold of myself during an average domestic sort of day. Those most difficult days stand out very clearly in my memory. There's nothing ho-hum about intensely

challenging times. You feel really, really alive.

I'm always wondering 'what next?' If I wasn't I might as well be dead. I love the lure of another adventure in the wilderness. My list of adventures in my head is way too long for just one lifetime.

PAULA CONSTANT
WALKED FROM THE UK TO AFRICA

The first big trip was the three-year walk which started from Trafalgar Square and then went out and down through Europe. The first year was 3,000 miles on foot with backpacks and then it moved into two years across the Sahara with camels.

It's been an interesting journey in the last few years to look back at what was driving me then and what drives me now, and how that differs. I'm ambitious; I think that is never going to alter. But the way it manifests is interesting. At the time I was quite clear about what I wanted. I wanted to make a living doing something I loved, and to see the world through other people's eyes. I wanted to write books and I wanted a big adventure. That was pretty much it. I didn't want to be stuck in a 9-to-5 working for people I didn't really respect. I had a strong desire to make my mark in some way. To live an extraordinary life, if you like. And for me that was what success meant: to succeed meant to lead an extraordinary life. So, that was my sole ambition, really.

I am so grateful for that walk. I can never describe it. It's taken me a long time to be grateful for it. I loved it. I just loved it. Loved every step of it. But, I have learned that it's OK to stop, to say 'what do I want now?' and go in a totally different direction, which I've now done. But I wouldn't say it scratched the itch. I'd say if anything it fired my brain synapses to really understand that anything I dream of is doable. The important part for me now is to be discerning about what I dream of.

I had a really specific desire that was related to the Sahara. I was fascinated by the way that cultures and religions have moved across that part of the world and up into southern Europe. That was my big drive, wanting to see the world through those particular eyes and to walk the same pathways that various people I admired had taken. But the adventure for adventure's sake never held any appeal to me.

I wanted the physical experience of moving through countries and through people. I wanted to meet the people and understand other people. To see the world through other people's eyes. That was really my only goal, I think at the time when I left.

The leap off the cliff of quitting my job as a teacher and committing to this was a relief and one I never looked back from. I think that daily, because it put a barrier between me [and my past life]. It created a life for me that I'm grateful for. It made me a platform from which to springboard into the rest of my life.

There was not a day, not one dawn, not one night that went by in the desert, outside of towns, where I didn't think I was born to do this and I'm so lucky to be here. Not one day.

RACHEL BESWETHERICK
WALKED A WORLD WAR II PRISON ROUTE
WITH HER BROTHER

We had planned on camping along the way. On our first night a local family took us in and allowed us to sleep in their house. They then suggested that for the remainder of the trip we sleep in the local *wats* (Buddhist temples). This became our daily task, to find the local *wat* as we walked and ask to stay. It was incredible. We slept in an array of different temples and got a unique insight into the life of monks. I had always wanted to do something that was unique, out there, crazy, different, difficult, testing, challenging. I wanted to know that I had done something with my life that had pushed me past all my boundaries, comfort zones and limits. I love to travel, I love to walk and I love other cultures.

While doing this walk I discovered the importance of family. I spent the expedition with my brother (testing at times) and I spent the time away from my new husband of only five weeks at the time (testing every day).

Completing an expedition you plan yourself is doable. Having an adventure isn't hard. You just have to do it. I wish I'd known that years ago.

ED STAFFORD
WALKED THE LENGTH OF THE AMAZON

I massively shouted about my trip before I left and made a big song and dance. I had a big website, got loads of people involved, told everyone I was going to have a big launch party. And then I felt the sensation that a lot of people describe when they set foot on the expedition: I had no idea what I had let myself in for!

There are a few things that I try to live by and I think it's good to be true to your word. If you say you are going to do something then you do it. It got so much harder and so much more dangerous than I thought it was going to be, but I just thought, 'You know what, I really want to do it.' My very core wanted to do it and said, 'I'm not an arrogant person at all but I believe I'm going to get to the end, I believe I can see myself running down the beach.' So we just kept going, really, and it was as simple as that. It wasn't enjoyable all the time. To a large extent it was a prison sentence, but I definitely had something stubborn within me that wanted to prove that I could do it. I think stubbornness isn't necessarily an amazing attribute but I think it was worth it. It's what got me through it. It was very much a boys' adventure. Cho and I would say to each other, 'if we die, we die – *si morimos, morimos*', and then laugh. It was one of our main jokes – we didn't have many. We accepted it as a potential consequence.

I look back now and I could never do it today. The amount of risks and the remoteness with

the lack of insurance and lack of evacuation plans and stuff like that. It was so out on a limb. The dangers of malnutrition, illness, injuries, African killer bees, wasps' nests, snake bites, anacondas, piranhas, caiman, jaguar, drowning and upsetting the locals. The hardest thing was sticking with it, dealing with the monotony rather than the dangerous bits. In the dangerous bits the adrenaline kicks in and suddenly you are flying and you've just had the most amazing life-changing experience. But the boring bits you get no credit for getting through at all. They are not fun, you don't remember them half the time and yet they are the bits that dominate most of your time. The

monotony was what I found harder than any of those so-called obstacles.

I guess it's no different from a hard workout or something that makes you feel good at the end. You've suffered for half an hour and then you come out the other end and you feel really good about yourself. I think expeditions are that, they are doing things that we were meant to physically do – exerting yourself, overcoming obstacles, thinking outside the box, having slight dices with danger. I think all that stuff is so important to keep growing as a soul.

If you have nothing in your life that challenges you, nothing that takes you outside your comfort zone, then you are just going to wither and waste away. However, I personally think that, in terms of massive expeditions, if I haven't proved what I wanted to prove to myself by walking two and a half years through the Amazon then I'm probably going to be forever chasing it if I don't look for a slightly different option [in the future]. I think to try to do a bigger expedition, then a bigger expedition, and then a more dangerous expedition isn't the way to prove that to yourself.

LEV WOOD
WALKED THE LENGTH OF THE NILE

It was a fascinating way of exploring Africa in the twenty-first century, with its diverse peoples and cultures.

Before I left, I thought 80 per cent would be dreadful and 20 per cent would be interesting. Actually what I found was that it was probably closer to 50-50. I'd say half of it was miserable, boring and just generally crap and the other half was really interesting and good fun. On a journey like this, where you've got so many different landscapes and cultures, every day is different and it was fascinating. For me, that's what spurred me on and gave me the motivation to wake up each day and walk for 20 miles, all the little adventures along the way.

It wasn't just about the physical challenge, it wasn't just about the extreme athleticism aspect, it was about meeting the people and finding the happy medium.

If you try to explain to a villager that you're walking the Nile, they just look at you blankly, whereas if you tell them you're walking to the next village, which is three miles away, they'll almost faint, 'No, you can't do that!'

I've always been fascinated by that river. Not just because it's the longest river, but because it does pass through some very diverse areas. And walking is how humans left Africa all those hundreds of thousands of years ago, and I thought it would be a

really raw and visceral way of meeting the people along the way. You're really putting yourself at their mercy and kindness, which for me was an important draw.

I like to test myself and challenge myself and I thought walking was a good way of doing that.

Walking the Nile has given me a huge respect for Ed Stafford [who walked the Amazon]. I had a big respect for him beforehand, of course, but doing it myself... Wow! It took him two and a half years. In the Amazon there are no roads, it's just hacking through swamps and bush the whole way in the jungle and it must have been really shit, to be honest.

So, 20 years from now, what are you going to regret? You're not going to regret the things that you have done, it's those that you haven't done. So don't put things off, go and take those risks, because some risks are worth taking. And by doing so, you're going to come away with some amazing memories and experiences.

NICK HUNT
WALKED ACROSS EUROPE

I walked 2,500 miles across Europe, from the Hook of Holland to Istanbul. This was a dream I'd had since I was eighteen – following in the footsteps of Patrick Leigh Fermor. I followed two major rivers and crossed three mountain ranges, finding accommodation in the homes of hospitable strangers, wild camping in the woods, squatting in abandoned castles and sleeping rough when necessary. During the course of my journey I stayed in a Hungarian school, a Romanian nunnery, a Bulgarian monastery and a Transylvanian psychiatric hospital.

I learned to love the slow magic of walking, the gradual shifts in landscape, culture, language and understanding, and the joy of solitude: what Tove Jansson called 'one part expectation and two parts spring sadness', and for the rest just a colossal delight at being alone.

I did very little preparation – I didn't research the route, I didn't look on Google Maps, I deliberately avoided travel guides, and I didn't do any physical training. My idea was to use Patrick Leigh Fermor's books, eighty years out of date, as my only travel guide. I wanted to let the continent surprise me, to have as few preconceptions as I possibly could. A bit of physical training would have helped, though, as I went through a fair amount of pain on my travels!

Living cheap when walking is easy, especially if you're prepared to rough it a bit and use Couchsurfing for free accommodation instead of relying on hotels. Apart from food, wine, beer, chocolate and cigarettes (my psychological reward system at the end of each day) I didn't really have anything to spend money on!

Seemingly modern, built-up Europe can still feel surprisingly wild, mysterious and exciting if you're in the right frame of mind, if you open yourself to possibility and allow imagination to flow – whereas you could put yourself in the middle of the Gobi Desert with an iPod and experience nothing more exciting than you would in your own front room. The freedom and the wilderness are inside you, not outside.

There's a great paradoxical disappointment in the act of arrival. Reaching the Black Sea, or indeed Istanbul, were things I'd looked forward to and imagined as an enormous triumph – but so often, travelling is more fulfilling than the destination, and when I finally got to those places, I felt a great sadness to think that the process of getting there was now at an end.

One of my mantras is that the best adventures are simple adventures. Adventures on foot are certainly not easy, but they are simple! Good adventures, too, ought to be slow. To have the time to immerse yourself in your journey, in the geography and culture you pass through, and to look deep into your mind as you explore what you are physically capable of achieving and coping with.

A tremendous benefit of doing something simple is how easy it is to begin. Andrew got fired from a job, didn't have enough money for the adventure he had been planning, so figured he'd 'just start walking and keep it simple'. Likewise, Jamie had done little more than a wheezy five-hour marathon before setting off to run 5,000 miles. And Andy began 48 hours after drunkenly hatching the plan and 'beyond that the rest was a bit of an adventure'. In terms of logistics, gear and cost, nothing beats a journey on foot; chuck a few things into a rucksack and then you're pretty much on your way. It's all quite a contrast to something like Ben Saunders' South Pole journey that took ten years of preparation.

What is it that made these people stop daydreaming and begin their trips? It's one thing to know that you could walk out of your front door tomorrow morning and be on your way to China. It's quite another thing to have the courage actually to do it. Karl did it through the self-confidence the military had instilled in him, as well as being 'too ignorant' to know he might fail. A totally different personality, Rosie, feels that it's nothing to do with age or gender, it's just a frame of mind. Nick 'told ten people [he] was doing it. If you tell ten people you are doing something, you have no choice but to do it.' Rachel booked her flights – once she had done that she felt committed. Lev managed to get going despite thinking before he left that '80 per cent would be dreadful'.

And then comes the sensation that a lot of people describe when they set foot on the expedition. Says Ed, 'I had no idea what I had myself in for!' This can be unnerving, but Nick actively sought out this uncertainty, not researching the route or doing any training at all. He 'wanted to let the continent surprise him.' He does acknowledge that he suffered for his lofty visions and wished he had trained a little!

I've always been fit before beginning my long walks, but Andy preferred to see the first month as training, and Jamie liked suffering and the challenge. Like Rob, I've found that the reality of walking is really hard and I prefer to begin without the extra misery of having to get fit. Paula probably speaks for many of us with this summary: 'it was definitely an adventure, poorly executed and a learning curve'.

It's interesting to note that our pedestrians discuss the notion of failure more than the cyclists. I wonder if this is due to the daily pain of walking, or the inevitable introspection of moving so slowly for so long. Andrew didn't want failure to loom over his trip, so he tried to 'hold lightly' to the end point in order to better appreciate the moment. That is one of the wisest bits of expedition advice anyone could ever want. Jon's definition of success is also not linked to a finish line: 'failure to me is simply not having a go in the first place.'

If the aim of your journey is just to get to the end, you miss out on so much of the experience. Nick describes appreciating 'walking for its own sake, not for its usefulness in getting me somewhere. It became less a means to an end than an end in itself. There's a great paradoxical disappointment in the act of arrival.' I know this feeling so well. Every trip I do ends in a sense of emptiness and anticlimax. To focus on the goal to the detriment of everything else is a real shame. It's one of the main reasons I've never been interested in high-speed expeditions.

I think the prospect of failure and the insidious temptation to just jack it all in and go home lingers at times in the mind of most who have taken on a long walk. And the reason is simple: because it's hard.

Jamie was clear that the moment he took on the challenge was the moment that he accepted failure. ('Having said that, once you start, just don't bloody give up!') Ed has a similar stubborn streak that wanted to prove he could do it. It takes a while to grow into a big journey, to believe that you actually belong on it. Kevin remembers the moment when it felt right to say, 'I am running around the world' rather than 'I'm trying to run around the world.' It's a nice moment to anticipate on your own journey.

'You've chosen to do this so jolly well enjoy it! And remind yourself each day what you have achieved, and hold your head up high'

It's OK to take some time to feel that you truly belong on your journey, that you're not just full of hot air and unlikely boasts: these journeys are difficult and you are a novice. That is part of the point. Ed believes it is important to be 'exerting yourself, overcoming obstacles, thinking outside the box, having slight dices with danger. I think all that stuff is so important to keep growing as a soul.'

But let's not forget the exhortation from Rosie Swale-Pope: 'I can't stand it when adventurers complain about how tough and miserable things are – we choose to do it! It was fun!'

People will certainly think you are crazy on a long walk, with Rachel, Lev and Andy all attesting to how often people try to give you lifts to help you out. When I walked across India I found myself in a conundrum: tell people I was walking only to the next town and they'd try to give me a lift; tell people I was walking all the way to Kerala and they'd refuse to believe me. As usual, the kindness of strangers is almost universally lauded with heartwarming tales of generous strangers. Rosie always 'gets a lot of hugs and kindness out on adventures' (though I suspect someone as cheerful and outgoing as she is probably gets hugs even from her accountant). Andy's advice that if you're open and friendly to the people you meet you shouldn't get in much trouble is sound, particularly if balanced with a bit of streetwise common sense.

It's understandable that everyone's motivations for a journey are different. I walked across India for the people, across Iceland for the absence of people. Andrew walked across America to listen to people's stories. Jon's walks through the Australian outback were about leaving the world behind and really putting himself to the test. 'Every day was more difficult than my summit day on Everest', he recalls. It was worth it though, he feels, for 'there's nothing ho-hum about intensely challenging times. You feel really, really alive.'

If this sounds a little gruelling for you, take heart from Paula, who reflected daily how lucky she felt to be out there. So give it a go! Hatch your plan, then make it happen. If you're a beginner – so much the better! As Lev urges, you're not going to regret the things that you have done. For Andy, his trek was one of the best things he ever did, with implications for his future too: 'I was offered several jobs because of it, because people thought I was an interesting person'. And Rob looks back, wistfully, at how magical his first trip felt.

I'll leave the last words to the inspirational and eternally cheerful Rosie: 'Remember that it's fun – you've chosen to do this so jolly well enjoy it! And remind yourself each day what you have achieved, and hold your head up high.'

ANIMAL

I have never undertaken a journey involving an animal, though I would love to. I know the reasons why I have not done it: it's more expensive than just going solo; making it to the start line is more of a hassle; getting under way each morning is slow; you need skills to care for and control the animal; or you need to travel with somebody who has those skills; you need patience; and at the end of a long, hard day you have to put the animal's needs above your own, and to look after it before you look after yourself. None of these things appeals to me. (Or rather, some of them do appeal in theory, but I know my weaknesses!)

Every style of adventure has its pros and cons. And the benefits of a journey with an animal are huge. There is the satisfaction of sharing the journey with another soul (probably one more intelligent and sentient than some of my previous human companions...). There is the inspiring example of stoicism, minimalism, simple needs and living in the moment which all adventurers aspire to but fall pitifully short of compared to any dog or donkey. You are instantly more interesting if you're travelling with an animal, leading to conversations, opportunities and shared hospitality. Then there is the exciting link to adventurers of old. Paula is a committed romantic towards the 'good old days' of explorers; crossing the Sahara with her own camel train brought her closer to the experiences of the explorer Wilfred Thesiger, whom she greatly admired. Leon McCarron and I hauled a stupid cart through the Empty Quarter desert in our own homage to Wilfred Thesiger. We'd have been better off with camels. On a practical level, animals can assist your journey, but on that trip we couldn't afford camels, didn't know how to use them and we're a pair of daft masochists who liked the idea of making things physically hard for ourselves.

If you have the time, the patience, the money and the temperament for a journey with an animal you can be certain that it will make for a rewarding, entertaining experience and a fantastic story.

WISE WORDS FROM
FELLOW ADVENTURERS

PAULA CONSTANT
SPENT TWO YEARS CROSSING
THE SAHARA WITH CAMELS

It was complicated spending two years crossing the Sahara with camels. It was, but I didn't realise it would be when I set out. And because of that, it never seemed to be. There were a lot of times when I thought, 'Oh my god, people just wouldn't be able to do this.' [laughing] At the time it was a terribly ego-driven thought, but it was so peaceful on so many levels. Towns were a nightmare; every month when I walked into a settlement it was always a shit fight, to be fair, but the second I got out of them, and I'd know I had another 30 days or whatever in front of me... it was just so beautiful and so peaceful and I loved every single second of that.

HANNAH ENGELKAMP
WALKED A LAP OF WALES WITH A DONKEY

I had already had the idea of walking around Wales because the [new official] footpath had only been open for a couple of months, and I was ripe for adventure. I thought that I would do the thousand-mile walk and it would take three months or something and it'd just be a nice thing to do. And then I saw this film with a caravan of nomads heading out into the Sahara with horses and camels, and it was just that one moment, that one sort of romantic view, that vision and I thought, 'Of course, I'll be taking a donkey with me around Wales. That's perfectly obvious.'

I'd never actually walked very far carrying all my stuff, so I was a little bit daunted about that. I figured taking a donkey would sort that one out,

and then I'd be able to take luxury items like my ukulele.

In the end I didn't take my ukulele, there was absolutely no time for it. It didn't work out anything like the romantic vision I had from the beginning. In those early days when I was dreaming about it, I thought it'd be a calm, Zen-like walking meditation and that I'd take watercolours and books and a ukulele, you know, all these things that I thought I would do and learn. It actually ended up being mostly about scooping up poo and setting up the donkey's corral and checking his hooves. It didn't give me the kind of time and space that I was expecting.

I'm not terribly good at solitude, but I felt like I needed to do it not with another human being, so the donkey would provide companionship. But also, of course, most of all, I'm just a showoff and I knew that people would look at me if I had a donkey with me. The donkey was the way to get very quickly into people's stories. We'd quickly dispense with what I was up to and then I would get the opportunity to ask them about themselves. Maybe they would've been more cagey if it had just been a journalist walking up, but because I had something to swap, it was a very quick way to get the inside track on people and places.

The donkey had a moment-by-moment appreciation of the world. For him it was just about feeling like having a roll, 'I'm having a roll,' or feeling like having a bit of this plant and having a bit of that plant. Even as I was trying to do that – not thinking about yesterday or tomorrow – in actual fact I was constantly giving myself little promises of something nice to eat if I get to the next hill, wondering what I was going to have for supper, or looking forward to setting up the tent.

Everything was about marking my progress even as I thought I was living in the moment.

I often found myself saying, 'Oh, it's easy, you can do something like this.' But, actually, it is quite hard. It's not something that I'd want to complain about because it was the most fantastic six months of my life, but it wasn't a breeze. Maybe it comes down to the fact that something can be simple without necessarily being easy.

TIM COPE
TRAVELLED FROM MONGOLIA TO EUROPE ON HORSEBACK

I set off on the trail of Genghis Khan by horse to retrace, and discover the spirit of, the nomadic people of Eurasia. It was an amazing journey. The beauty of the Altai mountains, temperatures of minus 50, the Kazakh Desert, the Carpathian Forest...

On the one hand, the lure was the prospect and endless possibilities of what might happen in this environment, where there are no fences for 6,000 miles. You set off on the horse and, from day one to the finish, it's unpredictable. I really wanted to understand who these nomadic people were. It just really beguiled me about how they lived in this environment with an attitude that kind of debunks the way we live in settled Western society. The concepts of private property don't exist. People adapt their lives to the animals rather than the other way around. Both of them were key to my inspiration and the horse seemed to marry everything together. Because the horse gave me that insight into an ancient world, it allowed me to transcend the modern era, and it gave me the freedom to move away from the roads and experience what these nomadic people have always known: the freedom of that environment. Every time I got on my horse I had two pack horses behind me and my little dog, Tigon: it was like stepping into a folk tale each day.

When I arrived on a horse and met people who

had never ridden horses, or at least hadn't lived the nomadic life, suddenly all of the things that their fathers and grandfathers had told them about horsemen and the horse life [came rushing back to them], traditions like, 'You should never let a horseman pass your family home, you should always bring them in for three cups of tea, and if possible host them for three days.' The horse enabled me to experience a way of life that has slipped into the past.

This might sound strange, something I hadn't really anticipated before I set off is that on a horse I lost my independence. The journey completely revolved around the well-being of

and it hadn't been something that I was really fully expecting.

The flip side of that is that the horses, as a result, completely tied me to the environment. From Mongolia to the Danube in Hungary I can still recount in my mind pretty much every patch of grass along the way. You start to learn to look at the world through the eyes of a horse. The world looks very different from horseback than from other modes of transport. You start to look out for threats and problems. Cities appear particularly unfriendly when you're on horseback, and they can be extremely dangerous. One of the great things was that horses can literally cross raging rivers, through snow, up mountains, and on tracks as well. They are incredibly versatile and you can go a long way.

I think one thing that gets forgotten is that the horse is not really a mode of transport. It actually becomes your companion. The relationship with your animals becomes the essence of the journey. It's like you're all in it together, and you are travelling and you're moving, and you've got a goal, but ultimately the goal is to find enough food and shelter and water to keep everyone healthy and happy.

MARTIN HARTLEY
CROSSED THE ARCTIC OCEAN WITH
A TEAM OF HUSKIES

I can't remember if it was 86 or 99 days on the Arctic Ocean, crossing from Russia to Canada with 19 Canadian Inuit dogs. That was amazing. Without the dogs everyone would have killed each other for sure. That was the worst – the worst – expedition experience with a team I have had by a long, long way. The dogs were always happy and they loved working, and they just exude happiness when they are working, so that kept us together, I think.

'The relationship with the horse and your animals becomes the essence of the journey. It's like you're all in it together'

the animals. I could only travel as far as it was healthy for the horses to travel. If you see a beautiful hill with a beautiful view, you can't just go there and camp with a horse, because the horses need up to 7 gallons of water each day, and it needs to be a place with good grass and good shelter and all the rest of it. That was a challenge,

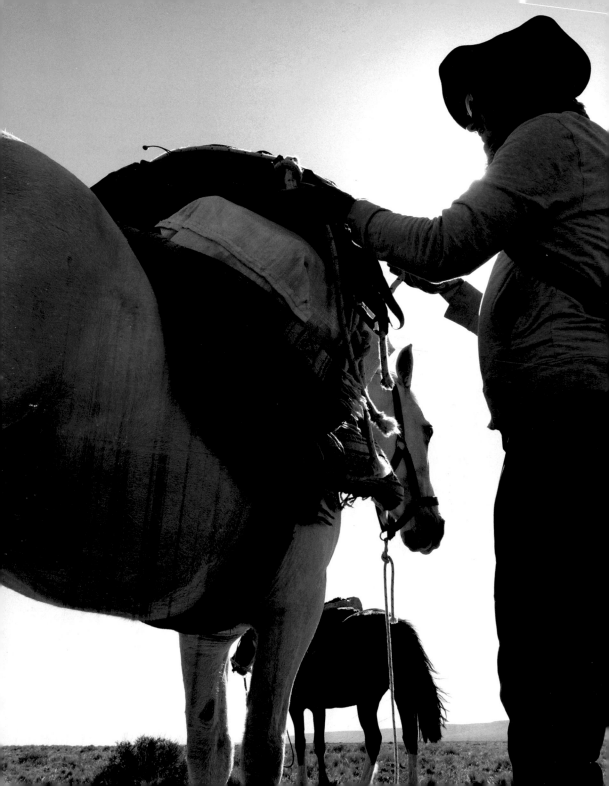

JAMIE BUNCHUK
RODE HORSES ACROSS KAZAKHSTAN

The basic idea of our adventure was to celebrate the centenary of an Anglo-Irish explorer's journey through Central Asia. Sir Charles Howard-Bury made his way overland to the furthest reaches of the Tian Shan Mountains in present-day Kazakhstan. We flew to Kazakhstan, bought three horses, and then rode south along the isolated desert steppe until we reached Almaty, 63 days later.

The highlight for me was taking my favourite and fastest horse for a ride one quiet evening on a rest day out in the steppe. We were in the middle of nowhere, the flat expanse of grass stretching on for miles and miles in every direction. Both the horse and I must have been bored from the enforced rest – due to bad weather – and I had barely hopped on him when he took off full kilter. We rode like the clappers, the ground becoming a streaming blur of colour. It was really a bit dangerous; I had no helmet on and, considering no one knew where I was, a fall would have been quite dodgy. But the risk added to the experience and I've never felt such a vivid sensation of being alive before. As we galloped full tilt into the glow of a setting sun, I knew that moment would stay with me forever.

I got completely attached to a romanticised notion that I could play the martyred hero, a modern-day explorer out on a brave quest through alien worlds on his trusty steed, trailing fame, fortune and adoration in my wake. Of course, the reality of the expedition turned out quite differently; it always does. Really, we were just two fools quite unprepared for the many hardships we'd eventually have to face. Indeed, we bumbled our way through it all without much of a clue.

The journey through Central Asia taught me so much about myself: about being confident in who you are and what you want your story to be, in learning true drive and determination and discovering that – ultimately – the banal things people always worry about don't actually matter in the slightest. You'll get round those inconveniences the same way you'll get across an unknown country. Granted, it will be with a lot of mistakes, mis-steps and more bumbling, but you'll always make it to somewhere new in the end. We'd never ridden horses before so we had to learn all about equestrian maintenance, purchasing, and indeed the riding itself.

Some people may say you can wing it, and once you're on the ground you'll probably have to. But don't skimp to do more, learn more and pursue a more coherent picture of the adventure in your head when you have the opportunity to do so beforehand. Not doing your research is lazy. You may still have an exciting trip 'on the hoof' and it may still be fun, but the scope of your achievements will increase tenfold if you don't dick around and you get working hard prior to leaving.

I wish I had learned more Russian before beginning our journey. The quality and experience of our adventure would have increased massively if we had been able to converse properly with the many colourful characters we met along the way.

HELEN LLOYD
CROSSED KYRGYZSTAN ON HORSEBACK

Travelling on horseback gives you the freedom to go almost anywhere and have a companion, too (one that doesn't answer back or get angry). It doesn't matter how tired you may be, or how much you may want to do something, always, always, the horse's needs must come first. For some, that may be a disadvantage, but personally I find it very rewarding. For me, the horse has been my favourite mode of travel – although to be fair I was riding in Kyrgyzstan, which is ideal horse territory.

LEON MCCARRON
BY HORSE ALONG THE SANTA CRUZ RIVER

I did a journey on horseback in Argentina, from the Atlantic Ocean to the Andes. I think I was interested in this relationship you build with an animal, where you're both totally reliant on each other to survive and make it through.

The best reason for taking animals on an adventure is that they let you properly get off the road. I needed to be near water, but that was about it. It's an amazing feeling to strike off into the steppe, or wherever, and know you don't have to rely on a road, or a town to resupply from. It was also amazing to start to understand my horse, and to feel like this huge animal was beginning to trust me. To begin with we were sounding each other

out, but after a few days we both had the other one figured, more or less, and settled into a good rhythm. I got on better with that horse than I have done with some humans!

It's quite hard work! Horses are clever beasts, and super hardy, but they do need to be looked after. I was lucky because I travelled with a guy who knew his stuff, but I didn't realise until after we started how much the horses would affect the arc of each day. I also never really thought about the fact that I'd be holding my horse's reins with one hand, and holding the rope for the packhorse in the other. That meant even simple things like scratching my nose or adjusting my hat required a bit of pre-planning because my hands were always busy. It was much more involved than if I'd been walking or cycling. It also limited my filming from the horse.

One of the recurring themes of this book is that everyone begins as a beginner, and inexperience should not impede your adventuring plans. The notion of learning on the job resonates through the stories of all those who have travelled with animals in this book.

Both Paula and Hannah found their journeys to be more complicated than they had anticipated when they began, their imaginations fired by romantic visions of carefree adventure. They were only walking alongside their four-legged companions; both Jamie and Leon also had to learn how to ride them. As someone who has often daydreamed about a long expedition with camels or horses, I shuddered a little at Tim's comparison that 'the easiest day on the horses was harder than the hardest days of any other journey.' Strong words from a man who has cycled and rowed thousands of miles in the wild. He loved the experience though, as did Helen, who has also travelled by many means. She ranks her horse journey as her favourite of all.

'I was interested in this relationship you build with an animal, where you're both totally reliant on each other to survive'

Something I always aspire to on my own journeys is to live in the moment, to take each triumph and disaster one at a time, and to enjoy each day as best I can. But I am hopeless at doing this. I am forever dreaming of the future, reminiscing about the past, or grumbling about the present. A journey with an animal is one long lesson in living in the moment. Hannah observed that her donkey had a moment-by-moment appreciation of the world. There's a lot of wisdom about the art of travel in that small donkey!

The key to the strength of feeling these kinds of journey generate is the relationship that develops between human and animal. Leon found it amazing how trust and understanding developed between him and his horse. Helen savoured a companion (an adjective used by several interviewees) that didn't answer back or get angry. It is an interesting relationship. Companionship and trust suggests equality in the relationship, though the human is in charge and the animal is working towards their goal. And yet, for the journey to succeed, the needs of the animal must always come first. Tim and Helen both appreciated learning to put their own needs behind those of their horses, and the daily search for fodder and water directed the rhythms of everyone's journeys.

Journeys with animals are hard work and slow. But they also allow great freedom of movement, which Leon, Helen and Tim all mentioned. It is worth noting that those three had each previously done long journeys by bicycle. Escaping from the man-made roads of the world is an intoxicating prospect not often possible on touring bikes.

Tim sums up the essence of journeys with animals: 'It's unpredictable. It was an unscripted life that I was looking for and a sense of freedom. That was what I was really looking for.'

WATER

Whether you choose a canoe or kayak, build a raft, or simply set out to swim, heading to the water is possibly my favourite way of guaranteeing an interesting journey. Pick a river, any river on Earth, follow it from source to sea and you have found yourself an exciting and fulfilling journey. I love the way landscapes and people change as I follow a river's meandering course.

As much as I loved cycling round the world, I was aware that virtually the entire journey, even in the wildest places, was done on a man-made road or track. Rivers, on the other hand, are wild and natural and ageless. Whether you follow a frozen river on skis in midwinter or paddle along it in the summertime, the river is the best sort of road to travel along.

One of my favourite trips was canoeing 500 miles down the Yukon River. My memories of being properly in the wild, of drifting peacefully even when I wasn't paddling, of camping on islands in the middle of the river, are some of my happiest travel memories. For day after day there was no sign of human life; just grizzly bears, millions of trees, and the quiet lapping of the river in motion.

Paddling a river can be cheap and logistically simple. You can build your own raft and paddle the great rivers of Europe or South America as two of our interviewees did, or you can buy a dugout canoe, emulating Olly Whittle as he set out to paddle the Mekong in search of something more life-affirming than his office job.

For many river journeys, however, kit, logistics and cash loom large on the horizon. I crossed Iceland paddling rivers using a packraft – an inflatable boat that overcomes some of the logistical hurdles of paddling. It was one of the most exciting adventures of my life. Packrafts are like an adult's rubber dinghy. They are brilliant fun, a super passport to the wilderness, and enable really creative journey planning. But they are not cheap, and the hike to get to the beginning of the paddle phase tends to be longer than the river part of the journey.

Journeys that require kayaks or canoes will typically begin and end with a tedious shuttling of large, cumbersome boats between your home and the river. That is not to say it is not worth it – far from it. Paddling a long river is an enriching, brilliant way to experience a landscape. Mark Kalch attests to that with his thoughts from midway through his long-term goal of paddling the length of the longest river on each continent.

And I, for one, have a dream to return to the Yukon and paddle that great river all the way to the sea.

At the end of every river lies the sea. I love using an ocean to bookmark the beginning or end of a trip. There is a great finality to arriving at the sea – unless, of course, you come up with the crackers

idea of trying to get across that ocean and seeing what lies on the other side!

Oceans beguile us with their scale, their mood swings, their unyielding and unchanging presence and power. Other than for Poppa Neutrino, who crossed the Atlantic on a raft made of junk, or Thor Heyerdahl's legendary balsawood raft, *Kon-Tiki*, with which he crossed the Pacific, ocean adventures are going to cost you considerably more than £1,000. That is not to say they do not have a place in this book, though, for *Grand Adventures* is about overcoming the barriers that get in the way of your big adventures, and rowers have many barriers to overcome. So read on for the inspiration even if you're personally planning a trip that will cost £1,000 rather than £30,000.

'As well as a good chunk of cash, you'll also need time, patience, persistence, courage and a sense of humour'

The tales in this book from those who have crossed oceans will reinforce the impression that tackling an ocean is not something to be undertaken lightly. As well as a good chunk of cash, you'll also need time, patience, persistence, courage and a sense of humour. What you do *not* need to be, at the beginning, is an expert seaman. None of the adventurers featured in these pages knew a thing about the sea when they began their long journey to the start line. And there *is* much to learn: out at sea you (or your crew mates) must be able to fix everything on the boat, to navigate through the doldrums, to safely weather a storm. It is not a type of expedition to undertake lightly, and the preparation phase will certainly take longer than the ocean crossing itself.

It is for this reason that I never harboured any ambitions to row an ocean. I love adventures but I hate preparing for them. I am too lazy, disorganised, short-sighted and generally incompetent to prepare to row an ocean by myself. The lack of detailed planning pages in this book would be horrifying to a task-oriented, diligent ocean rower.

I would love to row an ocean solo, but I know I am not up to the task of getting to the start line,

which is why, when I received an invitation to join a crew to row the Atlantic with just six weeks' notice, I jumped at the chance. The timing was tight and inconvenient. I had little time to prepare physically or mentally. I had no time to bond with my new team-mates. But in life you will never

'If you want a great adventure you must shoehorn it into life and make whatever compromises are necessary to make it happen'

simultaneously have lots of time and lots of money and lots of energy, so if you want a great adventure you must shoehorn it into life and make whatever compromises are necessary to make it happen. I skipped the long and laborious (yet undeniably rewarding, too) preparation phase and just embarked on the rowing phase. Consequently I was less competent than my team-mates and I was less invested in the whole long journey. They will have taken more from the overall project than I did. But what I *did* experience was the ludicrous feat of rowing all the way across an ocean.

I had already sailed across the Atlantic before I rowed it so I was interested to compare the two experiences. Rowing the Atlantic was a more visceral experience. Four of us, crammed into a 26-foot boat – little space, zero privacy, crazy sleep deprivation, every small task a hassle, boiling water on a wildly swinging stove, crapping into a bucket, changing from storm-soaked clothes in a cabin the size of a coffin, then putting those same cold wet clothes back on after the cruellest of short sleeps to return to the oars once more. They were hard times. Yet they are a price worth paying for the lunatic thrill of rowing down steep, fast waves in pitch darkness as tropical rainstorms lash down upon you; for the sunrise that signals the end of another long hard night and the ritual checking of the GPS to see how many miles we covered in the

last 24 hours; for the treat of a sliver of salami every 100 miles, food so appreciated that it actually made me cry; for the calm sea and sunshine after a frightening night of storms; for sitting on the cabin roof at sunset and chattering about the huge fish we caught that day; for laughing more than I have ever laughed in my life with these three strangers who became great friends, and for that first cold, crisp beer back on dry land after 45 days at sea. Life is rich on an ocean adventure.

Would I row another ocean? No. Am I glad I have rowed one? Absolutely. But for sheer happiness of days, I reckon nothing can top drifting down a big river in a cheap little canoe, catching your supper, and sleeping by campfires on the riverbank each evening.

WISE WORDS FROM FELLOW ADVENTURERS

TIM COPE
ROWED THE LENA RIVER, SIBERIA

Physically, the rowboat journey was not as difficult as riding a bike, or travelling with horses, although it was inconvenient that we rowed 24 hours a day on two-hour shifts, so sleep was always in short supply! It was a beautiful experience to float through the heart of Siberia watching the landscape and people change as we neared the Arctic coast. The boat itself was a story – we found the rotted hull of a boat on the shores of Lake Baikal and were told that the owner had been knocked off by the Mafia! We took the boat away and spent three weeks building a cabin, then spent four months or so rowing our way north, surviving on fish, mostly, navigating some rapids and – more importantly – the large barges that would appear from the fog. The hardest thing was simply surviving with four of us on such a small boat. When the coffee and chocolate ran low near the end, tensions built. I found it ironic that here we were, in the middle of Siberia, this land of endless horizons of tundra and forests, yet we were living life in what felt like a cramped glass bottle! To me, the way to cope was always to focus on the rich texture of the land, the moods of the weather, and the fascinating people. That seemed to calm me, and allow me to ignore some of the cramped conditions and lack of sleep and food. By the time we neared the end, the river was about 36 miles wide and the current was meaningless. When the wind blew from the north we simply had to point the bow into the swell and hope we could maintain our direction. We often got pushed back upstream. The land at the river's edges sprawled out in a sea of tundra with its brown, weather-beaten hues and was dusted with snow come the finish. We ended our journey in the Yenisei Gulf, on a small island where a couple of families of reindeer herders known as 'Nenets' live. They took us to the beach where scattered human bones could be seen protruding from the sand – the remains of the many hundreds who had perished here when Stalin deported ethnic Germans from the Volga River to Siberia during World War II.

OLLY WHITTLE
CANOED DOWN THE MEKONG

I was a management consultant in London – pretending I earned a lot, pretending I was important, pretending I was smarter than average. In reality I was none of those things and I was surrounded by a lot of unhappy people.

It took a while to find someone I could convince to sell me a canoe. Anybody who spoke English told me to get a ticket on a tourist boat. 'Why? You don't need a canoe – you can get on the tourist boat'. Yeah, but that's not the point, is it? I did find it hard for them to get the idea, and I did feel a little overprivileged at that point – because it seems like you have to have a certain level of comfort in your life before you actively seek hardship, danger and, well, adventure!

Anyway, I found a fisherman, and using a translation I had previously had written for me on my notepad, he knew I actually needed to buy my own canoe. I started at $80, he said $200 and we settled on $155 with a free wooden paddle. I threw in a few beers as a persuader, too, and he helped me fix it up (it was the runt of his fleet). This still remains the best hundred quid I have ever spent!

The only other kit I needed were some barrels for my stuff and a rope to tie them to the canoe. I got these for about $20 and then bought some food – rice and tinned fish. So the whole adventure cost me under 200 quid (I already had a tent and a stove).

I had imagined some sort of epic endurance adventure where I'd need to draw on mental strength for the possible monotony of day after

'The best bit was the sheer beauty of being alone on a powerful river with thick noisy jungle on each bank and feeling completely alive'

day on a dull river, but I soon found it would be a-thrill-a-minute action. There were rapids and it was a constant effort to keep the canoe facing forwards and out of the way of rocks.

I found quickly that the river was in charge, not me, that I could try to decide my course but only if the river would let me. Everything was on the river's terms.

But the best bit was the sheer beauty of being alone on a powerful river with thick noisy jungle on each bank and feeling completely alive in the universe as a natural part of it. I felt as if the planet were perfect and that there was nothing else I ever needed in life. *This* was it, right *now*. I'll never forget that feeling.

ROBERT TWIGGER
CROSSED THE ROCKY MOUNTAINS IN A HOME-MADE BIRCHBARK CANOE

A good expedition needs to have what a friend calls 'tilt'. For example, crossing Canada in a birchbark canoe is OK, but add in following a former explorer and you have tilt. Walking in the desert is OK, but add in a new mode of transport – a trolley – and you have tilt. Going to look for Antoine de Saint-Exupéry's crash site in the Sahara is OK, but backtracking on foot to replicate his experience has tilt.

Locals who are not actively going out into the wilderness are the biggest scaredy-cats in the world. Oasis dwellers will talk up the desert until you're scared even to go a mile from the oasis. Canadians who don't go into the wilderness properly (i.e. without a massive RV) will talk up bears and every other kind of problem. The real local bush experts are the ones you can rely on, though sometimes you get bullshitters who just pretend to know. The best kind of advice comes from people you meet really far into the wilderness – who by their very presence have proved they know what they are talking about.

Negativity is everywhere. I don't feel ready until someone has told me my trip is impossible, and then I *know* I can do it! People who are negative don't really know that they are behaving automatically, and my response is to automatically dismiss them.

When you're in the desert all you can think about is getting out; when you're in the oasis all you can think about is getting back out into the desert. Man is a restless beast! By going in a canoe or on foot you naturally brake any desire to rush, so I don't feel the mere presence of the urge too much. I believe self-managed adventures are one of the best ways to grow as a person, to develop judgement and to see the world.

TIM HOBIN
PADDLED THE GANGES IN A £50 INFLATABLE KAYAK

My plan was simple: buy an inflatable kayak off eBay for £50, jump on a plane to India, then paddle between Haridwar and Varanasi. It would be my very own Ganga Yatra, a sort of modern-day pilgrimage on the holiest river in the world. What could possibly go wrong?

There isn't much information on the internet about such a trip so I took my second-hand inflatable kayak down to the local canal, paddled it for an hour up and down, packed it up, went home and ticked the box marked 'trained and tested'. Simple, really.

My solo kayak trip down the Ganges covered 600 miles over 26 days. It cost me £750, including flights and all my equipment.

After a couple of weeks on the water you really start to understand the nature of the river; what certain ripples mean and where the sand bars are likely to be. And those moments when you have a pod of Gangetic dolphins swimming alongside or watching the sinister crocodiles on the shoreline seemingly smiling benevolently back at me. Children would shout out greetings to me or swim out to intercept me. No tourist ever goes that way so there was a real sense of adventure surrounding the journey. It was magical!

I did the trip because I like trying to come up with ideas for solo journeys that I can undertake with little or no prior knowledge of the technical skills needed to be successful, and without it being too dangerous. I'm 51 years old now so I haven't got loads of spare years to acquire all the relevant knowledge for remote adventure! I was looking for a self-powered expedition that would take me far enough out of my comfort zone so that it was exciting and adventurous, but not so far that I wasn't able to enjoy the experience.

This trip has given me the confidence to know that even in your fifties you can work hard for

8–10 hours a day, every day, for a month. So I know that I can still get out there into the remote parts of the world under my own steam and thrive. You are only limited by what you think you can do rather than what you can do.

Turning this adventure from a dream into reality was simple, really. The idea came to me and, rather than thinking too much about the pros and cons of a journey like this, I just got on and started planning what kit I needed. I hit the internet to try to do as much research as possible, as I knew there would be many unknown factors along the way that I couldn't foresee.

MARK KALCH
KAYAKED THE AMAZON, VOLGA AND
MISSOURI/MISSISSIPPI

Sometimes I forget that 22,000 miles is sort of a lap around the Earth. And when I think of that in terms of paddling, I think, 'Yeah, that is a long way.' A lot of that isn't easy paddling. There is a fair portion that is quite difficult. The project has been so interesting and I am not even halfway yet. The three big ones I have done so far are the Volga, the Missouri/Mississippi and the Amazon. I think the differences between the three are pretty stark. The lower Amazon is a super-highway for big boats,

but it still felt quite isolated. On the Missouri and Mississippi that wasn't the case. As I have done more of these trips, I have become less focused on isolating myself from people. I think both being isolated and being amongst communities can be a good thing.

Initially, going to do the Amazon was a chance to do this massive adventure and be sponsored, showing people how hardcore I was and that sort of thing. But now, seven or eight years on, the idea of being this death-defying adventure-type person is largely removed from my reasons for doing these things. Anything that I do now is because I want to do it.

There's some other guy trying to paddle the seven longest rivers as well. He's a nice guy, but it definitely takes away from the experience. To be totally honest, all it does is cause me stress. It weighs on me to think that it feels like there's sort of a wolf chasing me, so to speak. That's not a feeling that I like. I just want to go about paddling rivers, not competing. It got me thinking a while back about paddling the second-longest river on each continent – maybe I should have gone for that. I could have the same amazing experiences and very little fear of some guy thinking of doing that same project. It's not an enjoyable feeling.

If I look at the impact that the Amazon had on the direction of my life, it's been huge. There were multiple, multiple times when I thought we were going to die. I cried more than once – I think twice, to be fair.

It did really feel that we went through something that was so ridiculously hard at the beginning and managed to come out the other side. That has to change you in some way. And a big part of that was learning that if you don't do something, if you don't get up and do it, then it's not going to happen.

We sat above these rapids after we made camp at night, and it was just so loud. And even when it turned pitch black, they're so loud that you can't hear anything else. Either side are these steep canyon walls, which, even if you had climbing gear, there's no way to climb out of. So you're faced with the fact that to get out of there and to live, you're going to have to run this rapid. If you don't do it, you can stay here and die. Or you can do it and then see what happens when you come out the other side. That is not to say that, now, I don't sit in my air-conditioned apartment in Buenos Aires and get distracted by stuff on the internet and not get anything done!

JASON LEWIS
SPENT 13 YEARS CIRCUMNAVIGATING THE PLANET UNDER HUMAN POWER

I think the main thing is just to immerse yourself in the experience of the outdoors. In the early 90s, technology wasn't a factor and I remember crossing the Atlantic with just a sextant and no GPS, no sat phones, so you really were out in the environment. And then the digital age caught up and now you almost *have* to have a connection to the internet. And then you're beholden to the technology and having to worry about charging batteries through solar panels and all the bazillion leads that you need and suddenly it becomes a whole different monster and you're no longer really connected with your environment. You're blogging about your environment, you're not just enjoying it. If I were to give advice on a first-trip adventure, I'd say, save up the money before you go and don't think about making a career out of it and, ideally, don't take any gadgets, nothing that needs to be charged other than a camera maybe to take photographs. Just keep it massively simple.

On my first crossing, it was a real wilderness immersion experience. Having left England's cold wet island as a guy in his early-20s wanting just to get away, it was what I needed. You go through that sort of 40 days and 40 nights experience and you do, finally, genuinely forget about land. You stop missing everything about land, then you can actually make that shift to your universe being

on the boat. I found that incredibly rewarding and quite lovely and very spiritual, just being in the present, the here and now. And even with the rowing (or for us it was pedalling), you just get into the present more so that it becomes almost a meditation. But you can't do that when you have technology that is demanding that you think about writing a blog post.

You don't need to be an expert climber or have hundred of hours of caving experience under your belt or yachting experience, whatever. Any idiot can get on a bike or get on a boat that's powered by pedals and cross an ocean or cross a continent.

SEAN CONWAY
SWAM THE LENGTH OF BRITAIN

I wasn't a very confident kid. I was quite small at school, really tiny, and I grew up in a big, rugby-playing South African high school which meant that, if you weren't massive, you didn't feature in sport at all. So I just like the idea of trying something I can't do and going through all the baby steps of training and getting fitter, and I love documenting that process, you know?

I'm pretty slow. In my first training session in the pool I got seasick from all the waves generated by the swimmers in the lanes next to me. First you come up with the idea and for this one it actually was really tough because I struggled to get useful advice. If you go online and search 'Sean Conway swimming Britain forums', there's a lot of negativity. A lot of people thought it was a PR stunt. A lot of people just sort of thought, 'oh, this is so daft, I'm not even going to bother replying to your email.'

Then I had to find a crew. I managed to find four amazing crew members who believed in it. Then there was the logistics of route, food, boats I was going to use, and you just try to ask people who are willing to help. [I learned later that Sean bought his battered old support boat – unseen – on the eBay app on his phone when in a pub!]

I'm not going to lie to you, doing a 'world first', something that no one has ever done before: I would be lying if I said there wasn't a part of me that wanted to go, 'yeah, you know what? I did do it, and all those people who said you couldn't do it: in your face!'

Part of me really wanted to tell my story and inspire other people and that sort of thing, too. Being a professional adventurer, it's almost like an oxymoron in a way, because the whole idea of being an adventurer is to go and challenge yourself and get away from it all. But to become a professional adventurer you have to be in the middle of it all [with sharing your stories online and spending time at a computer].

JAMIE BOWLBY-WHITING
PADDLED THE DANUBE ON A JUNK RAFT

I had only managed to save a few hundred pounds, but I was desperate to be outside and to explore. We asked around until we were given eight 200-litre barrels, some old billboards, and some billboard plastic: all materials that were being discarded. I had always dreamed of being a pirate, so we assembled these bits into a recycled pirate ship and rafted down the Danube for a couple of weeks. Each day we swam, we read, we enjoyed the sunshine. Every evening we pulled up on the shore and cooked dinner on an open fire using the seemingly endless supply of driftwood. We stayed on the raft for a couple of weeks through Slovakia and Hungary.

Now that I have done this journey, all I want is more. More adventures, more nights outside, more memories of every single day of my life. Once you know how fantastic the world is and how easy it is to make experiences that most people think are impossible, the world feels like a pretty exciting place.

HENRIK FREDERIKSEN
RAFTED DOWN THE AMAZON

One evening we sat down and started doing all the initial calculations for how to float down the Amazon on a raft. We sat and pieced together some Excel sheets on how much the raft would weigh, how much flow speed is in the Amazon, how much buoyancy we would need, how we would construct it, and a lot more basic research. Within two hours we looked at each other and smiled and said, 'This could maybe, possibly, be done.' Then we just kind of said, 'Well, let's at least try; let's just throw all our effort into it and see if we can get going with it.'

We started in a little town in Ecuador in the very western part of the Amazon rainforest. We spoke to tons of different people at dump yards to find used scrap metal and all kinds of fun things. It was such a good experience just constructing it. The raft didn't cost a whole lot to construct. I think we spent around $1500 on the raft, and that's two people.

It was a big challenge at the beginning, getting the whole thing together. Then there was also some fear about what was going to happen once we set off. That's when things got a bit more scary. There was definitely a good ounce of fear in it.

It was such a crazy, crazy experience because we didn't have any oars or engine or anything, we just had some long sticks that we figured that we'd kind of navigate with and push ourselves off the shore in case we got too close. But it turned out that the raft is a heavy structure so we didn't have much control with these sticks. So the first day was very chaotic but it was a crazy, wild feeling, standing there and pushing it off the shore and thinking, 'Well, I hope this goes well. I hope that we don't get lost or stuck in the jungle.' But it was also a wonderful, wonderful feeling to see the raft floating and slowly moving down the river.

We would normally park the raft for the night, then we would wake up at sunrise, start floating again, and we would be fishing and playing chess and cooking food and taking photographs and meditating and all sorts of things. We had a lot of good times on the raft. We managed to construct some oars that we used in order to avoid collisions with tree trunks and the side of the river. There was quite a lot of work in the first month fighting with the

oars to avoid the raft colliding with the tree trunks, and once in a while the river was also very low so the raft would get stuck on some shallow banks.

After that month we bought an engine for the raft because a lot of container ships use the Amazon and it would have been dangerous not to have a little bit of control. So things got a little more relaxed, but, both with the oars and the engine, we didn't use them unless we were about to collide with something. So for the majority of the day the raft would just be floating down the river in complete silence through this untouched wilderness.

It was so wonderful, it was so great. Every morning we would wake up to these beautiful

sunrises and go to bed to unbelievably beautiful sunsets. You had those beautiful jungle sounds all day long. From insects, birds, howling monkeys – all parts of nature, which was very special, in the way it should be in the jungle. The vegetation itself was also very, very unspoiled. I didn't see a whole lot of big clear cuts and stuff like that until the later part of it, when we got deeper into Brazil.

We would often park the raft at the side of the river during the day and just walk straight into the middle of nowhere. It was such a wild feeling knowing that you were probably the first man ever to set foot on these square feet and just walk through this unspoiled, wild, overgrown endless wall of vegetation.

When we reached a town, we would have some beers, but we'd also drink some home-distilled booze that we would buy in actually quite large quantities – maybe like a gallon at a time – both to have our own supply but also because it was a very valuable trading commodity with the locals down the river. They wanted to trade booze with us.

I wasn't going to say this, but once we got deeper into the journey, actually on the Brazilian part of the Amazon, things got quite dangerous, lots more than I'd ever imagined. I think both of us underestimated this danger. I mean, there were tons of local people who told us that there were pirates there, drug smugglers, and that they would kill us and things would be very, very scary and dangerous. But we kind of just waved it off. I think after travelling for so many years, both of us, we've got used to people warning us about every single thing on this planet. And what I've seen throughout my years of cycling around the world is that this planet is not that dangerous, violent and evil, so I think we were almost immune to these constant safety warnings. The problem was, though, that here on the Amazon, the warnings seemed to be true.

At the end, when you're supposed to be all whooping and, 'Wow, we're done. I can't believe it!', you just stand there and think quietly, 'Hmm, that was the end'. It's such a weird feeling. Then, slowly, the whole thing comes tumbling down on you and you start thinking about all the things that have happened and you break into a smile every ten minutes when you think about all those experiences.

DAVE CORNTHWAITE
SWAM 1,000 MILES DOWN THE MISSISSIPPI

I love river journeys. I've kayaked, SUPed [Stand Up Paddleboard] and swum them. I think a source-to-sea adventure along a good-sized river is as close to perfect as an adventure could be. Every stage prepares you for the next one and you're sharing the journey with the waterway.

'It's not about having a massive level of experience or skills to start with. You can learn those things as you go along'

There are several reasons why I love adventures on the water. They're never the same two days in a row, they are powerful and industrious – even small streams can move mountains, given time – and they often pass through very varied landscapes. I also feel that the peace, tranquillity and connection that wild places offer humans are taken to another level when water is close (this goes for the ocean too). The water can test reactions (whitewater and fast currents) and mental strength (low flow, lakes, plodding into a headwind) and is always a great challenge – you can't switch off when you're on the water! One great thing about being on a river is that you can't get lost!

When I embarked on my swim, I couldn't swim, but by the end I had gills! I would recommend that anyone wanting to do a similar adventure should learn to swim before they start! A few bits of kit will aid the swim, a nose plug makes long-term breathing easier and protects you against inhaling water, and ear plugs will reduce the risk of constant exposure to river water. If you're pulling a raft with gear on, use a waist-mounted towline.

Safety is paramount, of course, so whether you're solo or not, do whatever you can to make yourself visible to motorised craft. If you are travelling down a river with industrial traffic or regular recreational motorboats, consider wearing small flippers to enable faster evasion of danger.

SARAH OUTEN
ROWED SOLO ACROSS SEVERAL OCEANS

My first big expedition was when I rowed solo across the Indian Ocean. It took me four months to get from Australia to Mauritius on my second attempt. On my first attempt I basically went around in a 400-mile loop for ten days all the way back to land, because weather and various things had made the trip a little tricky.

You don't need to be a rower to head out on an ocean rowing expedition. I think the most important thing is just being able to manage yourself in a challenging environment, emotionally, keeping on top of your personal admin, keeping things going. So it's more about seamanship. I always say to people that it's not about having a massive level of experience or skills to start with. You can learn those things as you go along. You seek out people who have that experience and knowledge and are willing to share it, and who will let you learn in an environment where you can ask the questions and make mistakes and have a bit of support.

When I said that I wanted to row the Indian Ocean and said, 'I'm going to do this in three years' time', I was 21 and really fuelled by grief at my father's death. It can be daunting and massive to pull something off, particularly something like an ocean row, where you're out there and you're committed. It's an unforgiving environment and there are big consequences if you screw up. So you need to get everything in place. The other side of it is that financially it's huge and that can be daunting, too.

SVEN YRVIND
CELEBRATING HIS 50TH ANNIVERSARY AS A SMALL-BOAT SAILOR BY DOING A NON-STOP CIRCUMNAVIGATION OF THE WORLD, SOUTH OF THE CAPES, IN A TEN-FOOT BOAT

It will be difficult. It will take me between 600 and 800 days. I will not touch land in that time, nor get a resupply from anywhere. I enjoy sailing, I enjoy life, so I'll be OK. It's about 30,000 miles, at a speed of 2 knots. I will carry 880 lbs of food on the boat, giving me 1,500 calories per day. I will carry 200 lbs of mathematics books, also books in French and German: books that will take me longer to read.

I don't like people making big things. Boats, everything, becomes bigger and bigger. It uses up our precious resources. I'm an idealist. Also, [a small boat is] all that I can afford! A bigger boat does not make you happy. I'm not really adventurous. My voyages are a practical solution to my life's problems. I am very dyslexic. Teachers used to beat me. I did terribly at school. I was strong, but I couldn't really advance in life. Setting out to sea in a small, cheap boat – my house – was the answer. I had no rent. I could see the world. I could find knowledge. I was curious. Now I live on a small pension. I'll do this journey, maybe sell a few books, and who knows what the next journey will be.

In 1980, I sailed from east to west around Cape Horn. That's the 'hard way' to do it. It was winter, my boat was aluminium and it had no heating. I was cold. This journey was tough. It was dark most of the time, so navigating with only a sextant was very difficult. I had to concentrate just one hour at a time. Just to survive. I thought 'don't look sideways, don't look backwards', just keep going. I wanted to show people what small boats can do.

I'll have no entertainment on this trip except my books. No radio. I'm trying to get more like the mood of an animal. It's simple out there. It feels nice. Building the boat is the same. The years pass so quickly, and then suddenly, one day the project is done. I don't put time pressures on myself. I just do it so I can enjoy each stage of it. You must not hurry a journey. Don't hurry if you want to do a job well or get the best possibilities.

I take care of my body. I exercise twice a week, running for 90 minutes. I only eat twice a day so that I don't get fat. If you exercise your body you also look after your mind. The 'Comfort Zone' is the problem in life. Imagine you wake on a rainy morning; the rain bangs on your windows – it's easier to stay in your nice bed than go for a walk in the rain. But in the evening you think 'what a boring day'. If you do it, if you get out of bed and walk in the rain then you will look back on the day and think 'what a wonderful day'. Comfort really is a bad thing. We are striving for comfort all the time. But it kills you.

RIAAN MANSER
ROWED THE ATLANTIC, KAYAKED ROUND ICELAND AND MADAGASCAR

You know that to cross an ocean it should be from the biggest piece of land to the next big piece of land. That is what I was hoping to achieve by rowing from Africa to New York, to have no regrets. I have been fortunate to have been to some exotic places on the planet. If I look back now, I realise that what draws me, like a moth to the flame, is the travel aspect of it. People just love the fact that we stopped at the Canaries, then the Bahamas, where Christopher Columbus landed in 1492. I loved seeing the swimming pigs at Staniel Cay.

People say, 'Hey, well done. Well done on rowing across this massive piece of water, it must have been fun?' The rowing bit wasn't fun for me. It was fun getting to the finish and now having a story to tell.

HARRY GUINNESS
SAILING ADVENTURE ON THE BALTIC

We sailed down through Denmark to the French coast, then sailed across the Biscay which was the highlight of the trip.

Despite the forecast we had huge waves and force seven winds. We were tearing along at almost ten knots with feck-all sail up and dolphins playing in our wake. At night we were the only thing around, so being on deck by yourself with huge waves that could kill you, 10,000 feet of water beneath you, perfectly clear stars millions of miles above and a meteor storm going on is a little bit humbling!

BARRY HAYES
ROWED THE PACIFIC

I was walking home from the pub in the early hours of the morning, staring through blurred vision at my phone, taking far less notice of the pavement than I should have been, or the hedge that I kept falling in on my merry way home. I was, bit by bit, reading Alastair's latest [blog] offering, in which a crazy guy called Philip was looking to form a team to row across the Pacific Ocean. In particular, I was attracted to one line that said '*You do not need rowing experience*'.

'Perfect,' I thought. 'I've never rowed a boat in my life', and with that I applied.

Extremely long story short: of the hundreds of applicants, I was the successful one. Philip and I found two more people and a boat, and we rowed across the Pacific in the world's first rowing race on the world's largest ocean. We came second and returned home with two world records – we were one of only seven boats that made it across.

You may know exactly what it is you want to achieve, or, more likely, you do not know what it is that you want to do yet, you just know that you want to do something epic. Keep your eyes open. Don't be afraid of failure. I am just a post-room worker who ignored the naysayers and put every ounce of determination into doing something cool. Absolutely *anyone* can do what I did. You can do what I did, and you can do far more. There have been pensioners and paraplegics who have rowed oceans. The one thing they had in common was complete determination to pull it off.

When I got involved in the rowing project I became friends with a great bloke called John Haskell who rowed the Atlantic in a wooden boat. He showed me a poem called 'The Dash' which talks about the fact that when someone looks at a gravestone they always look at the birth and death dates. The poem says that these dates are irrelevant and that the only bit that is important is the dash in between the dates.

So then, what will you do with your dash?

A
dventures inspired by water are always alluring. Anyone casting around for an adventure idea would do just fine by heeding Dave's notion that a source to sea journey along a good-sized river is as close to perfect as an adventure could be. And the urge to look out at an ocean and imagine crossing it must be as old as curiosity and humanity itself.

Crossing oceans, however, is an expensive game, certainly costing more than the £1,000 notion this book is loosely based around. Ocean rower Sarah acknowledges that and prefers the idea of cheaper, simpler trips. But she was sufficiently captivated by the idea of rowing an ocean that the hard work of fundraising felt worthwhile. You have to feel inspired to pull off an expedition like that. I've often pondered the nature of people who are willing to work hard for so long at launching a trip that takes longer to prepare than to execute. My slapdash, impatient nature leans more towards trips I could begin tomorrow but that would last for ages. To succeed at a journey that requires a great deal of planning and learning new skills requires a personality which will relish the entire project, not just the playing on boats bit at the end. Sarah concedes that it can be daunting to pull off something massive like an ocean row. But veteran

'Adventures inspired by water are always alluring. The urge to look out at an ocean and imagine crossing it must be as old as humanity itself'

adventurer Sven encourages us to contemplate the bold and difficult, railing against a society that strives for comfort all the time. 'Comfort kills you!' Having responded to an ad on Twitter looking for volunteers to row the Pacific, Barry echoes this sentiment, 'take the opportunities you are presented with, however slim an opportunity that

may be. Hang yourself out of your comfort zone.'

Remember, as always, that everyone has to begin somewhere. Jason pointed out that 'any idiot can get on a boat and cross an ocean'. That simplicity appealed to him. Sarah offers reassurance that you don't need to be a rower to row an ocean, advocating the importance of asking people for help and being willing to learn.

Rowing an ocean is definitely not for the faint-hearted (my 45 days at sea were amongst the toughest, yet most rewarding, of my life). Riaan felt that '99.9 per cent of the time it was mental torture' and Sarah cautions that there are serious consequences to face 'if you screw up'.

The love of water and the challenge to tackle a long journey may overlap, but the practicalities of river journeys are very different to the sea. The biggest difference is that, though the journey is on water, it passes amongst changing lands and landscapes. When rafting the Amazon, Henrik enjoyed meeting indigenous people, chatting and trading with them in their dugout canoes. That is an entirely different experience to spending months at sea alone. Tim, in his £50 kayak, also enjoyed chatting with children each day.

You have a choice on river trips how much physical exertion you wish to incorporate into the trip. Dave's 1,000-mile river swim was gruelling, and some stages of Mark's expeditions have been exceedingly difficult. But Henrik drifted gently and enjoyed the slower pace of travel that meant he got to see a small section in extreme detail. Robert also commented on the slowness of his canoe trip. He liked it because it removed the urge to rush matters too much.

That doesn't mean it is easy. Robert's birchbark canoe trip was constantly difficult. Olly, a novice paddler, set out 'utterly bricking it'. Tim found the greatest challenge to be claustrophobia, confined with other people in a very small space for so long. And Henrik underestimated the dangers of rafting the Amazon.

Amidst the enormous variety of these river tales, however, one thing is consistent: everyone looks back on their journeys with great satisfaction.

For Riaan, getting to the finish was the fun part, a sentiment shared by James in an earlier chapter, who fondly remembers rowing into harbour after a whopping 110 days at sea.

Ocean journeys are not all preparation and Type 2 fun, however. Sven talked about the pleasant simplicity of the life. And Sarah loved the idea of spending so many months at sea by yourself in that environment. If you are willing to take on the enormity of an ocean row you will reap your reward.

The allure and challenge of the water is not only from the sea. Many of my interviewees had adventures on rivers, and these trips are more in the realms of affordability.

MOTOR

I have never done a proper motorised adventure. My personal preference for adventure involves human-powered, physical and masochistic means of transport. If I'm having fun, I often feel, then I'm on holiday not an adventure. But that's certainly not to everyone's taste. In fact, I can completely see why you might say that it's a pretty dumb way to operate! The machines I've driven, whether it's skidoos in Siberia and Nunavut or Land Rovers in Iceland and Africa, have always been really fun.

I can absolutely see the appeal of the freedom and fun of being out in the world with your own motorised transport. I've ridden on the roofs of crowded buses in the Philippines, hitch-hiked in a pick-up full of beer from South Africa to Victoria Falls, risked life and limb at the hands of lunatic bus drivers in India, China and the Andes. And I have had wonderful times hitch-hiking to run with the bulls in Pamplona or through the night to reach Lake Malawi in time for sunrise. But with your own motorbike or car you are no longer at the mercy of vague bus schedules, railway pickpockets or lunatic, sleep-deprived bus drivers and their hideous blasting pop music.

Indeed, a man with a motorbike could argue to me very strongly that cycling round the world is a mere fool's exercise compared to the fun and the freedom of zooming along with the warm wind in your face and all the world within your reach.

Your adventure might be by big motorbike, tiny tuk-tuk, a pizza delivery bike or a London taxi. But a few common threads run through these tales of motorised adventure: you can do a big journey like this on a relatively small budget, you do not need to be an expert mechanic, you have total freedom to maraud across the planet, and it is a lot of fun. If journeys like this appeal, then I'd urge you to consider a motorised adventure of your own.

WISE WORDS FROM
FELLOW ADVENTURERS

AUSTIN VINCE
MOTORBIKED ROUND THE WORLD

I have ridden round the world but I would consider myself neither a petrolhead nor a 'biker'. I am not interested one iota in motorcycles and can barely read the motorcycle journalism that we have today. However, motorcycling is tremendous fun.

Add to that the chance to actually travel and go somewhere and it's pure dynamite. Take your bike on unpaved deteriorating trails and the thrills and skills are quintupled.

I think tweets, blogs, etc. are a nice touch for friends or family. However, if you are doing something that you think is special then you need to make a proper film about it or write a book. It will live on long after the trip is over. Making a decent film about your exploits is a huge ask, but the results are well worth it if you are prepared to make the sustained effort.

LIAM MARTIN
CROSSED EUROPE ON A PIZZA DELIVERY BIKE

We're all musicians and we worked in a music shop at the same time. We were all getting a bit tired of it, as you do with jobs that are quite repetitive. We would joke about doing crazy things or getting our big breaks as musicians and that sort of thing. Our boss would joke with us, saying, 'You're not going to do it, you're not going to quit', because it seemed like a stupid pipe dream, although it's not like a terribly ambitious thing. We weren't saying we were going to walk around the world or do something really, really difficult. But we just really got caught up in the romance of it, of leaving our jobs to do

that, to do something completely stupid.

Jamie was the last person to convince, even though it was his idea. Because when he said it, it was a joke. It wasn't a real thing. But me and Bon, we just bought our bikes and just started getting really into the idea. Eventually we all had bikes but with still no commitment to actually doing it. We went to and fro a little bit, as in somebody would start to drop out and be like, 'Actually, this is stupid, I need to do this, I need to do this, I've got a job, I've got a band.' Then the other two would take on the role of encouraging them. And then it would swap around like that. We'd all have a go at dropping out.

It went on for about two months. Then we had a little meeting. I called everyone round to my house and we got a map up on the screen. We basically decided that if we were going to do it, we'd have to hand in our notice the next day and all at the same time, which wouldn't be great for the shop! It was like, 'Well, we've got this far, we have to do it. It would be so lame to back out now.' We went in the next day and handed our notices in.

One of the worries was that we were going to be killed immediately. That's quite a common reaction. 'You're going to die, you're going to die.' Leaving a job is another thing. It wasn't the most exciting job. We had no careers to speak of, but none of us was necessarily in a position to do that in terms of how much money we had to spend. That was an obvious thing. The idea that we'd come back and have nothing. That was definitely a thing, a fear.

Our lives *have* changed since the trip. It was a catalyst for change because when we all went back, we all had a different head on. So in that respect, I think it can be really, really positive and really enriching to do something and be like, 'I can actually breathe now and not be stuck in my routine.'

PAUL ARCHER
DROVE ROUND THE WORLD
IN A LONDON BLACK CAB

Myself and two buddies from uni decided it would be funny to try to drive a London taxi to Australia and break the world record for the longest ever taxi journey. We set off from Covent Garden in a taxi we bought off eBay for 1,200 quid. It repeatedly broke down the whole way.

It started in a pub, and obviously we visited a few pubs on the way. It was designed to be fun, it wasn't designed to be arduous. It was designed to be an adventure with two buddies in a truly ridiculous vehicle.

We decided we wanted to do it, so we told people we were going to do it and nobody believed us. We re-built the taxi with some modifications though none of us knew what we were doing, but we blagged it. Then we set off.

There's a really delicate balance between planning and not planning. Certain things you need to plan, especially with vehicles. You've got logistics, and some countries that you have to get to because of visa restrictions and meeting people and things like that.

If you look at a map, you can drive from France to Singapore without taking a boat or shipping it. Shipping's where the big, big expense is. Basically, as long as you don't go to China where it's incredibly expensive to have visas for a vehicle, you can do a vehicle expedition very cheaply.

We drove 43,000 miles through 50 countries and raised £20,000 for the Red Cross. We also racked up £80,000 on the taxi fare meter, which was on the whole way.

Just thinking about the £1,000 idea, if you get four buddies that's actually £4,000. If you save up for two years, that's £8,000. You buy a vehicle for a grand or £1,500. And you certainly now have a budget that you can run away and have a three-month adventure driving around.

ARCHIE LEEMING
MOTORBIKED THE LENGTH OF AFRICA

Everyone now assumes you have to buy the best motorbike and gear. The motorbike I bought to go across Africa cost me £750 and the rest of the gear was second-hand off eBay. When you take an old motorbike, you're going to break down, and when you break down, it sort of changes the path of where you're going that day to somewhere unknown. I like that. We just kept being picked up by friendly locals in the garage who then gave us a place to stay. I think we met more people through breaking down than we would have if we hadn't broken down. It's amazing how things work out when they go wrong.

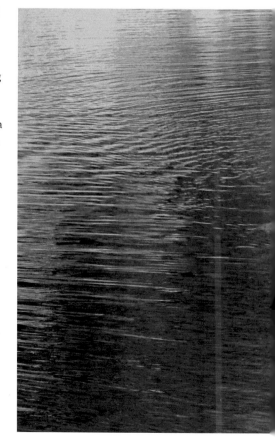

I don't think you need to have any particular skill set. You just need to be open-minded, and always have a smile! With that attitude I think you can go anywhere and do anything.

ANTS BOLINGBROKE-KENT
MOTORBIKED THE HO CHI MINH TRAIL

I set off from the heaving, cacophonous streets of Hanoi on a solo motorcycling adventure, riding a 25-year-old neon-pink Honda Cub dubbed the Pink Panther. Battling inhospitable terrain and multiple breakdowns, it was a journey that ranged from the hilarious to the mildly terrifying, during

which I encountered tribal chiefs, illegal loggers, former American fighter pilots, young women whose children had been killed by unexploded bombs left over from the Vietnam War, eccentric Aussie bomb-disposal experts and multiple mechanics. It really was the most awesome adventure.

Travelling alone was definitely the highlight of my experience – the feeling of being completely immersed in my environment without the distraction of companionship. I'd always wanted to do this journey solo in order to test myself and see what I was really made of, and I'm so glad I did. Oddly, it was on the really tough days, when I was forced to confront my fears and weaknesses, that I really relished this solitude and learned the most about myself. I was terrified about sleeping alone in the jungle, with its countless unexploded bombs, huge spiders and venomous vipers. But the feeling of being woken up the next morning by shards of sunlight hitting my hammock and the howl of a distant gibbon will stay with me forever.

Every adventure wakes you up, shakes you out of the torpor of routine and everyday life. This was no different. Although I didn't have any major epiphanies or 'find myself' in the Southeast Asian jungle, I did gain insights into my personality that could only have come from travelling alone. In times of adversity, when the mud and the mountains had conspired to beat me, I had faced myself and passed the test. I hadn't cried or given up, I'd kept plugging on, mile after muddy mile. For someone as self-critical as me, it was a good realisation to have!

MATT PRIOR
MANY MOTORISED ADVENTURES ACROSS ASIA

I have driven a London taxi to Everest Base Camp and a rickshaw from the bottom of India to the Himalayas. I've also driven from London to Mongolia in a £150 car for charity. The most life-changing of these experiences was the drive to Mongolia in a crap car. (We actually returned to England in a £100 bright yellow Fiat with no roof...) This was the first big trip, and I suppose that's why it had such an impact. My favourite countries on this trip were Iran, Turkmenistan, Uzbekistan and Russia.

I love the unpredictability of trips like this. I deliberately very rarely research anything and just take what comes around the corner. The realisation that a lot of what you hear in the media is utter rubbish means that it's really important that you go and see the world with your own eyes and form your own opinions.

My initial plan was to go backpacking across the United States, but after a conversation with a friend over a few beers, I realised I needed a proper adventure, something different, something challenging. So that was that: find a really crap car and head east.

Honestly, this first adventure completely turned my life upside down. It changed the way I view the world, the people, the endless possibilities, as well as realising that something that initially sounds almost impossible is actually quite doable even for the 'average Joe'. Commit to something. Put your balls on the line. Then figure it out.

Believe it or not, this will take you most of the way. A key thing is to tell other people your plans as this will almost force you to make it happen.

On this particular trip, there were two of us and so we looked at our respective strengths and split the tasks up from there. It seemed to work well. You also help each other out and learn from each other in the process.

ANTS GODDARD
DRIVING ROUND AMERICA WITH HIS FAMILY

My wife, my son and I left home on a whim and decided to see some more of the country. We're driving round the USA. We knew we wanted to experience living in a different town after being in the same place for the past six years, but we didn't have much of an idea where we wanted to move to. We thought if we took our time finding a place, then in the meantime we would have the opportunity to have an adventure and see a lot of the country. So far we've driven around 12,400 miles. That's the distance from the North Pole to the South Pole.

I've always been much more fascinated by smaller towns than big cities. I love arriving in a town and getting a feel for the place, finding out what makes it different and what flavour the locals have put on it. There's a small town we stayed in, north of Santa Fe in New Mexico. Some houses had no electricity, and there were wild dogs roaming the streets. After passing through big cities, it was mind-blowing to see just how different places in the same country can be.

One of my favourite things about travel is when there's no real destination. With everything we need strapped to the car, we've been able to change our minds daily depending on what looks interesting on the road ahead.

We set off with a laughable amount of stuff piled so high in the car I couldn't see anything while driving. When we got to Washington, DC, we took a day to sort out what we really needed, and worked on storing things better.

You also don't always need a destination for an adventure. Just think about where you want to be tonight, tomorrow, maybe for the rest of the week, and repeat that process. You can stop at any time that way and not worry about 'not making it' to where you thought you were going.

In fact, we just finished our road trip because we've decided to stay in the Rocky Mountains for the next year. We were literally driving out of the town we were in, with the Rockies in the rearview mirror, but in two minds about leaving because we liked the place so much. So on the way out of town we stopped at a coffee shop and grabbed a local paper, saw a rental in it, called the guy up, went over, signed the lease and then moved in the next day.

I enjoyed interviewing people about their adventures with cars and motorbikes, not least because I have never done a trip in that style. It's always interesting to get a fresh perspective on the adventure world. One thing in particular shines through all of these tales: motorised adventures are fun! That by itself is reason enough to get involved.

Austin, Liam and Paul were all drawn to motorised adventures with a sense of silliness and fun, seeking out great driving roads and occasional pubs. I am sometimes guilty of taking the world of adventure rather too seriously and having a rather austere, masochistic approach to things. Perhaps a sensible balance might be that of Ants' latest ride through Southeast Asia which 'ranged from the hilarious to the mildly terrifying'.

'The detours, the breakdowns, the unexpected things are part of the appeal and help lead to all sorts of spontaneous adventures'

There is a cavalier approach to many of these journeys: 'find a really crap car and head east' was Matt's advice. Several bought their machines from eBay – Matt drove to Mongolia in a £150 car – and few had much knowledge of or interest in mechanics. The detours, the breakdowns, the unexpected things are part of the appeal and help lead to all sorts of spontaneous adventures. Indeed, I got the sense at times of a mischievous desire for things to go wrong. It is the grit in the oyster that makes a pearl, and perhaps heading out into the world in a crap car with little mechanical knowledge or planning is just a technique for gritting life's oyster. The thirst for uncertainty, surprise and unusual interactions is strong.

The important thing, as always, is just to go. Ant and his young family left 'on a whim' to see

more of the country they lived in, with scant regard for destinations or detailed plans. Paul cautions that there's a balance to be struck between planning stuff and winging it. My own maddening encounters with the world's petty bureaucrats would ensure, at least, that I had all my paperwork in good order before beginning a trip like this. But Archie points out that you can't prepare for everything and it's important not to get bogged down with the minutiae of preparation. 'Just get a light simple bike, shove your bag on the back and head south or east.' That refrain again – just head east! Or south! And, as Liam pertinently reminds us, 'compared to all of the other stuff we do in life, this is actually one of the easiest.'

TRAVEL

Adventure is a broad brush; it's not just climbing death-defying mountains or gasping with thirst in the Sahara. One of the most adventurous moments of my life was when, aged 18, I over-filled an inappropriately massive, shiny, new rucksack with all sorts of things I would never need and flew to Africa to spend a year living in a small village there. It was the happiest and most important year of my life. One adventure is not 'better' than another. The important thing is only the way it makes you feel and what it teaches you.

Travelling by train is a sedate, civilised way of seeing the world. Certainly there may be moments of chaos, particularly if you choose to sample the rare delights of the cheapest classes of train carriages. I once travelled by train through Pakistan, from Islamabad to Karachi. We were virtually out of money, for we were returning home at the end of a long trip. At one of the many lengthy delays at a small station, my friend headed out clutching the very last of our rupees to spend it wisely on the largest amount of food he could find. We were both extremely hungry. We were hot, too, suffering and sweating in the stifling heat in a crammed budget carriage without air conditioning or fans. I waited eagerly and impatiently. He returned, looking delighted with his haul: a big pile of battered balls that looked filling enough to fuel us to the end of the journey. Biting into them, though, our faces fell. The last thing you want in a hot, sweaty train so crowded that even the disgusting, stinking toilet had a family permanently perched in there, was a bagful of deep-fried red hot chillies... It was a deeply unpleasant 40-hour journey as our mouths burned, our bodies sweated and our bowels gurgled!

Our delight at eventually reaching the end of this train torture was dampened considerably by our bicycles no longer being in the luggage carriage we had stored them in. 'Don't worry,' the station master reassured us, 'they will perhaps arrive on the next train. Tomorrow. *Inshallah.*'

Full of doubt and out of cash, we could do nothing but wait. We slept amongst the rats and homeless people on the station platform until the next morning when, to our great surprise, our bicycles arrived on a totally different train.

It was a memorable train journey, though considerably less enjoyable than the night train I once rode from South Africa to Zimbabwe, the delightful experience of crossing southern India by train, or even the brilliant British adventure of riding the overnight sleeper train from London to the Scottish Highlands. In India I had just walked from one coast to the other and was returning by train in order to fly home. I was exhausted after the walk, jubilant to have succeeded, and enchanted with India. I sat in the open doorway of the train, watching India unfold before me. I drank sweet tea and grazed on the little snacks sold at every village station we stopped at. My bare feet dangled from the carriage, the warm wind ruffled my hair, and I had one of those special feelings of realising that this was an experience that I would remember and treasure for the rest of my life. Not bad for the price of a very cheap train ticket!

'My bare feet dangled from the carriage, the warm wind ruffled my hair, and I realised that this was an experience I would treasure for the rest of my life'

Hitch-hiking can be an even cheaper way of seeking out adventure. The vague, unofficial 'rules' of hitch-hiking vary from continent to continent. In some places you'll be expected to contribute to petrol costs or buy the driver coffee. Sometimes, though, you'll find the drivers buy you food and your only duty is to provide interesting conversation to help pass the time on a long journey. I've cadged rides in Africa, Asia, Latin America and Europe and enjoyed the experience

everywhere. I hitch-hiked around Spain and France in the summer I graduated from university. My two friends and I often hark back to the glorious randomness of that experience, the frustrating delays in places you'll be happy never to see again, the gambler's rush of excitement and action when a car stops and you run up to the window hoping you've scored a lift in the right direction, hoping that the driver isn't too weird, but too caught up in the thrill of crossing the next horizon and the vast possibilities of the endless road to care too much.

And off you go! Revelling in being in motion once again, starting a new relationship, a new conversation, leaning forward to the next crazy venture. At first you follow a formula to and fro – where you're from, where you're going. And then, just like the infinite twists and turns of the road, you'll be off on all sorts of new conversations, about politics or work or football or music or heartbreak. It's all there, every story there ever was. Just waiting for you out there in the world...

WISE WORDS FROM FELLOW ADVENTURERS

STEVE DEW-JONES
HITCH-HIKED FROM THE UK TO MALAYSIA

This was my first major adventure. I set off with my best friend and hitch-hiked from England to Malaysia. We set ourselves a couple of rules: never pay for transport (to make sure we were hitch-hiking rather than getting on a bus here and there), and never refuse an offer (to make sure we were open to people's invitations to stay with them and things like that).

Hitch-hiking is all about the interactions. The beautiful thing is that you're thrust into the arms of the people you meet on the way. That shapes your trip completely and gives you amazing insight into the places that you go through and the people there. I just love hitch-hiking as a form of transport – as long as you have time in hand. That's probably the major drawback: you're completely reliant on other people to get you places and you don't know how long it's going to take.

I tend to have a *laissez-faire* attitude to life, and I'm a hopeless optimist; it comes from being a Tottenham Hotspur fan. But there were certainly others who were worried on our behalf.

I think we probably arranged the trip about a month before we went. We ended up looking into visas just a week before we went, which is ridiculous and ended up costing us quite a bit of money to fast-track the applications for Pakistan and Iran. That was it really. We budgeted £10 a day, each. It was £1,500 each to get us to Malaysia, and it took six months.

All along the way we kept meeting people who took us into their homes. One time, my friend needed the loo and decided he wasn't going to go by the side of the road because it was a bigger job than that. He knocked on someone's door and sure enough, a couple of minutes later – well, maybe ten minutes later – he came back with a big smile on his face saying, 'You'll never believe this, follow me.' We ended up having a night in their home, just because he needed the loo. That was in Croatia but it could actually happen anywhere.

GRAHAM HUGHES
THE FIRST PERSON TO VISIT EVERY COUNTRY IN THE WORLD WITHOUT FLYING

In the first year I went to 133 countries and in the second year I went to about 50. I think the real trick, and the reason I finished the trip, is I didn't just have a plan A. I had a plan B, and a plan C, and a plan D. Sometimes it ran to like the seventh plan I had in order to get to this frickin' island or wherever I needed to get to. I think that's the main thing.

I always tell the story about being on this overnight bus in Iran and this little Persian grandmother sitting

in front of me; she must have been in her eighties and she was talking on her mobile phone, and then she gave me her mobile phone. She didn't speak any English. So I put it to my ear and the guy on the other end said 'Hi, my name is Syed Hussain and you're sitting behind my grandmother. She's called me because she's concerned about you.' I said, 'Why?' 'Because the bus gets in very early tomorrow morning and she's worried that you'll have nowhere to go and no one to make you breakfast. So if it's OK with you, she'll take you home with her and make you breakfast.'

If you go to university these days it's £9,000 a year. For £9,000 you could travel like a king. If you're doing law or medicine you need to go to university to do that. But if you're contemplating doing drama or philosophy, just go travel, because an employer's going to look at it and go, 'Drama, philosophy, so what?' To be able to say you single-handedly went to every country in Africa, that's something that's pretty impressive to anyone, I think. I mean, that shows initiative, logistical skills, bravery – what else could you really want from an employee? Then again, you might piss off on another adventure halfway through your tenure...

CHRIS HERWIG
TRAVELLED ROUND THE WORLD WITH HIS WIFE, THEIR THREE-YEAR-OLD AND A NEWBORN BABY

The plan was that there was no real plan. We would buy our tickets as we figured it out and if it felt that it was not working out we would take a break or just end it and fly home.

We got a lot of looks from people when we told them. I think people thought it was irresponsible. Our answer was always that if it doesn't work we can come home and we tried to keep an international hospital close by in the beginning. In many ways it was much easier. Malin just laid around for the first while, breastfed and got cheap massages on the beach.

ROLF POTTS
WORLD TRAVELLER, ONCE CIRCLED
THE GLOBE WITHOUT LUGGAGE

I consider my main 'vagabonding years' to be the eight-month trip around North America and the two-year trip around Asia, back in my mid-twenties and early thirties. These are the journeys that taught me how to travel, and taught me how easy and cheap and safe travel could be. Before then I had assumed that travel was something you saved for much later in life, something you did in much smaller doses. Travel is now an instinctive part of my life, and a normal part of my yearly cycle.

Simplicity is your ticket to travel. At home, it allows you to focus on what's important and save money for the journey to come. On the road simplicity allows you to travel lighter and focus your attention on the world before you, instead of the things you drag behind you. In short, it makes both travel and life at home more affordable and enjoyable. I think modern life is cluttered with far more objects and distractions than we really need. Simplicity allows you to find identity in experiences rather than in things.

I'm a fan of physical endeavours and adventures that put you in the world in a challenging way; I have nothing against things like mountaineering and kayaking and cycling. But it feels like these kinds of adventures are fairly easy to find. To me, a more compelling adventure is anything that puts you out of your comfort zone. It could mean trying some new food in a street market in Myanmar, or visiting a provincial town in Bolivia that's not listed in the guidebook, or chatting up a random stranger on some street corner in New Zealand. It's about overcoming fears – not just physical ones, but psychic ones. It's about seeking daily challenges that you might never try at home. Travel, in putting you so far away from home, allows you to find adventure in almost every aspect of the unfamiliar.

TEMUJIN DORAN
TRAVELLED ROUND THE WORLD
WITHOUT A PLANE

'After I finished my degree at art school, I was really interested in the idea of travelling somewhere without an aeroplane. I got a job as an intern in St Petersburg, in the Hermitage Museum. I figured that the cheapest way to get to Russia was on one of those horrible Eurolines coaches, which lasts about 40 hours and costs about 50 quid. It was pretty gruelling! I thought that if I'd got that far to Moscow and then carried on to Beijing, that's a huge chunk of the world which I'd travelled through without flying. The Trans-Siberian Express is regarded as one of the great train journeys to have taken, and I had always wanted to do it. I also began to look into the options of getting across the Pacific and the Atlantic without catching a plane as well. Some of the big cargo ships have about two or three passenger beds on them.

It's interesting because you are travelling from A to B, but you also feel quite trapped in a way. It's not like if you were cycling and if you see something you can pull over and take a look at it. It just whizzes past. Much of the time was spent looking out the window at these amazing sights which are then gone – they're very fleeting. I guess that's one of the drawbacks of travelling on a train. But also it's quite enjoyable. It's like a long tapestry from Moscow to Beijing. You can see the landscape; woodlands or scrubland grow into big mountains, and then dip into vast lakes. I stared out of the window a lot, mesmerised. It was incredible.

I think the Tibet-Beijing was my favourite train journey I've ever been on. Just like in Europe, Chinese trains have lots of different classes, and I was at the bottom rung. But it actually felt a bit better than most of the other trains I'd been on in China. For sleeper trains there's three beds in a tier and someone at the top bunk is snoring and then every now and then leaning over to spit. If you are stuck in the middle rung or the bottom one, you're praying that you're not going to get any splashback and hoping that they have good aim.

If you're walking or if you're cycling, there's a physical element to it, and you have to ask yourself 'Am I up to it? Can I do that challenge?' I guess with trains, it just relies on managing yourself well, and managing money and things.

The ocean crossings were incredible. They seemed so profound when I was there and still feel like that now. This huge cargo ship that was leaving port at Hong Kong: it felt enormous. It would take ages to go under bridges spanning the Hong Kong Harbour and I thought, 'This is huge!' And then as soon as you're out for half a day into the middle of the Pacific, you feel like a toothpick. Seeing the water all around you, extending on to the horizon and these enormous waves, rolling across the horizon towards you, which care nothing for the concerns of the captain or any of the crew. It sounds like a cliché, but you feel tiny. But it's also a really nice feeling. It's satisfying somehow.

ED GILLESPIE
TRAVELLED ROUND THE WORLD
WITHOUT A PLANE

I went around the world without flying, taking anything but a plane to circumnavigate the globe; buses, trains, cargo ships and the odd belligerent camel! It was a 381-day, 33-country, 45,000-mile trip. I intended to rediscover the romance and adventure of overland travel when you move slowly through the world, enjoying the transition of landscape, culture, people, language and cuisine rather than just soaring over it at 35,000 feet.

Crossing the Pacific by cargo ship from New Zealand to Mexico, a 16-day voyage across the world's biggest ocean, was a true traverse of our blue planet. They were glorious, lazy days of sunshine, blue skies and gently rolling waves, with flying fish skittering alongside the huge ship we were on.

The trip had a huge effect on my temperament and disposition. The frenetic, frantic nature of London life and the business of creative communications was exhausting and high tempo, but the relaxed rhythm of slow travel soon dissipated that mania. I became much more at ease, more level-headed and probably easier to work with. My business partner certainly said so!

IAN PACKHAM
SOLO CIRCUMNAVIGATION OF
AFRICA BY PUBLIC TRANSPORT

This was my first big solo adventure – riding battered bush taxis, flatbed trucks, dugout canoes and a van delivering freshly made meat pies, among countless other vehicles, following Africa's coastline for 25,000 miles through 31 countries, equivalent to circling the Earth at the Equator. I feel I experienced Africa at its most raw and real. And I loved it.

The idea for Encircle Africa seemed to develop spontaneously after studying a world map. The more I looked at Africa and the ready-made route of the coast, the more I knew had to give the journey a go.

Africa was so unlike the way it is portrayed in the mainstream media. I struggled to reconcile what I was seeing first hand to what I had been expecting. I didn't have a clear idea of what I would do on my return (or after failure). Learning some of the language spoken in the area is perhaps the most important practical step. Knowing about three words in Portuguese and another three in Arabic really helped. Hand signals and loan words got me the rest of the way.

the Fianarantsoa to Manakar train, a 12-hour journey across some of the world's most incredible landscapes, all seen by sitting in the open carriage door of an ancient train. Amazing.

You'll meet people who say that they'd 'love to come with you', or say 'that sounds amazing, I wish I could go...' but they never do. I just didn't want the trip to always be a dream, a conversation in the pub or at dinner. And so I simply committed. I booked the flights, and then I worked towards the day of my flight with all of the planning and additional money saving.

African adventure travel is like no other adventure travel. It takes patience, and an understanding of TIA – 'This Is Africa!' But if you can just embrace it and smile, it has so much to offer.

BRENDAN LEONARD
LIVED AND WORKED OUT OF HIS VAN

I was working from home for a big software company. I was living with my girlfriend and that ended. So I just packed my stuff in my car and said, 'Oh, the hell with it' and hit the road for a little while. After five weeks running around climbing and hiking and backpacking and meeting with my friends, I realised I could probably just work from the road. I took conference calls from coffee shops and turned in all my assignments. Just as long as I had internet, I could make it happen. In America, we always think you're married, you have two kids, a house, probably two cars and that's what the goal is. There's so many people who were making it work differently than that, in a different model. I started thinking, 'I'm 32. What's happening? I don't have this in my life. Am I going to be OK?' I mean, geez, everybody's got their own path to happiness, I guess. After six months of living in my car, I bought a van and then continued to live in a van. That lasted almost three years. Just bouncing around the West, driving around, doing fun stuff and trying to find places to work, places with wi-fi. It was a blast.

MARC LAMBERT
TRAVELLED THROUGH MADAGASCAR

I set myself a realistic and quite fun target of saving enough cash to get myself to the island of Madagascar, and off I went! I flew to Madagascar with a map, a tent, a camera, a whole lot of patience (much-needed for African adventures!), and spent five weeks solo travelling around the great island, trying to hitch-hike and walk as much as I could.

I've always found solo travel to be so rewarding. Not speaking English to anyone for most of the trip was a real challenge but such a great experience. My favourite memory has to be getting on board

MATT EVANS
TRAVELLED OVERLAND FROM THE UK TO ASIA

One day, we were tramping around in some fields near Penrith when my friend said, 'If we don't do it soon, we won't do it at all'. And he was right. We'd been pontificating and dreaming about it for a few years, but hadn't actually done anything about it. Every time we met up for a beer we'd talk wistfully and hopefully about our plans – and by last orders, we'd *really mean it* – but nothing firmed up, and in reality, the Silk Road dream didn't seem to be getting any closer. So right there and then we made a pledge, we set a date and with a firm, manly handshake got the ball rolling for real.

It wasn't easy. We had to persuade our girlfriends that, a) We all needed to quit our jobs; b) It would be *fun* travelling through barren desert and inhospitable mountain ranges; c) There really *are* romantic restaurants and funky bars in Tashkent and Ashgabat.

We packed in our jobs, rented the house out and set forth to travel from St Pancras to Xi'an overland. It took five months of our lives, created unforgettable memories and changed us all for the better.

We made a decision to live lives we love to live, and have never looked back. In the end, it was a 'it's now or never' moment that made us take the plunge. We'd all travelled plenty before, but had got side-tracked by the minutiae of everyday life. We'd had a whimsical goal for a while, but it needed some refocusing and lifestyle changes to mould it into reality. At times, sure, we ate nothing but yak meat and stale bread for nine days straight. But it honestly feels as though in five months of travelling we created five years' worth of memories.

JAMIE FULBROOK
HITCH-HIKED TO SOUTH AFRICA

I guess I've hitch-hiked around 20,000 miles so far in my life, bringing me into all sorts of terrific mischief. Perhaps the most defining journey was from England to South Africa via the Middle East.

I was a 22-year-old, bored stupid but otherwise eager and hungry graduate. One evening, something just broke. Out came the atlas and the following morning I walked to the end of my street, stuck my thumb out, and pretty much off I popped. I hitch-hiked from there to South Africa.

You could do it quickly. If you actually wanted to do the journey quickly, you could knock it out in a month, especially if the 'mission' element is your driving force. What was really nice at the time, though, was that I was rich in the most valuable of currencies – liberal time. That allowed me to move super-slow, and I only moved on from a place when it stopped being a stimulus. If I found a spot I liked, be it a village or at times total isolation in the desert, I'd stay and settle in for many weeks. When my gut spoke, and it was time to move on, I just walked to the edge of town and stuck out my thumb again.

You know, I didn't set out to hitch-hike all the way to South Africa. That wasn't the deal. It actually came about because I wanted to hitch-hike to Syria – that was my goal. It seemed within reach.

What I really like about hitch-hiking is the mutual audacity of it. You [the hitcher] are bold enough to say, 'Hey, stranger. Take me with you.' In the same vein, the driver has to be willing to say 'Hey, stranger. I trust you. Jump in.' These two personality types often align, and more often than not you get along very well.

I f I say that going on a hitch-hiking or overland adventure is a good idea for young or inexperienced travellers, I certainly do not mean that they are inferior to other types of experience. Visiting every country on Earth, hitch-hiking to Malaysia, or circumnavigating the globe without using a plane are fabulous adventures. The reason these trips suit first-time adventurers is that they are incredibly easy to begin and do not depend on previous hard-earned skills. This is the

'It's important to remember that adventures are not a one-way ticket to Mars: if it turns out that it's not for you then just come home and do something different with your life instead'

sort of adventure that the Lonely Planet empire was built upon, proof enough of its popularity. Jamie demonstrated this perfectly, aged 22, 'bored but eager', by browsing his atlas, walking to the end of his street, and hitch-hiking to Africa. Brendan packed his stuff in his car, said, 'Oh, the hell with it' and hit the road, and journeys like these first taught the best-selling travel writer Rolf how easy, cheap and safe travel could be. Temujin contrasts the physical requirements of a journey by, say, bicycle with travelling by train which 'just relies on managing yourself well.'

Neither Steve nor Ian did much planning for their debut but epic adventures. Chris and his wife, Malin, were already very experienced travellers when they set off to travel round the world during Malin's maternity leave. This, plus a simultaneously relaxed yet proactive approach to life's adventures, meant that they saw a young baby as an opportunity not a constraint. They ignored the naysayers who thought that they were irresponsible, hit the road, and had a fantastic time

together. They remind us of an important detail about planning for daunting journeys: there are hospitals, shops and people who can help all over the world. Plus, if things really don't work out or are not enjoyable, you can always return home. Remember that adventures are not a one-way ticket to Mars: if it turns out that it's not for you after all then just come home and do something different with your life instead.

In contrast to Chris and Malin, Graham felt a lot of organisation and back-up plans were necessary to deal with the complex logistics of his record-breaking challenge to visit every country on Earth without flying. Once again, within one specific niche of adventure style, there are many different ways you can approach things according to your plans and personality.

The key ingredient you need for hitch-hiking is time, what Jamie describes as 'the most valuable of currencies.' All of our hitch-hikers make the same point: if you are lucky enough to have no pressing schedule in your life then hitch-hiking is a great way to travel. What makes it so unique, educational and fascinating are the people that you spend time chatting with along the way. I am quite a shy person, I don't really like meeting new people, I detest small talk and chit chat at parties. And yet I absolutely love the chaotic randomness of hitch-hiking, nattering away about life and the world to the colourful characters I've met on the road.

More structured than hitch-hiking, but with different advantages and appeals, is travelling overland without using planes, Phileas Fogg style. Jump on the Number 47 bus at the end of your street and you're on a continuous network of public transport that could carry you to Cape Town or Qingdao. Whether you are watching Madagascar trundle past, sitting in the open carriage door of an ancient train as Marc did, or hoping the gentleman clearing his throat and spitting from the top bunk above you has good aim, like Temujin in China, public transport is always memorable. Matt felt as though his five months on the road filled him

with 'five years' worth of memories'. Ed found that the relaxed rhythm of slow travel had a significant effect on his disposition since returning home and reminisced fondly about the slightly old-fashioned, romantic notion of slow travel. Both Ed and Temujin were particularly enamoured with the experience of crossing oceans by cargo ship, an adventure that seems more unusual these days than rowing across an ocean! I once crossed the Pacific Ocean on a cargo ship and the slow rhythm of those long days at sea are quite unlike any other travel experience I have had.

So how do you make an adventure like this happen? Rolf emphasises that simplicity is the ticket to travel, both in terms of the journey itself (Rolf once travelled round the whole world with no luggage at all) and in the preparation phase. And, as in every chapter, our travelling adventurers stress that the hardest part is committing to beginning. Marc didn't want the trip to always be a dream, 'a conversation in the pub', and Matt realised that 'if we don't do it soon, we won't do it at all.'

CLIMB

Mountains produce the best adventure stories. Actually, that's not quite true. *Climbers* produce the best stories, mountains don't give a damn. And that, of course, is part of the magic. These vast, beautiful beasts soar above us – secular cathedrals, perhaps – tempting us to raise our eyes upwards, wondering if it's possible, if it'll 'go', wondering if we are up to the task. They do not care about our feeble, futile efforts on their flanks. And yet the sacrifice, the suffering, the efforts, the guts, the risks that mountaineers pour forth in their desperate attempts to reach the top (and then back down again) is nothing short of the very limit of human potential and zealous fanaticism.

The rewards are preposterous: to stand on the highest bit and get a slightly nicer view than you do a little lower down seems a crazy thing to risk so much for. For the risks are always there with climbers. All top-level climbers have tales of when they nearly died doing what they love. They all have friends or colleagues who have died in the mountains. And some of them will die themselves in the same way. There is a dark side to the mountains. They know that, but still they do it.

And a love deemed worth dying for is a powerful love indeed. It's a love affair based upon risk and ego and ambition. But it is one made possible and sustained by effort, hope, collaboration, empathy, patience, persistence and caring, as well as by serving an apprenticeship, mastering your craft and the good bits of pride. It's totally bloody daft. It is, as Yvon Chouinard put it, pointless but meaningful. I prefer that explanation to the hackneyed 'because it's there'.

Pointless but meaningful: that might just be a perfect subtitle for this book, for my life, and one which all the other tramps like us will surely understand.

I am not a mountaineer, though I wish that I was. I'm not a mountaineer because I have been reluctant to put in the time necessary to learn the skills to climb something exciting and stay alive.

So I admire mountaineers for being something that I am not. I like the way they can choose between solitude and camaraderie. I love the untouched simplicity of mountain tops, and how beautiful they look from down in the valley as well as up on the windy heights.

From my own few mountain experiences, I have happy memories of rasping for breath with each small footstep, kicking crampons into the snow to create a small step for my partner, roped to me below, in the Andes. '1-2-3-4-5-6-7-8-9-10'. I counted the steps in my head as I struggled for breath, and after the tenth I treated myself to a little break. Gazing down from almost 20,000 feet, the world below looked so small and unreal. And then turn, kick, climb once more. The high camp, with your tent teetering impossibly, is a special place to be. So, too, is the thrill of rock climbing, though the fear of what climbers call 'exposure' (the bloody big drop beneath your feet) is enough to cripple any rock-climbing aspirations I may ever have. I'm intrigued by this fear and I enjoy challenging it. After all, if you are securely tied to a rope then you are very safe. But the mind struggles with the difference between perceived risk and actual danger. I like learning that lesson. Even Scotland's Inaccessible Pinnacle had me clinging tight to the rock with fear (though simultaneously whooping with delight). But whilst rock climbing to a serious level is out for me, I do harbour an ambition to climb a large mountain in Greenland or Central Asia. I don't care about world records, yet still the prospect of a first ascent – a mountain never climbed before – really captures my imagination.

Mountaineering and climbing require skill, commitment and time. But that is no reason not to begin. Every climber once had to learn how to use a karabiner, first climbed a small hill, first trekked up an easy mountain. You can, too. You just have to begin. Just bear in mind as you do, though, the crazy, obsessive affair that you might just be opening the door to.

WISE WORDS FROM FELLOW ADVENTURERS

TIM MOSS
CLIMBED IN THE ALTAI MOUNTAINS,
AN EXPEDITION FOR UNDER £1,000

The Altai is the best mountain range you've never heard of. I found it on Google ('world mountain ranges'), and the more I asked around, the more I realised that no one seemed to know much about it (at least not from a British mountaineering perspective).

The expedition was pretty standard in mountaineering terms: fly to an unfamiliar country, spend a few days cobbling together supplies from whatever shops you can find, take a bus to a tiny village in the middle of nowhere, hike into the mountains with some packhorses, pitch your tents in a good spot and climb as many mountains as possible before it's time to go home again.

My personal highlights were finding bear prints in the snow, tweeting from the top of a previously unclimbed mountain (something to be celebrated or not?), and the long evenings huddled around the stove beneath the stars in our big base-camp tent.

We recruited our team by just running an advert in the Royal Geographical Society's Expedition Bulletin and soon grew from two to six. Not having anyone to go with is no excuse – you are not alone. Try also Explorers Connect and Escape the City.

We made first and first-British ascents *without undertaking technical climbing*. In fact, one of our team had never even climbed before. These days, mountains are usually unclimbed not because they're really hard but just because no one's tried. Technical expertise need not be a barrier to a great expedition.

We achieved this in two weeks' holiday from work. I went a few days early and stayed a few days longer but most of the team were in and out within 15 days. Virgin peak glory and a summit photo without upsetting the boss.

It cost £1,000 all in for a proper expedition, including flights to Russia, insurance, supplies and logistical support.

GRANT RAWLINSON
TRAVELLED THROUGH NEW ZEALAND
TO THE HIGHEST POINT OF THE COUNTRY

Together with my climbing partner, Alan, we started at the highest point of the North Island of New Zealand and made a continuous, human-powered journey to the highest point in the South Island of New Zealand. Our journey involved climbing to the summits of Mount Ruapehu and Aoraki/Mount Cook, a 153-mile kayak descent down the Whanganui River, 600 miles of road cycling and a 44-mile sea-kayak crossing of the notoriously dangerous Cook Strait.

Our aim was to have a unique and challenging adventure on a shoestring budget, without having to travel to the ends of the Earth, and fitting it into our annual leave entitlement. Our total budget was £1,000 each. I borrowed my wife's bike. We used our own climbing gear on the mountains and rented a sea kayak to cross the Cook Strait.

The fewer resources and support I use, the more I tend to enjoy the experience. Things have a habit of sorting themselves out, especially if you want it bad enough and make it your priority. If you really want to go on that adventure you *must* move it to priority number *one*. It must be the top of the list. All other reasons not to do the trip must be relegated to the *excuses* category. Every reason

not to go is an excuse. Don't make excuses. No one likes people who make excuses.

If you make it your priority you will find the money to do it. A simple question I like to ask people is, 'could they come up with x thousand dollars tomorrow if they had to?' Most people say no – they could not. Then I ask again, 'could you come up with that amount *if* the person most precious to you would die if you did not come up with the money?' A lot more people put their hand up the time.

So what's changed?

The only different thing is that it has suddenly become a much higher priority.

Of course, adventure is not as important as life or death. The point is simply that if you really, really want to make something happen, you can do it.

PAUL RAMSDEN
TWO-TIME WINNER OF THE
CELEBRATED PIOLETS D'OR AWARD

I've been lucky to do a lot of climbs in the Himalayas, and they've tended to be successful. Most hard climbs in the Himalayas fail.

I guess the two Piolets d'Or climbs are the most well known. Certainly the second of those, in India, was the best climb I'll ever do. It was hard, but enjoyable. I got to lie down every night. It was absolutely brilliant! Most people climbing in the Himalayas rush, they stress. Alpine climbing is all about speed, but in the Himalayas you need to relax, and just be slow and consistent. People treat mountains like an enemy that needs to be 'beaten', but you can't beat a mountain. They don't care. So relax. I love being in the mountains so I want to take as much time up there as I can manage.

I do one expedition a year, every year. I go away for a month. I can't justify a long holiday on my own, but I can delude myself that an expedition is useful and will make me a better person!

It's a bit brutal. There's no compromise. My wife has to work much harder when I'm away. I get a lot of heartache from the family, I'm in bad books for a while, my daughter sulks for about two weeks before I go away. It's selfish, a huge disturbance. It's hard. I've learned to be a bit of a bastard. To not think too much about it otherwise I'd get too guilty! But on the other hand, these are things I just have to do. And my family understand that. I'm a nicer person for it [laughing].

I'm lucky, because I climb with Mick [Fowler: Assistant Director, Shares and Assets Valuation at HMRC/climbing legend] who is really famous. People always send him ideas and photos. So we'll be in the pub and he'll pull out some photos and

we'll think 'that looks fun', and off we go again.

On Google Earth you can 'fly in' to the mountains and study them. You can also see how they change with the seasons and the time. You see where the mountain catches the sun and where it is in shadow, so you can now know a lot about the climb in advance. The downside of this is that the sense of exploring decreases a little. But we can squeeze a lot more adventure into our short time away now.

Time spent on Google Earth is seldom wasted. Actually, make that 'A fuck-load of time on Google Earth is seldom wasted.' Mick prints out all these views on his printer at home and off we go. It works

great, except for the time when we were in the Tien Shan and a baggage mule fell over in a lake, soaked all our maps and all the colours ran! It's quite interesting then to spend a month in the mountains without any map at all!

Scrape together a grand and we could do something good. The expedition where I won my first Piolets d'Or cost me 850 quid.

ANDY KIRKPATRICK
CLIMBED EL CAPITAN OVER 20 TIMES

I think people often focus too much on the pinprick of an outcome – the summit, the finishing line, the road ahead – and they ignore the tapestry of the experience. The best climbs I've had have often been the ones where we didn't get to the top.

I've always done trips on a very tight budget. I've always put climbing before a career as a climber – if that makes sense. This means I've never really had a big budget for trips. Usually it's about £800, and half of that goes on flights.

My trip to Antarctica this year was paid for by Norwegian sponsors. It cost a huge amount of money, which I find hard to square in my head when I saw so much poverty in South Africa, from where we flew to Antarctica, not to mention that it would have been enough to fund me for the rest of my life for my trips away!

I often joke that I never go on expeditions, only holidays, and I made a point of going on 'Alpine-style' trips where one expedition rucksack and a big holdall was all you needed. The aim was never to pay for excess baggage – and I never did!

This approach works well in South America (I've had five Patagonian holidays) and Alaska, and I've never personally been interested in doing trips involving dozens of blue storage barrels, porters, LOs [Liaison Officers] etc. People often get hung up on gear and think you need to be sponsored to climb in the big mountains, but there is endless dirt-cheap kit that still allows you to be better

equipped than superstar teams were in the past. Plus you've probably already got most of what you need, or can borrow it from your sad mates who buy kit but will never be brave enough actually to use it!

When I was on £13,000 a year, working in a shop, taking a month's unpaid leave each year to go climbing, people with real jobs (doctors, architects, lawyers) would come up to me after my talks and ask how I could afford to do it. If you want to do something, money should not be the limiting factor. Even living on £27 a week on the dole I could still hitch to the Peak District or the Lakes and have adventures as cool as going to Antarctica. I always had this idea of getting on my bike after signing on (which you did every two weeks) and seeing how far I could cycle in that fortnight. Money is no excuse.

When I came back from Antarctica this year, I hadn't worked for two months. I had about £20 in my bank and an ex-wife who was pissed off at me for not having looked after the kids for all that time. This is the reality. But if you work hard and are motivated you can always find the money; maybe not fifty grand to climb Everest, but enough to get you to Bolivia or Morocco.

I'd recommend starting off by doing the 14 peaks in Wales over a weekend, then the Bob Graham in the Lakes over a longer weekend, and then the Ramsay's Round in Scotland. After that, try ticking off all the Munros and all the routes in Classic Rock. While undertaking this, try reading as much about the history of British climbing as you can – all the classics. Then try to tick off all the classic Scottish winter routes, especially those on Ben Nevis, as well as the more remote ones in the Highlands.

By now you'll be pretty solid, so it's time to go to the Alps. How about ticking off all the 4,000-metre peaks over a few years, as well as throwing in some ice climbing and ski mountaineering in Norway?

The north face of the Eiger, Matterhorn and Grandes Jorasses should come next (at least one of them to be climbed in winter), giving you a boost for a trip to Alaska to climb Denali, and one to climb Aconcagua. You could tick off some more of the seven summits if you want, but you've just done the cheapest two, so I'd leave it at that (all the other tick lists are simply shorthand for amazing climbs and adventures).

By now you'll be ten, maybe twenty years down the line from starting up Snowdon, and you'll have had enough climbing and incredible days on the hill to know that Everest is a waste of time.

You're no longer a clueless dreamer, but someone who understands the harsh reality of the mountains as well as their joy. For most people, no real happiness can come from climbing Everest, only heartache. Spend the cash on climbs for your soul not your ego.

'Even living on £27 a week on the dole I could still hitch to the Peak District or the Lakes and have adventures as cool as going to Antarctica'

WILL COPESTAKE
A YEAR-LONG ADVENTURE
ROUND SCOTLAND

I set off on an adventure that would last one day shy of a year; to kayak solo around Scotland then cycle home via the 282 summits over 3,000 feet. These peaks are an infamous list known as 'The Munros'. I wanted to explore the landscape and culture that lay upon my doorstep. The Machair to Munro expedition was designed as a personal journey to prove you don't have to go far to have a big adventure.

I discovered the rewards of the winter in countless summit sunsets and ferocious gales. The long nights spent reading and eating balanced against the struggle against cold and wet. In 12 months I felt elation, I cried, I found friends in strangers and an intimacy with my country unlike anything I had experienced before.

KYLE DEMPSTER
PROFESSIONAL ALPINIST AND WINNER
OF THE CELEBRATED PIOLETS D'OR

While I do call myself a professional climber, I realise that the occupation is finite and at some point I may not want to be climbing at the level that I do at the moment. Instead of being an old burnt-out climber still talking about the past, I want to move on to other things. The coffee shops we own will someday support those activities and adventures. I also really love coffee.

I'd done four trips to Pakistan, three to remote China, several to South America, and the Canadian Arctic twice. I knew what I was getting into before I set off [on my cycling and climbing journey in Kyrgyzstan]. Central Asia is like the modern-day Wild West: all the amenities are available but they are few and far between. Happiness and hard-lived lives seem to be in unison.

Being a climber, I have a ton of admiration for the folks who are true specialists. But I also greatly admire and respect the folks who do many different things at 90 per cent efficiency. Specialists seem so focused on one thing that it really blinds them from enjoying all the other cool things that one can pursue in this life. Jack-of-all-trades accomplish a variety of things but they will never contribute to the true progression of a sport or activity or know what it is like to do something at the upper reaches of possibility.

BRENDAN LEONARD
A SELF-PROCLAIMED EVERYMAN
CLIMBER AND ADVENTURER

I think there are a couple of types of inspiration in the outdoors. For example, if you want to watch a climbing video, it's inspiring to watch somebody who's really good at it like Alex Honnold or Chris Sharma. Rock-climbing media is always about the high end of the grading scale. I like climbing a lot but I will never get to 5.13, 5.14 [the very highest standards]. I felt there was this huge emphasis on the elite stuff even though there aren't that many people who are achieving that level. I thought, why don't I try to speak about what people feel when they're out there? Because everybody understands what it's like to climb something that's really challenging to you, regardless of the grade. It may not be K2 or Everest, but it's challenging to me to go up a 12,000-foot mountain. There's not a lot of air up there. It's really tiring. So if you can capture that feeling or the things all these people have in common, then you're speaking to everyone.

I love being in the mountains or in the desert, just in these huge places to experience awe and kind of push the limits a little bit and get a little scared and be out in the elements.

KYLE HENNING
TREKKED AND CYCLED FROM THE LOWEST
TO THE HIGHEST POINT OF AFRICA

I spent 68 days travelling solo from the lowest point of elevation on the African continent to the summit of the highest mountain, using only my own power. Beginning from Lake Assal, Djibouti, at 516 feet below sea level, I cycled 1,900 miles through Ethiopia and Kenya to the base of Mount Kilimanjaro in Tanzania. Leaving the bike behind, I trekked to the summit of Uhuru Peak at 19,340 feet above sea level.

The journey began in a hot, rocky desert and ended on a glacier four countries away. In between the extremes were forests, lakes and massive cities.

Honestly, I wish I had known even less back then than I actually did. The best part was discovering new things with an open mind. Knowledge can bring prejudice, unmet expectations or personal doubt. A little naivety helped me push on and allow people into my life without over-thinking the project.

JON MUIR
CLIMBER AND ADVENTURER

I only summited Everest once and I've gotta say I just don't get all the hype about Everest. Sure, it was my boyhood dream, but as things panned out in my mountaineering career I'd summited some seriously technically difficult mountains before summiting Everest. I mean, Everest is just a high-altitude hill walk, essentially. You don't have to be a mountaineer to get to the top. You just have to really want to do it and have plenty of money. The Sherpas are the true mountaineers on Everest. Most of the people who climb it these days are adventure tourists with very little skill. There's also so much media hype about things like 'The Seven Summits' or the fourteen 26,247-foot peaks (isn't that a magic number!) [more commonly described as 8,000 metres]. These mountains, climbed by their normal routes, don't even justify the word 'climbing'. Everybody is wanting to join the crew or, if it's polar walking, break a record by doing the same old thing but just a little faster. Australian mountaineers climbed more new routes in the Himalaya in the 1980s than in all the time before or since. There remains no shortage of new routes or unclimbed mountains but everyone seems to want to climb the ones the media tells them to. There's a serious lack of imagination out there.

With the exception of trophy peaks such as Mount Everest, climbing adventures are often not as expensive as you might imagine. Many of our interviewees describe exciting climbs for under £1,000. 'Spend the cash on climbs for your soul not your ego', urges Andy. He champions the notion of saving hard then heading for cheaper mountain ranges in places like Bolivia or Morocco.

If the budgets in these stories are similar, the climbers certainly are not. Tim would not mind me saying that double Piolets d'Or winner Paul is a far better climber than he is. And Brendan's enthusiasm for encouraging fellow mere mortals to climb is inspiring, freely admitting that he finds a 12,000-foot mountain challenging. After all, it is important to remember that there is more to climbing than the summit. Andy feels people often ignore the 'tapestry of the experience'.

'It's OK not to know how you are going to achieve certain things at the start. You cannot expect to have all the answers at the beginning'

Tim is adamant that technical expertise need not be a barrier to a great expedition. His refreshingly simple approach to climbing expeditions ('Google for 'world mountain ranges'') is inspiring for anyone tempted to dabble with the world's high spots. Mountains are relative things, anyway: Britain's peaks, for example, are pitifully low but beautiful and challenging in their own way. They made a superb backdrop for Will's year-long exploration of his own country, a journey that proved you don't have to go far to have a big adventure.

At the other end of the planet, Grant did the same thing, using his imagination to come up with a multi-discipline adventure across New Zealand.

Kyle's trip to the summit of Africa was similar, and also achievable for non-experts. I like these ideas of combining modes of transport on adventures. (My favourite example of this was the late Göran Kropp who cycled from Sweden to Nepal, climbed Everest then pedalled home again.)

The pull of the mountains is a common theme, whether it is an annual return for Paul, or the sense of purpose – mentioned in a previous chapter – that was so cathartic for Jimmy after he broke his back. For Kyle, 'happiness and hard-lived lives seem to be in unison'.

In working out how to begin a climbing expedition, Grant reminds us that 'you don't have to come up with all the answers when you initially plan your trip and commit to it. It's OK not to know how you are going to achieve certain things (money, fitness, equipment, etc.) at the start. You cannot expect to have all the answers at the beginning.'

EVERYDAY

What is adventure anyway? One man's adventure is another man's holiday. One man's adventure is another's god-awful miserable penance, or another man's daily lot. So I always try not to define the word too tightly. Adventure means different things to different people.

I suggest that adventure involves doing things that are new and different and difficult. It's about challenging yourself, taking risks, leaving behind the ordinary. It's about being curious and open-minded.

For some this means pushing human potential in a specific way. For some it's about heading round the world on wild and ambitious journeys, unwilling to limit themselves to one environment or one mode of travel. For others it means carving a career out of travel and their creative loves, or going to live in a different culture. Still others look to share the world with their children. And some do not go anywhere: they make adventurous choices at home, living unconventional and inspiring lives.

WISE WORDS FROM FELLOW ADVENTURERS

NICK WESTON
LIVED IN A TREEHOUSE FOR SIX MONTHS

I've always been interested in adventure, but never really thought I would be someone who would do something like going to the other side of the world to do an adventure. I wanted to do something quite close to home, something that was more of a lifestyle project, I suppose. With the recession hitting London, I decided I wanted to get out. I was doing freelance work, and there was hardly any around. I started looking at ways in which I could simplify my life and do a lot of things for myself rather than having to pay for certain things like electricity, rent, food, and so on. The idea of going off and living in a wood and being self-sufficient was something that was quite appealing. I was quite a feral kid, so I grew up doing a lot of that anyway. It was a bit like going back to being a kid again. That whole side of not actually having the kind of responsibilities you do as an adult. You're put back into a mind-set where anything's possible. That was a big part of it for me. I think the idea of having a treehouse rather than just sleeping in a tent made it a bit more permanent. Also, a treehouse is a child's dream, so it was something that slotted in quite nicely.

I left London and moved into the woods. I lived under a tarpaulin while scrounging for various pieces from barns, garages and skips – whatever I could find. I did a few sketches. I think it took about six weeks to build the treehouse. It was a bit of a mishmash of recycled natural materials. It cost about £300 in total. It was quite taxing, the build and all the rest of it, whilst also digging a vegetable patch, doing all of that. The idea of the project was to do six months from April through till the end of October, and hunt and fish and forage for my food.

I got into a routine. I knew where all my resources were. I knew how to go and get fish. I knew where to go and get mushrooms. I knew where to go and get different types of food. The vegetable patch was chock-full of things. Yeah, that was a real sort of high point, because I was settled in and I knew where everything was. I think that was definitely when it was at its best.

I can see why hunter-gatherers lived in groups, because you could delegate and do different things. But one person having to do all of the different things was very busy. Wood was always the main thing, for fire. And getting water and food. That's it. That's all you have to worry about [each day]. It kind of cuts your life right back. I'd be lying if I said that some nights I didn't go to bed hungry, but yeah, that was part and parcel of it.

It is that kind of slowing down and adjusting to a new set of rules. Not rules, exactly, just a new lifestyle.

KIRSTIE PELLING
ENCOURAGING HER FAMILY TO LIVE ADVENTUROUSLY

As a family, we have hiked, biked and paddled in more than 20 countries. We aren't an itinerant family; we fit our adventures around work, school and home life. We have travelled and had outdoor adventures with toddlers, tweens and now teens. And, contrary to popular belief, we have found that it is possible to get a teenager out of the bedroom! Indeed, as our children enter the teenage years we

feel it's even more important for us to find ways to connect with them, and help them keep in touch with us, the outdoors and their environment.

It has shown the kids there are many ways to live, and many ways to make a living. It has taught us many things about ourselves. It has taught us resilience and stamina. The children have learnt skills for life and my daughter and I have become more brave. It has also turned the boys into adrenaline junkies, who are perhaps a little too keen on making fire!

CANDACE ROSE RARDON
MAKING HER LIVING FROM ART AND TRAVEL

At the moment I am just going where opportunities pop up. I never expected for the travel to become my work as well. It's all melded together now so there's no huge distinction. When I go on a trip, it's work, play and life all rolled in together, so I'm very grateful for that.

I started off right after college and didn't know anything at all about what I was doing, and I've just learned as I've gone along.

I am far from a millionaire. I think people would

be shocked if they knew how much money I don't make. I support myself through freelance writing – writing for websites and for a few in-flight magazines – and I also sell custom artwork through Etsy.

PHOEBE SMITH
FIRST WOMAN TO WILD CAMP SOLO AT ALL THE EXTREME POINTS OF MAINLAND BRITAIN

About ten years ago I left uni wide-eyed and desperate to see the world. I went travelling for two years, cut my teeth as a journalist, met some incredible people and experienced some truly once-in-a-lifetime encounters. But then I came home. And, as is typical post-travel, I had no money left and I felt that there was nothing

exciting to do here. Then I started going walking. Short walks became long day walks, walks on easy-to-follow paths became expedition-like forays into wilder and wilder places until eventually I was on my own, wild camping (that is, camping away from campsites, toilets and shower blocks) my way around the UK, seeking out my wilderness wherever I could find it – until I set myself my Extreme Sleeps Challenge to camp at the extreme points of mainland Britain.

The best thing about my love for seeking out the wild places to sleep in is that it's an adventure with no end date – and one I can fit in regularly around my full-time job as a travel editor. I was an instant addict. From surviving my first solo camp I started to seek out more quirky and unusual places to lay my head – from bivvying on mountain summits,

'We wanted to immerse ourselves completely in this way of life for a while, focusing in on the process of living, moment to moment'

It's hard to summarise a chapter of characters such as these. Perhaps the one thing they all have in common was a desire to follow their hearts, to do the adventure that felt exciting, important and meaningful to them, and to crack on and do it rather than worrying about behaving in a way that society may deem unconventional.

It may be seeking a new lifestyle, whether under canvas like Jen and her family, or up in a treehouse like Nick. Or it might be a concerted effort to fit adventure into a normal busy life like Phoebe or Kirstie and her family. Kirstie and her husband made a pact to keep adventure in their lives when their first child was born. Nick grew disgruntled with his London life of 'Go to work. Do work. Come back. Eat' and wanted to get back into a more excited, exciting mind-set where 'anything's possible'.

Candace turned her love of art and travel into her work. There are many examples of people who find a way to earn a living from their adventures, with most of the interviewees in this chapter carving out their own niche in this way. Candace offers this encouragement to anyone who likes the sound of this: 'I think anybody can pick up the skills and the routines that you need to make this lifestyle happen.' She may not be a millionaire, but now when she goes on an adventure, 'it's both work and play. And life. All rolled in together.' Could you ask for any more than that?

to nestling underneath boulders, sleeping in the wreckage of an old World War II Superfortress and bedding down in bothies – the wilder the better. And the best thing about it is that other than the transport costs of accessing some of the places from where I walk in, it costs me nothing at all. In the UK we are blessed with some of the best mapping in the world, and OS [Ordnance Survey] maps hold the key to showing you wild areas to explore. Once you've planned your first wild sleep, pack your bag and keep it either by your front door or in the boot of your car. I call this my 'go bag'. That way, when you get the weather window, you have no excuse. You're ready to go.

JEN BENSON
SPENDING A YEAR UNDER CANVAS WITH HER HUSBAND AND TWO YOUNG CHILDREN

The idea of a year under canvas combined our desire to take on a properly testing challenge and explore Britain's wild and beautiful places with the need for our adventures to be possible as a family. On occasions in the past we've found ourselves wondering whether a challenge is possible with small children. We'd proved, with a bit of creativity and chocolate, that many, surprisingly, are. We've conquered mountains, camped wild, climbed trees, jumped into lakes, swum in rivers, foraged our suppers and been on multi-day walks with our kids as company. We wanted to immerse ourselves completely in this way of life for a while, stripping away the parts that aren't really real, and focusing in on the process of living, moment to moment.

GRANDER

Polar journeys are not cheap. You certainly cannot do one for £1,000. They are logistically daunting, too. You will need to overcome these two huge hurdles if you have a yearning for the big white world at the Poles of our planet. But it's good that there are barriers to entry, for polar journeys – proper ones – are difficult and not suited for someone unwilling to rise to a challenge and to persevere.

I mention 'proper' polar journeys for, unlike any other kind of adventure described in this book, it's possible to slightly con other people (and, perhaps, yourself) with what you've actually achieved with your polar exploits. Here then, is a basic explanation of such journeys:

North Pole: the Geographic North Pole is the axis the world spins around, the top of the world, and, in adventuring terms, the purest spot to head for. There is no pole at the North Pole, only your GPS knows that you have arrived. It's in the middle of the Arctic Ocean, so to travel there you are travelling on frozen sea ice. This makes travel very difficult. Gaps in the ice ('leads') need to be detoured around or crossed by jumping, swimming or paddling on your sledge. Sea ice jumbles up into huge fields of ice rubble which have to be crossed. Ocean drift can carry you maddeningly off course. Polar bears are a hazard. The air is moist so kit gets wet and then freezes. The Arctic Ocean is a tough, tough environment to operate in.

The North Magnetic Pole is the spot that your compass points to. It's a long way from the Geographic North Pole and is mostly of interest to adventurers because it's easier to get to, but you can still, if you don't mind a bit of story-fudging, impress people that you've 'been to the North Pole'. The location of this Pole moves from year to year. People still often enjoy going to the 1996 location of the North Magnetic Pole because that's really easy to get to (even I've been most of the way there). Disingenuous adventurers (and Jeremy Clarkson) sometimes claim to have got to the North Pole when they've visited this spot.

South Pole: down at the bottom of the world, Antarctica is where the penguins live. Penguins and polar bears only ever meet on Christmas cards. Antarctica is a continent, so the South Pole lies on land, albeit land crushed beneath a couple of miles of ancient ice. The Geographic South Pole is at an altitude of 9,000 feet, and Antarctica is the coldest, driest, windiest continent on Earth. Travel in Antarctica is generally easier than on the Arctic Ocean. There are some areas of crevasses, but much of a South Pole journey is up on the flat, featureless polar plateau. The Geographic South Pole, scene of the heroic and tragic tales of Amundsen and Scott, today houses the Amundsen-Scott South Pole Station. This American monstrosity has turned the South Pole into a series of big warehouses. There is a pole at the Pole, with a gaudy brass shiny ball on top for you to pose for your picture with. There's also ice cream, a cinema and a gift shop.

A despoiled wilderness aside, a journey to the South Pole is made special by the great footsteps that you are walking in. There is also a South Magnetic Pole that you can head for, a Geomagnetic Pole (in the Southern Ocean) and a Pole of Inaccessibility (the spot right in the middle of Antarctica – the Geographic South Pole is actually fortuitously close to the edge of the continent for trekkers).

The way you travel to the Poles also has a significant bearing on its ranking of achievement:

Flying straight to the Pole. Congratulations! You are very rich. Your flight has helped contribute to the melting of the polar ice caps. Proceed to the gift shop inside the South Pole Station.

A 'last degree' expedition. Many people undertake paid journeys to walk the final degree of latitude to one of the poles. The journey is about 60 miles and involves several days out on the ice, hauling your gear, and camping. For many people this is either their first Polar journey or the most they are able to commit to, limited perhaps by time, expertise or fitness. It's a great trip to do and a really good achievement. Just resist the urge when you return home to omit details of flying most of the way to the Pole and to lead people to believe that you are the next Ranulph Fiennes! You've done something cool – no need to bullshit about it.

Next up are 'full length' journeys to the Poles. Generally, and simplistically, this means travelling from land (Russia or Canada) to the North Pole. Global warming is making this impossible to achieve in some seasons. In Antarctica it means travelling from the sea to the Pole (as Scott/ Amundsen had to do). But many people interpret it as walking from the Continental edge (where Antarctica would meet the sea if all of the ice

Will you go solo or in a team? Will you have a paid guide? Does that differ from just having a really experienced team-mate? Will you use kites to assist you when the wind is favourable? Or dogs (though they are not allowed in Antarctica)? Or skidoos? Or even a bloody tractor – for someone has driven one to the South Pole. Is nothing sacred any more...? Will you haul all your gear and food for the whole trip, or will you arrange for a resupply of food to be positioned along the way? Supported versus unsupported is fertile fodder for a pub argument. Getting a resupply makes the journey easier, but it makes the fundraising harder, for a resupply flight will cost well upwards of £10,000 a time, even if the weather is too bad for the plane actually to land on the ice and make its delivery. And if you walk the whole way to a Pole, hauling all your own food and gear, but then get a plane to pick you up and fly you home, should that count as unsupported? When Captain Scott got to the Pole he was but halfway home, and the hard times all lay ahead.

Let all this complication not put you off a polar journey. If you can summon the money, if you can learn the skills to stay alive and to move through these hostile lands, then you are in rich adventure territory. The books of journeys past are inspiring. The landscapes are spectacular. The low midnight sun, the lambent light, the warming glow of slurping a hot meal in your sleeping bag after a hard day's work: these are memories and lessons that will live with you all your days. I've spent time on the frozen Arctic Ocean and in Greenland and they are quite simply some of the best adventure memories of my life. I spent five years planning, preparing and dreaming for a South Pole expedition that, in the end, I was unable to go on. It gnaws hard as an unfulfilled ambition.

And, finally, if even the utmost ends of the Earth are not enough to satisfy your wanderlust, there are the very, very few who make the boldest leap of all: to boldly leave our planet behind and take their adventurous spirits off into space. Perhaps the grandest adventure of all?

'The low midnight sun, the warming glow of slurping a hot meal after a hard day's work: these are memories that will live with you all your days'

somehow melted) to the Pole.

As you can see, this all begins to get rather convoluted and the potential for petty arguments about who did what is large. So now let's throw this into the mix: how you choose to travel to the Pole.

WISE WORDS FROM FELLOW ADVENTURERS

MARTIN HARTLEY
SEVERAL EXPEDITIONS TO THE NORTH POLE

You get really excited by the whole preparation for the trip. But then when it actually comes to getting onto the plane you are desperately hoping there is going to be a bad weather delay so you don't have to get on the plane! And then you get on the plane and it takes off, and you are hoping, 'I really hope the weather is bad and we can't find a place to land and we have to come back. I just want one more warm night in a bed.' And when the plane does land you think, 'Shit! I'm here again. Oh my god.' The plane door opens, freezing air comes in, the pilot always says, 'Welcome to the middle of nowhere.' Then there is a bit of panic, everyone piles off the plane, hauls all the kit out. When the plane leaves, everyone just stands still without speaking and watches it, watches it and watches it and then the plane disappears and you can still hear it and you are still looking in the sky for it and then the sound goes.

Once the sound is gone, that's probably the best part of the expedition because then that's when the adventure begins – everything is open and that's the best part of the expedition by a long shot.

The other thing that happens, and it happens pretty consistently, is if you're on a trip and you know you are going to be out on the ice for 60 or 70 days, the first ten days are really exciting because you are getting to be experts in adventure and after ten days have gone then you start to think, 'Damn. I've got another 30, 40, 50 days of this. Oh my god.'

When you get to day 50 or 60, then you are counting down the days that you have got left and you are hoping there is going to be bad weather delays so that the plane can't come in because you don't want it to come and get you. Then when it does get you, the second you're back in civilisation you start thinking about going back out there again. It's freakish psychological behaviour that doesn't make any sense. It doesn't matter how dirty you are or how smelly you are, you just don't care, it doesn't matter. It's not important.

Photographically, Siberia wins hands down, because it's just a lot weirder. There's less new stuff around and a lot more character and also it seems – although it's probably not true – that there is a lot more colour in Siberia than there is in Canada. The Arctic Ocean is the best place, nothing on Earth can touch it. It's like a frozen version of a lava flow – that's probably the best way to describe it.

The Americans have successfully destroyed any sense of remoteness of the South Pole. It's just an industrial site, really. If they'd built the South Pole base over the horizon, three or four miles away, you could still stand at the South Pole and wonder what Scott was thinking, or Amundsen, when they were there. But you can't have those thoughts now, because there's a great stupid building there. But I think Antarctica has a lot more romance associated with expeditions than the Arctic. When you go to Antarctica you have feelings of nostalgia. When you go to the Arctic... you're just cold.

BEN SAUNDERS
SKIED TO THE NORTH AND SOUTH POLES

I'm most proud of the last expedition, the Scott Expedition. Even now I can't put it into words. It was so much harder than I ever thought it was going to be and it just took so much to get it off the ground.

There were so many years and years and years where it seemed like everyone was doubting. I was doubting whether this was actually going to happen [it took ten years to raise the sponsorship]. Just to get down there and start felt like a triumphant achievement really. So it was an extraordinary experience. Was it worth it? I'm not really sure how to answer that.

I've always dreamed of having some sort of secret benefactor who gives me huge chunks of cash and then I could just have a stealth expedition with no sponsors, no social media, plain clothing, no logos, no flags, and just go and do it for the hell of it, really. I'd love that, but sadly I don't have enough money and the niche that I've chosen is ridiculously expensive. I've always had to find sponsors.

I'm still sort of chewing over this now, but for a long time I imagined that once I did this trip, everything would somehow change. It would miraculously transform my life. And, of course, when we reached the end of the trip, nothing changed. Nothing happened. There wasn't a magic wand that just ended the trip and cast a spell. And in some ways, it was a giant anticlimax. So for me to expect the layman to be able to look at what [my expedition partner] Tarka and I did and somehow evaluate it objectively is totally unrealistic. That's why Tarka was such a great team-mate because he has zero ego. He just doesn't care about external

validation. He's got no interest in any sort of public recognition or fame. He's just totally unfazed. He doesn't even own a mobile phone. He was the perfect team-mate. He's got no Twitter, no Facebook, nothing.

[Before the expedition] we went to Greenland for three weeks as a little dress rehearsal. I was really at the height of the sponsorship [phase], with tons of money going in and out, and we had huge contracts with lawyers. Everything was nuts. I had inadvertently become the CEO of this bizarre business that was turning over tens of thousands of pounds a month. We also had lawyers, accountants and PR people, and we had an intern, eight people in the office, a huge payroll to meet. It was just bonkers. I was thinking, 'What on Earth is going on?'

And suddenly to be transported to Greenland for three weeks with Tarka and to be with someone who is driven purely by this genuine love of the wilderness: it was perfect timing because it reminded me why I started down this path in the first place. If I was doing it for public recognition or something then I was barking up the wrong tree, because I was doing something that was so specialised in such a weird niche that no one's really going to appreciate it.

I think one of the biggest lessons is that, earlier on, there was a lot of ego involved and I wanted to make a name for myself and prove something, I don't know, do something that I'd be proud of. The biggest lesson of this last expedition has been the importance of being able to de-couple achievements or praise or criticism or any of that stuff from self-acceptance and self-worth.

Quite a lot of my expeditions have failed. I'm extraordinarily proud of those trips, even though the last North Pole attempt didn't even start! We didn't even get a weather window. We raised the money, did the training, flew out there, and the weather was so crap that we couldn't even start. We waited for three weeks and then you're too late in the season.

I was trying to do something that mattered to me and that I felt was genuinely chipping away at the boundaries of what was considered possible. It would have been a lot easier to do a normal-style North Pole trip with a longer time window and more food and to be one of the list of people who have done that. But I wanted to do something that was in some sense pioneering.

So I'm kind of proud I kept bashing away at that, and, each time, I managed to pick myself up and go back and try again. And of course with each of those attempts and with the months and years of planning and training, I was learning stuff that actually meant that we got to a position where the Scott Expedition was a viable undertaking. Looking back at each of those trips, even the biggest failures, even the ones that didn't start, they were all crucial stepping stones to getting to where I wanted to be.

Ironically, I don't think I've ever had a completely successful expedition. On every journey I've done, I failed to achieve everything I've set out to do. In that process, though, we've done some cool things. I've genuinely raised the bar in this weird little niche. And I've done that through failing over and over again.

Looking back, it sounds clichéd, but the only failure would have been not to try in the first place. That, to me, is the only acceptable definition of failure, just to not actually try.

Looking back, certainly there's something about the scale of the places, the remoteness of them, the intensity of the conditions and therefore the kind of experiences and emotions that you go through. They're enormous highs and lows, and I think there must be something almost addictive about that kind of intensity, because as humans we seem to seek out experiences of intensity. We go to big rock concerts, or we go on rollercoasters, or we like having fast cars, we like spicy curries or getting drunk, or whatever it is. We seek out experiences and stuff that's intense. To me, hanging out in a cold tent in Antarctica, for some reason, that's the thing that does it for me.

JAMES CASTRISSION
COMPLETED A RETURN JOURNEY
TO THE SOUTH POLE

I thought the Antarctica trip was harder than crossing the Tasman Sea in that there's something about the cold and the wind that you just cannot escape. The ocean – regardless of whether you're one mile or 500 miles off the coast – is beautiful. The birds are out, your shirt's off, you're getting some sun. There's fish in the water. It's really, really pleasant. Whereas I found in Antarctica you just didn't get the same time off and the same respite. It was just constant and incessant. At sea, though, I felt that you could (on a nice day) relax.

SCOTT PARAZYNSKI
ASTRONAUT, SPACEWALKER
AND EVEREST SUMMITEER

I really don't like to brag, Alastair, but I too have circled the planet on a bike. On my first shuttle flight back in 1994 we had a bike ergometer on the flight desk, with the shuttle's overhead windows much like a glass-bottom boat. I pedalled one lap around the planet in 90 minutes, clicking in at 17,500 miles per hour. Sorry to burst your bubble...!

I think the initial motivation for all explorers is the adventure of it. As a little kid, my father worked on the Apollo missions, so I had model rockets and posters on the wall and dreamed of becoming an explorer myself, wanting to actually set the first boot prints down on Mars.

Although it didn't turn out exactly like that, I was very fortunate to get a chance to fly in space on a number of occasions. I think what initially attracted me was just the audacious nature of breaking the bonds of gravity and seeing the planet from those altitudes and being in a place where very few could go. The experience of weightlessness, looking at your planet from that extraordinary perspective, is, I think, life's greatest adventure.

I think that's a common thread as an adventurer, going to a place that is difficult to get to, to see a place that is out of the ordinary. I love your idea of the microadventures. You don't need to go all that far to get to places of beauty that are out of the ordinary.

Great things in life are never going to be handed to you. I was five years old when I established that I really wanted to fly in space. My first trip, I was 33.

I've also climbed Mount Everest. The similarities are the physical/mental preparation, the training and the equipment. I remember leaving my tent at high camp, Camp Four, at 8,000 metres, in the darkness. I was covered in protective clothing. I had a waist harness with a lanyard that would clip onto fixed lines. So when I crawled out of the vestibule, I felt almost as if I was floating out of the hatch of the space shuttle or the International Space Station, because you're really going out into the void. It struck me that this was very similar to an EVA [extravehicular activity]. The physical threats are not dissimilar, either. If you make the wrong decision in space, you could go floating away or not make it back into the air lock-in. And the Summit Day on a big mountain is very much like the big day of floating out of the hatch on the space walk.

There are a lot of dissimilarities as well, though. When you're in space or on a shuttle mission or any type of spacecraft, you feel the threat of the launch, in particular. But once you get up into space, you're floating around, just in short-sleeves. You don't really appreciate the fact that on the other side of that thin aluminium hull is the vacuum of space. So you feel very comfortable and secure.

However, when you're in the Himalayas or on any other big mountain, it's very cold. There's hypoxia. You're very far away from any kind of rescue. You feel an element of threat all the time.

I think it's important to find exciting challenges in our down-to-earth lives. Like you're saying, you don't necessarily need to go climb Everest and spend two months out there. You can go climb Ben Nevis or whatever. There are all sorts of really cool adventures that can be done on a shorter scale, too.

The grander adventures with which I have finished the book are included to set our imaginations racing. The North Pole! The South Pole! Space! Which of us has not imagined blasting off on a rocket? Of course, a trip into space pulverises the prospect of a £1,000 adventure. There's the good old tale of NASA investing millions in developing a space pen (the Soviets, the story goes, simply used a pencil). But an interview with an astronaut serves a useful purpose for our own rather cheaper adventures: it gets us excited, reminds us to dream big, and cajoles us into action.

Exciting though polar journeys may sound, they are undoubtedly difficult. Martin recounts how the pre-trip excitement turns to a secret wish for a bad weather delay when the moment of departure draws close. James found his Antarctic expedition much harder even than crossing the Tasman Sea. And Ben's South Pole journey was also so much harder than he had anticipated. Hardship at the Poles, though, is an inevitable consequence of striving for something pioneering.

Polar journeys are so complex and expensive that even getting to the start line is phenomenally difficult. Ben remembers the many, many years of doubt – from himself and from those around him.

'My bucket list has never been fuller. I think if you have the will, you can find a way. You can craft opportunities, rather than excuses, to do big things'

Is the suffering worth it in the end? Ben ponders this: 'I'm not really sure how to answer that.' But Martin is certain that the Arctic Ocean is the best place: 'nothing on Earth can touch it.' Nothing on Earth, perhaps, but Scott trumps all of us in this book by breaking the bonds of gravity and seeing the planet from a place that very few have ever visited.

And so I will leave the final words to our astronaut adventurer. 'People ask me all the time, "You've flown in space. You've climbed Everest. What else is there left to do?" My bucket list has never been fuller. There's so many different places I want to visit. I think if you have the will, you can find a way. So I think you can craft opportunities, rather than excuses, to do big things.'

BIOGRAPHIES

TOM ALLEN
ADVENTURE TRAVEL
WRITER AND FILM-MAKER
Cycled, packrafted, walked,
hitch-hiked and rode horses on five continents.
@tom_r_allen tomsbiketrip.com

PAUL ARCHER
ENTREPRENEUR AND
INTERNATIONAL TAXI DRIVER
Drove around the world in
a London Black Cab.
@paul_k_archer daredevilproject.com

MARK BEAUMONT
ADVENTURER, CYCLIST,
AUTHOR, BROADCASTER
Cycled around the world, length
of the Americas and Africa. Also rowed through
the Arctic and survived capsize whilst rowing
the Atlantic.
@MrMarkBeaumont markbeaumontonline.com

RACHEL BESWETHERICK
ADVENTURER AND AUTHOR
Walked 325 kilometres in memory
of World War II Prisoners of War
who built the infamous Death Railway in Thailand
and Burma.
@intrepidgirl
intrepid-girl.com, deathrailwaywalk.com

ANTONIA BOLINGBROKE-KENT
TRAVEL WRITER
Numerous slightly silly vehicle-
powered expeditions around the globe.
@AntsBK theitinerant.co.uk

DAVE BOUSKILL
AND DEB CORBEIL
TRAVEL AND ADVENTURE
BLOGGERS
Six years of non-stop travel and adventure to
more than 100 countries on all seven continents.
@theplanetd theplanetd.com

JAMIE BOWLBY-WHITING
LOW-BUDGET EXPLORER AND
AUTHOR: I WANT TO LIVE A LIFE
FROM WHICH I DON'T NEED A HOLIDAY
Hitch-hiked tens of thousands of miles,
rafted the Danube, and walked across Iceland.
@jamierbw greatbigscaryworld.com

JAMIE BUNCHUK
JOURNALIST, ADVENTURER
AND DISTANCE RUNNER
Ran across the Steppe of Misfortune,
rode horses across Kazakhstan, lived with
indigenous hunters in Tajikistan and Mongolia.
@bunchuk jamiemaddison.com

KARL BUSHBY
ADVENTURER
Global journey on foot.
@bushby3000 bushby3000.com

KEVIN CARR
ULTRA EXPLORER, ADVENTURER
AND MOTIVATIONAL SPEAKER
The fastest man around the world:
ran coast-to-coast across four continents, closing
a continuous loop around the world in record time.
@hardwayround hardwayround.com

JAMES CASTRISSION
ADVENTURER
Kayaked the Tasman Sea and first
unsupported return journey from
the coast of Antarctica and back.
@MyAdventurGroup myadventuregroup.com.au

NIC CONNER
NORMAL GUY WHO WENT CYCLING
Cycled from London to Tokyo with only £1,000.
@aroundinagrand facebook.com/aroundinagrand

PAULA CONSTANT
AUTHOR
Walked the Sahara with camels.
@PaulaConstant paulaconstant.com

SEAN CONWAY
ENDURANCE ADVENTURER
First person to complete a length of Britain triathlon.
@conway_sean seanconway.com

TIM COPE
AUTHOR, LONG RIDER, FILM-MAKER
Three years on horse from Mongolia to Hungary, Russia to Beijing by bike, Siberia to the Arctic by rowboat.
@timcopejourneys timcopejourneys.com

WILL COPESTAKE
FREELANCE OUTDOOR LEADERSHIP
Kayaked around Scotland and climbed the winter Munros in a year. Walked across Iceland, kayak guided in Patagonia.
@WillCopestake willcopestakemedia.com

DAVE CORNTHWAITE
ADVENTURER
Expedition1000: 25 non-motorised journeys over 1000 miles.
@DaveCorn davecornthwaite.com

KAREN DARKE
ATHLETE AND ADVENTURER
Two decades of expeditions by bike, sea kayak and sit-ski, and six years as a Paralympian (British Cycling Team).
@kdarke karendarke.com

KYLE DEMPSTER
COFFEE SHOP OWNER
Professional alpinist who once rode a bike through Kyrgyzstan.
kyledempster.blogspot.com

IAIN DENLEY
DREAM CHASER
Cycled Europe and South America.
@DennersHQ dennershq.com

STEVE DEW-JONES
JOURNALIST, AUTHOR AND SEMI-PROFESSIONAL HITCH-HIKER
Hitch-hiked from England to Malaysia in 2008, then Argentina to Alaska in 2014.
@stevedewjones theruleofthumb2.wordpress.com

TEMUJIN DORAN
FILM-MAKER
Childrens' book illustrator and expedition film-maker.
@studiocanoe studiocanoe.com

HANNAH ENGELKAMP
WRITER AND INEPT DONKEY OWNER
Walked 1,000 miles around Wales with an eccentric donkey called Chico.
@hannahengelkamp seasidedonkey.co.uk

MATT EVANS
NURSE, TOUR GUIDE AND KEBAB ENTHUSIAST
Travelled from Nottingham to Saigon overland.
@mattyevans75

ANDREW FORSTHOEFEL
WRITER AND LISTENING FACILITATOR
Walked over 4,000 miles across
the USA.
@aforstho walkingtolisten.com

HENRIK FREDERIKSEN
ENGINEER AND ADVENTURER
A bicycle journey around the world
with two surprising detours.
@worldonbike_com worldonbike.com

JAMIE FULBROOK
FILM-MAKER, HITCH-HIKER
AND TROUBLEMAKER
Ten years bouncing about,
hitch-hiking continents and seeking balance.
@onlybloodyhuman onlybloodyhuman.com

DOMINIC GILL
FILM-MAKER
Global tandem cycling and climbing
expeditions.
@domgill dominicgill.me

ED GILLESPIE
ENVIRONMENTALIST, SLOW
TRAVELLER, AUTHOR
Around the world without flying.
@frucool onlyplanet.co.uk

ANTHONY GODDARD
ADVENTURE MAP MAKER
Road-tripped all over the USA.
@anthonygoddard zerosixzero.org

JIMMY GODDARD
YOUTH WORKER AND HAND-CYCLIST
Hand cycled up Kilimanjaro.
@jimmygoddard1
jimmy@jimmygoddard.com

ALICE GOFFART AND
ANDONI RODELGO
LONG DISTANCE CYCLISTS
AND FILM-MAKERS
Family cycling around the Earth for seven years.
mundubicyclette.be

CHRIS GUILLEBEAU
AUTHOR AND TROUBLEMAKER
Visited every country in the world.
@chrisguillebeau chrisguillebeau.com

HARRY GUINNESS
LOCATION-INDEPENDENT WRITER
Works from a laptop in lovely
locations.
@harryguinness harryguinness.com

ÁRPÁD HARKÁNYI
AND ZITA ZÁRUG
CYCLED ROUND THE WORLD
FOR A HONEYMOON
@360fokbringa 360fokbringa.hu/en

MARTIN HARTLEY
EXPEDITION AND ADVENTURE
PHOTOGRAPHER
28 expeditions globally; four full
expeditions to the Geographic North Pole.
@martinrhartley martinhartley.com

BARRY HAYES
OCEAN ROWER
Rowed 4,000 kilometres across
the Pacific Ocean from California to
Hawaii as part of the world's first human-powered
race across the world's largest ocean.
@Barry_Hayes barryhayes.co.uk

TIM HOBIN
OPERATIONS OFFICER
Paddled the Ganges on a £50 kayak from eBay.
tim.h@wwdas.com

ANNA HUGHES

LONG DISTANCE CYCLIST
AND AUTHOR

Cycled and sailed the coastline of Britain.
@EatSleepCycle annacycles.co.uk

GRAHAM HUGHES

MAN OF THE WORLD

Successfully completed the first journey to every country in the world without flying.
@EveryCountry grahamdavidhughes.com

NICK HUNT

WRITER AND STORYTELLER

Walked from the Hook of Holland to Istanbul in the footsteps of Patrick Leigh Fermor.
@underscrutiny nickhuntscrutiny.com

**ADAM JONES AND
SUSAN WELFORD**

STUDENTS

Mountain bike tour of Iceland.

MARK KALCH

EXPEDITION PADDLER

7 Rivers, 7 Continents: source to sea paddling descents of the longest river on each continent.
@markkalch 7rivers7continents.com

JAMES KETCHELL

SERIAL ADVENTURER
AND SPEAKER

Climbed Everest, cycled the world, rowed Atlantic Ocean.
@CaptainKetch jamesketchell.net

KU KING

PERPETUAL NOMAD
AND TRAVEL WRITER

Exploring the planet with a progressively smaller backpack since 1985!
@JourneyJunkies journeyjunkies.co.uk

BELINDA KIRK

FOUNDER OF EXPLORERS CONNECT
AND BASE CAMP FESTIVAL

Two decades running filming, scientific and youth expeditions in jungles, deserts, mountains. World Record for rowing around Britain.
@explorerstweet explorersconnect.com

ANDY KIRKPATRICK

CLIMBER AND WRITER

Not playing it safe or easy.
@psychovertical
andy-kirkpatrick.com

MARC LAMBERT

CORPORATE INVESTIGATOR,
PART-TIME MOUNTAINEER

A solo walk around Madagascar.
theatlasdiaries.com

ARCHIE LEEMING

PHOTOGRAPHER

Motorcycled across Africa. Canoed and cycled through the Congo.
@archieleeming archieleeming.com

BRENDAN LEONARD

ADVENTURE WRITER

Bicycled across America, traversed Colorado's Sangre de Cristo Range.
@semi_rad semi-rad.com

ROB LILWALL
ADVENTURER, AUTHOR, SPEAKER
Cycled from Siberia to London via Papua New Guinea and Afghanistan; walked the length of China.
@roblilwall roblilwall.com

HELEN LLOYD
MODERN-DAY NOMAD
Long-distance adventure-cycling and journeys by horse, river and on foot.
@helenlloyd helenstakeon.com

TOM LLOYD-SMITH
CONSTRUCTION PROJECT MANAGER
Cycled from the UK to India.
@tomlloydsmith tomlloydsmith.com

ANDY MADELEY
TRAINEE POLAR EXPLORER
Cycled from London to Sydney for War Child, now training for Last Pole expedition.
@agmadeley andymadeley.com

RIAAN MANSER
PIONEERING EXPLORER
Four world firsts in modern exploration.
@riaanmanser riaanmanser.com

LIAM MARTIN, JAMIE HYATT AND BONAMY NORMAN
C90 DREAMERS AND ACCIDENTAL FILM-MAKERS
Rode some knackered old Honda C90 pizza bikes to a Greek island on a whim, shot some video footage, then learned how to make a film.
@C90Dreams, *@LiamMartinFilm*
c90dreams.wordpress.com, liammartinfilm.com

LEON MCCARRON
ADVENTURER, FILM-MAKER
Human-powered storytelling.
@leonmccarron leonmccarron.com

JAMIE MCDONALD
ADVENTURER, SPEAKER, (PART-TIME) SUPERHERO
Ran 5,000 miles (or 200 marathons) across Canada.
@MrJamieMcDonald jamiemcdonald.org

CHRIS MILLAR
FULL-TIME THERAPIST, PART-TIME ADVENTURER
Cycling, running, hitch-hiking or just blagging it.
@chrisjsmillar goo.gl/qaY1FN

TIM MOSS
ADVENTURER
Cycled world, climbed new mountains, crossed a desert.
@nextchallenge thenextchallenge.org

JOHN (JON) MUIR
MOTIVATIONAL SPEAKER AND WILDERNESS GUIDE
Four decades rock climbing, mountaineering, desert traverses, polar exploration, sea kayaking and sailing.
@suzanmuir jonmuir.wikispaces.com

KERRY O'NEILL
TAKER OF EXTENDED SOJOURNS
Cycled from home (Bristol) to Rome; good at going somewhere for a weekend and staying for a year.
@kezoneill howtobeanadventurer.com

SARAH OUTEN
EXPLORER BY LAND AND SEA
Cycled, kayaked and rowed around the Northern Hemisphere.
@SarahOuten sarahouten.com

IAN M PACKHAM
ADVENTURER, TRAVEL WRITER AND SPEAKER
Circumnavigated Africa by public transport, now seeking off-beat adventures across the globe.
@ianMpackham encircleafrica.org

SCOTT PARAZYNSKI, MD
ASTRONAUT, SPACEWALKER, PROFESSOR, INVENTOR, HIMALAYAN CLIMBER, DIVER, DOCTOR AND DAD
5x Space Shuttle Astronaut, 7x spacewalker, Everest climber.
@AstroDocScott parazynski.com

KIRSTIE PELLING
JOURNALIST AND FAMILY TRAVEL WRITER
Over 20,000 kilometres of family cycling on several continents, plus lots of other family adventures and microadventures.
@familyonabike familyadventureproject.org

TEGAN PHILLIPS
LONG-DISTANCE CYCLIST AND ADVENTURE CARTOONIST
Cycled through Spain and Africa.
@Unclippd unclippedadventure.com

ROLF POTTS
TRAVEL WRITER AND AUTHOR
World traveller, once circled the globe with no luggage or bags of any kind.
@rolfpotts rolfpotts.com

MATT PRIOR
PILOT
Various places in various vehicles for various reasons (mostly fun)!
@mattprioruk mattprior.co.uk

MENNA PRITCHARD
WRITER, FILM-MAKER AND CLIMBER
Family adventures all over the globe.
@Menna_Pritchard
magneticmountains.com

PAUL RAMSDEN
Health and Safety Consultant. Lots of big mountains.

GRANT 'AXE' RAWLINSON
HUMAN-POWERED ADVENTURER
Peak-to-peak expeditions: human-powered expeditions beginning and ending on interesting mountain summits.
@axeoneverest axeoneverest.com

CANDACE ROSE RARDON
WRITER AND SKETCH ARTIST
Drove an auto-rickshaw 3,000 kilometres across India.
@candacerardon candaceroserardon.com

BEN SAUNDERS
POLAR EXPLORER
The first to complete the Antarctic expedition that defeated Sir Ernest Shackleton and killed Captain Scott, a 1,800-mile trek that broke the record for the longest human-powered polar journey in history.
@polarben bensaunders.com

PATRICK MARTIN SCHROEDER

ADVENTURER

On a mission to travel to every country in the world.
@world_bicyclist worldbicyclist.com

PHOEBE SMITH

EXTREME SLEEPER, AUTHOR AND SPEAKER

First woman to sleep at the extreme points of mainland Britain, wild camping aficionado and author of the only guidebook to British bothies.
@PhoebeRSmith phoebe-smith.com

ED STAFFORD

EXPLORER

Walked the Amazon.
@Ed_Stafford edstafford.org

JOFF SUMMERFIELD

PENNY FARTHING BUILDER/ ADVENTURER

Cycled around the world on a Penny Farthing, twice!
@JoffSummerfield pennyfarthingworldtour.com

ROSIE SWALE POPE

ROUND THE WORLD RUNNER, SOLO SAILOR, WRITER

Five decades of voyages and adventures.
@RosieSwalePope rosieswalepope.co.uk

SHIRINE TAYLOR

WANDERING PHOTOGRAPHER

Two-year cycle tour through Asia and South America.
@awanderingphoto awanderingphoto.com

INGRID, SEAN AND KATE TOMLINSON

TREE PLANTERS AND SCHOOL STUDENT

Family cycling expedition from Arctic Canada to Patagonia. Kayaked the coast of BC and Alaska.

ROBERT TWIGGER

POLYMATHIC ARTIST, WRITER, ADVENTURER

Followed old explorer routes along rivers and through deserts.
@roberttwigger roberttwigger.com

SATU VÄNSKÄ-WESTGARTH

TRAVEL PROFESSIONAL, WRITER AND LOCAL ADVENTURER

White water kayaker turned long-distance cyclist, currently wondering what adventure to take on next!
@SatuVW todestinationunknown.com

AUSTIN VINCE

CURATOR: ADVENTURE TRAVEL FILM FESTIVAL

Multiple circumnavigations of the globe by dirt-bike.
@AdvTravFilmFest austinvince.com

ANDY WARD

POLAR EXPEDITION MANAGER, PHOTOGRAPHER AND FLY-FISHING BUM

Walked from London to Istanbul. Managed five North and South Pole Expeditions. Adventures with rod and packraft around Scotland.
@ward_andy andyward.me

JANYIS WATSON AND CHRIS SZCZERBA
BICYCLE TRAVELLERS
Cycled over 16,000 kilometres together in Europe and Africa.
thespokeandwords.wordpress.com

KRISTEN ZIPPERER
WRITER AND EDITOR
Lived and worked in India and Nepal.
@kristenzipperer
kristz.portfoliobox.me

JESSICA WATSON, OAM
SOLO SAILOR
Around the world solo sailor.
@watsonjessica jessicawatson.com.au

NICK WESTON
FOUNDER AND DIRECTOR OF HUNTER GATHER COOK
Lived in a treehouse, now runs a foraging and cookery school.
@HuntrGatherCook huntergathercook.com

OLLY WHITTLE
ANALYST
Paddled the Mekong and crossed the frozen Lake Baikal on foot.
@OllyWhittle ollywhittle.com

COLIN WILLOX
USER EXPERIENCE DESIGNER
Slow traveller.
colinwillox.com

LEVISON WOOD
AUTHOR AND EXPLORER
Former Paratrooper. Walked the length of the Nile and Himalayas. Expeditions on five continents.
@levisonwood levisonwood.com

SVEN YRVIND
SMALL BOAT SAILOR
Sailed round Cape Horn in a 20-foot boat.

INDEX

PICTURE CREDITS

All photos © Alastair Humphreys except:
pp8–9, 62, 82–83, 87, 171, 178–179, 180 (top),
181 (bottom) © Archie Leeming; pp12–13 (top), 138,
140 © Leon McCarron; p21, 89 © Alice Goffart
and Andoni Rodelgo; pp22, 84–85, 102, 104–105
© Tim and Laura Moss; p33 © Anthony Goddard/
Linda Martini; p55 © Shirine Taylor; p58 © Daniel
Munoz/Reuters/Corbis; pp61, 86, 107 © Ingrid
and Sean Tomlinson; pp73, 127 © Ed Stafford; pp90
(top), 158–159 © Henrik Frederiksen/worldonbike.
com; p90 (bottom) © Tom Allen; pp92–93
© Mark Beaumont; p95 © Joff Summerfield;
p99 (top) © Anna Hughes; pp99 (bottom), 201
© James Ketchell; p125 © Luke Nowell and Rachel
Beswetherick; p135 (top) © Rhys Thwaites-Jones;
p135 (bottom) © Hannah Engelkamp; pp152–153,
156 © Mark Kalch; p155 © Jason Lewis/Kenny
Brown; p157 © Jamie Bowlby-Whiting; pp166–167
© Dave Bouskill/theplanetd.com; pp174–175,
180 (middle) © Ants Bolingbroke-Kent; pp177,
180 (bottom), 181 (top) © Matt Prior; pp186–187
© Steve Dew-Jones; p188 © Rolf Potts; p192 ©
Jamie Fulbrook; pp198–199, 204–205, 206–207, 209
© Will Copestake/www.willcopestakemedia.com;
pp212–213, 216 © Phoebe Smith; p228 © NASA/
Handout/Getty Images; pp250–251 © Candace
Rose Rardon. Biography portraits kindly supplied
by the individual contributors.

ACKNOWLEDGEMENTS

My chief thanks must go to all the adventurers featured in this book. Thank you for your time, your expertise, your wisdom, advice, friendship, photographs and support. It's been a pleasure and an inspiring privilege. I apologise that I couldn't include every story.

Thanks to Rob Symington for first opening my eyes to the power of putting aside £20 a week, every week. Do it for long enough and anyone can escape the city.

Thanks also to Julia, Myfanwy, Helena and Myles for all your expertise and wisdom. Thank you, in particular, to Myles for having your 'annual good idea' early this year and helping so much with the structure of the book. I enjoyed watching you settle back and open the cheese and onion crisps with self-satisfied relish.

I urge readers to explore the websites of the adventurers listed in these pages and enjoy following all their future exploits.